Study Verse by Verse with Dr. Steve Schell

The Book of Acts

Written by Dr. C. Stevens Schell

A Registered Trade Name of
Pastoral Resource Ministry
Federal Way, Washington

ISBN: 978-1-7348135-0-0

A word from the author

This is the commentary I wish someone had given me before I began teaching through the book of Acts. It answers the questions—as well as I can—that I needed answered in order to understand what I was reading. And I wrote it with a particular perspective in mind: I pictured myself sitting down with you, with a Bible open before us, reading together through Acts, verse by verse. As we progress, we'll encounter words we'll need to define, places we'll need to locate and names we'll need to identify. When we come across quotations from the Old Testament, we'll turn to that passage and read it in context to see why that person chose it. Our goal will always be to understand what's being said in each passage and then to take the spiritual insight we find there and apply it to our lives today.

Of course, each of us will bring to our study of the Bible our own spiritual history which influences what we see and don't see in a particular passage, but as much as possible I tried to keep my personal opinions out of the way and to let the Bible say what it wants to say. I really believe it is a God-breathed book. I believe that every verse, once we properly understand it, is full of spiritual life. And I believe God wants to reveal His Word to us. He will help us understand it.

How did I come to write this commentary? The process began when the Lord asked me to teach through a book of the Bible, all of it, and to not skip over the tough passages. To do that meant I would have to do a great deal of study. So I began to write a verse by verse explanation of the text and handed it out each week to our congregation. Then I would preach from the topics I discovered in each passage. That meant I didn't pick my own sermon topics anymore–the Bible did. Sure, there were special seasons during the year when we focused on other subjects, but we would always come back to the book we were studying and pick up where we left off. Week by week I would diligently study the next passage and look for answers to the many questions that arose, which is why it took me three years to preach through the book of Acts. Now three years may sound like too long a season to spend in one book of the Bible, but instead of growing tired of Acts, the congregation seemed to grow in their love for it. Apparently, they too were tired of reading verses there that they didn't understand, and when we finally came to the end, many were sorry to move on. As long as we were learning truths we could apply to our own lives, no one seemed to grow weary of the journey. And because of that I owe an enormous debt of thanks to Northwest Church. Without their patience and sincere love of God's Word, this commentary could never have been written.

As you read, you'll come across internal notes at those places where I quoted from another author or included someone's special insight or information. However, you'll find large sections without such notes because each week I produced my own translation from the original languages, and that let me hear Luke's stories afresh. And as a result, I came to my own conclusions. So what you'll find here is not a familiar revisiting of what others have said. This is a new commentary.

Most of the direct quotations used in the comments are from my own translation and often read awkwardly in English. That's because I've tried to convey to you the literal meaning of what Luke wrote so that you can feel the full force of his words. You'll find all such quotations are indicated by the word "literal" after the quote. All other quotations are from the New American Standard Bible (1977 and 1995). And though I don't pretend to be a great Bible scholar, I have earnestly tried to be a diligent student, so I am reasonably confident in the work I've done. I didn't write things that I couldn't point to in the text. Yet I'm sure I must have made mistakes along the way and for that I apologize to you and to the Lord.

I hope you'll read this commentary with your Bible open beside you and take the time to read the verses being covered before you read my comments. Please don't hurry. Stop and picture in your mind the event being described. Ask yourself, "What truth is God teaching me here?" And remember that when you read the book of Acts, you are observing the first generation of believers who came fresh from the hands of Jesus. Yes, those first disciples had human flaws like we do, but in many ways they show us what Christianity is supposed to look like, and they challenge us to follow their example. Throughout church history whenever this book of Acts was allowed to teach God's people how to walk with Him and was not dismissed as a mere description of something that happened in the past, those believers experienced revival. And it still offers that same gift to us today. So I pray that the Holy Spirit will use this commentary to help a new generation hear those truths afresh.

Steve

Pastor Steve

Book of Acts
Table of Contents

Acknowledgements

A person doesn't simply sit down and write a verse by verse commentary like this. It's the culmination of study and writing, week after week, over the course of years. And when it comes time to gather all that information into a book, there is much editing, discussion and design needed in order to produce something that is actually useful.

I've been blessed to have people who have diligently worked with me on this project, not for a few weeks or a few months, but for years. They have corrected, advised, encouraged and prayed, believing as much as I in the irreplaceable role the Bible has on our lives. My name will go on the front cover of the book, but without these beloved friends, there would be no book. There aren't words enough to express my thanks, but I have to try.

To Marc Hagman, who carefully laid the foundation for this series of books and for the beauty of its design, thank you! To Lianna Greer for typing, improving and patiently laboring over handwritten drafts that were ridiculously late, thank you! To Leigh Harris who edited, suggested many needed improvements and proofread with a careful eye and a deep love for those who will read these books, thank you! To Katrin Hagman and Martina Cline, whose administrative skills have shepherded this project so that these resources are available to pastors and Bible teachers around the world, thank you! To Northwest Church who, instead of growing frustrated that we were moving so slowly through the book of Acts, loved the process of discovery as much as I did, thank you! You constantly encouraged me and generously allowed me to take the time I needed to study week after week. I will always be grateful God called me and Mary to be your pastors. In another environment this project would have been impossible. To a small village in South Africa named Ndibela where the idea to write such a commentary began, thank you! And finally to my family who gave up so much time to let me work, yet you never complained, but always encouraged me, thank you! You're amazing! And just between you and me, even if no one else reads this book, I wrote it for you.

How to Study Verse by Verse

The three study questions listed below are ones I use when I preach through a book of the Bible. I didn't develop them. I think they are very old, but hopefully the explanations I provide will make them a practical tool for you to use as well if you don't already. By the time you've answered all three about a particular passage, you'll discover you have prepared the basic components of a good sermon.

As you move through a book of the Bible, verse by verse, you'll notice that each author teaches on a certain topic and then moves on to another topic. Watch for these "logical limits of thought." Some can be quite long and contain numerous sub-points, but try to identify where each one begins, and where it ends. The best sermons focus on one topic at a time rather than attempting to string together many different topics.

1. What does it say?

As I reflect on each verse, or group of verses, I ask myself, "What do I need to know in order to understand this verse?" In other words, what questions does this passage raise that I will need to answer before I can understand what the author is saying? This quickly identifies where I'll need to focus my study. Which words need to be defined carefully?

Who was the author of this book and to whom was he writing, and why? Does he mention people or places that I'll need to look up so I can picture in my mind what I'm reading? Is there research I'll need to do on ancient customs, modes of transportation, clothing, food or family relationships? And are there other passages of Scripture which might help me understand this one? Answering so many questions might seem like a lot of work, but when I'm done, a fascinating story emerges that people will love to hear.

Before I move on to the next question, I want to emphasize the importance of defining words carefully. It's so easy to assume we know the meaning of a word because we use it often in daily conversation, but that does not mean we know what the author meant when he used that word. We need to remember that the purpose of this first step is to understand, as deeply as possible, what the author intended to say. What did the original recipients of this letter hear the author say when they read these words? Without doing this work, we can think we see meanings in a text that don't really exist. This has led to many unnecessary controversies. To avoid this pitfall try to identify the Greek (or Hebrew) word which the author originally used, and then look at other passages where that same word is used in a similar way. Give special emphasis to those passages in which the same author uses that word in the same book. We want to understand why the author chose that word. Most words, at their root, are based on a familiar action, object or experience which humans encounter in life. As I watch to see how this word is used in passage after passage, the root meaning of the word becomes clearer. Then when I return to the verse I am studying, what the author is saying becomes more apparent.

2. What does it mean?

Once I understand what the author said, the next step is to recognize what he meant. In other words, what spiritual truth was he teaching to the men and women who first read those words? Though many things have changed over the past 2000 years, the basic issues of being human haven't changed at all, and of course, God never changes. So the eternal truths which are taught in the Bible are just as true today as they were for those who first heard them. As I prayerfully meditate on what a passage says, the Holy Spirit is wonderfully faithful to show me what it means. Time and again I suddenly see something I never saw before, or at least never at that depth. Then I try to state that truth in one simple sentence. I want to use only plain, understandable language. I carefully avoid theological terms. I ask myself, "How would I explain this truth to someone who knows nothing about the Bible?" or "How would I explain it to a child?" This is usually much more difficult than it sounds, but it's in the struggle of choosing the right words to use that the practical application of the truth becomes apparent. I know I've finally stated it well when I can picture it in my mind. When that happens, it becomes easy to remember times when I've seen that truth at work in my own life or someone else's. Until then I realize that I need to keep meditating on that truth. I need to keep rewording the sentence until it really makes sense. Once I get it right, memories of watching God do that very thing begin to flood my mind, and my heart is often stirred by the beauty of what I'm seeing. This leads me to the final step.

3. What does it mean to me?

Now it's time to write out examples of where I have seen this truth at work. In some cases it may be easier to think of illustrations from the lives of other people, but it's important to ask the Lord to show me where this truth has been at work in me because that discovery produces a much deeper level of understanding. This memory brings with it all sorts of practical insights because I remember not only what I did in that situation, but more importantly, what God did. I am able to describe how He helped me overcome the emotions and obstacles that I encountered along the way. Such insights bring this truth alive to me and also to those I'm teaching. It awakens hope in them that they too can walk in this truth. There's nothing wrong with using examples drawn from the lives of others, but if I don't take the time to reflect on what a truth has meant to me personally, a depth of understanding will be missing.

Please don't skip this third step. It's the one that makes our preaching and teaching of the Word interesting to others. Truth by itself is dry. Spiritual principles without practical application seem lifeless and boring. But the moment people begin to see how God's Word will change their lives, they listen attentively. We all do. This is the step where faith and hope awaken. So again, please don't skip this step!

Here's a brief summary of the three questions:

1) What does it say?

What questions must you answer to understand this passage?

- Key words, information about the author, places mentioned, etc.
- What other Scripture verses apply?

2) What does it mean?

What is the main spiritual truth you would teach from this passage? Write this out in one sentence.

3) What does it mean to me?

Give an example of where you have seen this truth at work in your own life.

If you preach through a book of the Bible this way, what you'll discover is that you are allowing God to raise the topics you preach. As you study, the Bible first teaches you, and then you share with others what you have just learned. The process causes us to continue to grow in spiritual understanding. We are constantly learning new things which is exciting for us personally, but it also causes those we teach to continue growing as well. They come with expectation. They realize they are learning along with you.

It is my hope that as you study verse by verse through the book of Acts it will come alive to you at a deeper level than ever before, and that you'll have an opportunity to teach what you're learning to others. Whether you're preaching in a church, leading a Bible study, discipling a new believer, family member or friend, your journey through Acts will be a life-changing event. God's Word is full of life, and when we take the time to study and meditate on it, it will always transform us and those we teach. We become:

> "...like a tree planted by streams of water, which yields its fruit in its season and its leaf does not wither..." (Ps 1:3)

Book Abbreviations

Ge - Genesis
Ex - Exodus
Lev - Leviticus
Nu - Numbers
Dt - Deuteronomy
Jos - Joshua
Jdg - Judges
Ru - Ruth
1Sa - 1 Samuel
2Sa - 2 Samuel
1Ki - 1 Kings
2Ki - 2 Kings
1Ch - 1 Chronicles
2Ch - 2 Chronicles
Ezr - Ezra
Ne - Nehemiah
Est - Esther
Job - Job
Ps - Psalms
Pr - Proverbs
Ecc - Ecclesiastes
SS - Song of Solomon
Isa - Isaiah
Jer - Jeremiah
La - Lamentations
Eze - Ezekiel
Da - Daniel
Hos - Hosea
Joel - Joel
Am - Amos
Ob - Obadiah
Jnh - Jonah
Mic - Micah
Na - Nahum
Hab - Habakkuk
Zep - Zephaniah
Hag - Haggai
Zec - Zechariah
Mal - Malachi
Mt - Matthew
Mk - Mark
Lk - Luke
Jn - John
Ac - Acts
Ro - Romans
1Co - 1 Corinthians
2Co - 2 Corinthians
Gal - Galatians
Eph - Ephesians
Php - Philippians
Col - Colossians
1Th - 1 Thessalonians
2Th - 2 Thessalonians
1Ti - 1 Timothy
2Ti - 2 Timothy
Titus - Titus
Phm - Philemon
Heb - Hebrews
Jas - James
1Pe - 1 Peter
2Pe - 2 Peter
1Jn - 1 John
2Jn - 2 John
3Jn - 3 John
Jude - Jude
Rev - Revelation

Introduction

The book of Acts is the second installment in Luke's history of the ministry of Jesus Christ. His first was the book we call the gospel of Luke. There he focused on the person of Jesus Himself: His life, death and resurrection. Now, in the book of Acts, he picks up where his gospel left off to show us how the Risen Savior continued to minister through His church. Jesus had repeatedly encouraged His disciples to expect that after He ascended into heaven, the Holy Spirit would be given to them in far greater measure than it had ever been possible for human beings to receive. Jesus' resurrection and ascension would inaugurate a new era of God at work from within His people, and through His people (Lk 22:20; 24:49; Jn 7:37-39; 14:16-20; Heb 8:8-12).

As Lord of the Church, Jesus would continue to lead His church. To use Paul's metaphor, He would be our Head and we would be His Body (1Co 12:27; Eph 1:22-23; 4:4, 12, 15-16; Col 1:18). As Savior of the Church He would atone not only the sin that separated us from God, but our sinful, physical bodies as well, so that the Holy Spirit could dwell inside those bodies and empower us to function at a supernatural level, just as He had (Jn 14:12; Ro 8:3). He told His disciples that they should not be sorrowful when He ascended into heaven because His physical departure was not the end of His ministry, but rather the moment when there would a strategic transfer of that ministry to His people (Jn 16:5-7). He would continue to do everything He had been doing in the past, but in the future He would do it through them. What had been limited to Himself alone during His earthly ministry would soon be multiplied exponentially. His cross and resurrection would make it possible for the Holy Spirit to work through all believers. He further explained that when the Spirit came to them in that way, that from that moment on, He and the Father would also be present within each believer (Jn 14:18-20).

As we read Luke's account of the early church, we will see these promises fulfilled. We will see the arrival of the Holy Spirit in a new dimension and then watch remarkably transformed men and women boldly carry the message and work of Christ to Jerusalem, Judea, Samaria and into distant gentile nations, just as Jesus said they would (Lk 24:46-49; Ac 1:8). Thanks to Luke we will be able to see Christianity being lived out as it was intended to be. We will observe how the church functioned when it was led by the apostles themselves. We will be given a picture of the early church fresh from the hands of Jesus, before traditions, philosophy and politics sapped its strength. We will watch New Testament doctrine in action.

Every move of God tends to corrupt over time. Like a grapevine it needs pruning, and the book of Acts is one very important way God prunes us. By showing us how He intended His church to function, we discover what needs to change in our churches today. When the example of the first church is laid beside our church, the differences become obvious. Most of us will discover that our earliest forefathers and mothers functioned at a far greater level of guidance, spiritual gifts, relationships, boldness, evangelism and holiness than we do. Certainly the culture we live in varies widely from the culture of the first century, yet, the essential nature of what God wants to accomplish through His church does not change from culture to culture or generation to generation, nor will it until His Son returns in power (Mt 28:20; 1Co 13:9-12; 15:24). So, we should be preaching today the same gospel these early disciples preached; we should be seeing the same miraculous transformation take place within those who repent and believe that gospel; and we should be seeing the same sort of miracles and gifts of the Spirit that they saw because those miracles and gifts are available to us as well (Heb 13:7-8). If we will allow the book of Acts to show us what is possible, to show us what God intended to be normal, then it will become a powerful, prophetic voice calling us to repent where we have erred and filling us with hope in what God could do again in our day.

Some of the very first sermons ever preached are recorded here. Luke will allow us to listen while Peter preaches to thousands in Jerusalem (Ac 2:14-39; 3:12-26), and as Paul preaches to Jews in Galatia (Ac 13:14-41) or to Greeks in Athens (Ac 17:22-33). We will hear Stephen confront Israel's history of unbelief (Ac 7:1-60). We will hear Philip explain Isaiah 53 to a man from Ethiopia (Ac 8:26-39), and Peter evangelize a Roman household (Ac 10:34-43). The book of Acts is rich in apostolic doctrine and apostolic modeling. Here we will find the foundational truths that we should still be declaring today. Yes of course, we must communicate them in ways that those to whom we are speaking can understand, but the truths themselves are eternal. And here we will see a spiritual vitality with which we too should be ministering. If the book of Acts is understood this way and given the full authority it deserves, it has the ability to call each generation to "remember from where you have fallen, and repent and do the deeds you did at first…" (Rev 2:5). Luke has given us a great gift!

Acts Chapter 1

v1: Luke originally wrote this material for someone named "Theophilus"; just as he had the gospel which he wrote earlier (Lk 1:3). That name is probably a pseudonym meant to protect the identity of a man who held a high political or military position because Luke gives Theophilus the title "most excellent." Elsewhere in Acts he will apply this same title to Felix, the Roman procurator of Judea (Ac 23:26; 24:3), and Porcius Festus, his successor (Ac 26:25). The name "Theophilus" literally means "one who is loved by God," and is in itself an explanation of why Luke took the time to write this detailed history. Someone in high position was sincerely inquiring about Jesus Christ and His church, and because God loved that person (and us), He moved upon Luke to carefully investigate the reports of this newly emerging church and then to place that information in a clear, consecutive order so that Theophilus might know the exact truth about the things he had been taught (Lk 1:3-4). He was giving him reliable information so he could make an informed decision about becoming a disciple of Jesus Christ.

It's likely that Luke wrote the book of Acts in the city of Rome while Paul was under arrest waiting for a hearing before Caesar (A.D. 60, 61). During that two-year period of time Paul was permitted to stay in his own, rented quarters, accompanied by a soldier who was guarding him (Ac 28:16, 30-31). The Roman government gave him a surprising amount of freedom. He was allowed to teach and preach "with all openness, unhindered" (Ac 28:31). During those years Paul wrote Philemon, Colossians, Ephesians and Philippians, and Luke wrote Acts and possibly the Gospel of Luke; but we should note that he may have written his gospel during Paul's earlier imprisonment in Caesarea (Ac 24:27). In either case, both men turned what might have been wasted time into a season of research and writing which would leave an immeasurable gift to the church (Eph 5:16).

vs1-2: Luke tells Theophilus that his gospel was designed to record the things Jesus did and taught starting at the very beginning of His ministry, which for Luke extended back to events before Jesus' conception and continued until Jesus ascended into heaven (Lk 24:50-53). He reminds Theophilus that before Jesus ascended, He commanded the eleven apostles whom He had personally chosen (Ac 1:13, 26), to wait in Jerusalem "until you are clothed with power from on high" (Lk 24:49). After that power arrived, He said they were to proclaim Him "to all the nations, beginning from Jerusalem" (Lk 24:47).

v3: Luke tells Theophilus that before the ascension the resurrected Jesus appeared to His disciples on numerous occasions over a period of forty days. Eleven such appearances are recorded or mentioned in the New Testament, and there may have been many more. He says Jesus "presented Himself alive in many convincing signs." One delightful example of such "signs" was the occasion when Jesus took a piece of broiled fish and ate it in front of His disciples to prove to them that His resurrected body was real (Lk 24:41-43). Luke tells us that on that same occasion Jesus showed them "His hands and feet," meaning of course, His scars (Luke 24:40). John tells us that during the discussion which took place Jesus invited Thomas to touch the scar on His side where the spear had entered (Jn 20:27). Luke's point is to assure Theophilus that honest, reliable witnesses saw Jesus alive after His resurrection, and that what they saw was not a vision or a dream. He could be certain that there was a sound, historical basis for his faith. The proclamation that Jesus had risen from the dead was no myth or unconfirmed rumor. Many people had seen Jesus during that 40-day period, and some even touched Him and ate meals with Him. Those appearances were not momentary visions brought on by a state of religious ecstasy. People going about their daily activities, skeptical people who were not expecting to see Him alive, encountered Him. In other words, Theophilus was no fool for putting his faith in Christ.

Luke says that during these appearances Jesus spoke about "things concerning the Kingdom of God." By the phrase "Kingdom of God" he meant God's plan of salvation, particularly as it had now been revealed by the coming of Jesus. When we review the passages in the gospels which record some of what Jesus said during this 40-day period, we discover He focused on three topics: First, He explained how He fulfilled the prophecies of the Old Testament (Lk 24:44-47); second, He prepared His disciples to receive the promised baptism with the Holy Spirit (Lk 24:49; Ac 1:4-5); and third, He commanded them to be His witnesses and to make disciples in Israel, Samaria and all the gentile nations (Mt 28:19-20; Mk 16:15; Lk 24:47; Ac 1:8).

To speak about the "Kingdom of God" in the early church was to declare Jesus as the fulfillment of Old Testament prophecies and promises, and to call all who hear this message to believe in Him. What had been a mystery for centuries had at last been revealed. Now everyone could understand the truth: "that the Christ would suffer and rise from the dead on the third day, and that repentance for forgiveness of sins would be proclaimed in His name…" (Lk 24:46). And all who would respond in faith would become citizens of the "Kingdom of God."

v4: Luke next turns to the conversation Jesus had with His disciples prior to His ascension. It took place on the fortieth day after the resurrection. Luke described the same events at the end of his gospel, but here adds further information. This verse opens with a very unusual word which either means to gather together a large group of people or to eat together. When we read the account in his gospel, we see that both meanings can apply. The gathering was composed of "the eleven and those who were with them" (Lk 24:33), which sounds like the same group he mentions in Acts (Ac 1:13-15). So it may have totaled about 120 persons. And then when Jesus appeared in their midst, He ate broiled fish (Lk 24:41-43), so it sounds like a meal was taking place.

vs4-5: During that meeting Jesus commanded His disciples to remain in Jerusalem and wait for the "promise of the Father." He said this was a promise He had told them about earlier (Lk 22:20; 24:49; Jn 14-16). Then, so no one would mistake which promise He meant, He described what would happen when it arrived. He reminded them of how John the Baptist had immersed people in water and said that in a similar way they would soon be immersed in the Holy Spirit. That baptism actually arrived ten days later on Pentecost (Ac 2:1).

John the Baptist had already compared the coming of the Spirit with water baptism. Speaking of the coming Messiah he said, "As for me, I baptize you with water for repentance, but He who is coming after me… will baptize you with the Holy Spirit and with fire" (Mt 3:11). The "fire" to which he refers is God's coming judgment, but he also said the Messiah would baptize (dip, immerse) the righteous with the Holy Spirit (Jn 1:33). The preposition used here with the word "baptize" (Greek: en) essentially means "within." It pictures something inside of something else. We need only reflect on the image of baptism to determine what Jesus is saying.

John the Baptist immersed (submerged) people, or had them immerse themselves, under water in the manner of the Jewish ritual bath. The ritual bath was a common activity among observant Jews at that time. It was performed either in a place with a natural body of fresh water, such as a lake or stream, or in a "mikvah," which was a special tank containing at least 85 gallons of water located in homes or near religious sites. This bath was meant to cleanse people physically and spiritually in order to prepare them to approach God in worship. In a mikvah, a person would walk down a series of steps into the water, totally immerse themselves under water, and then walk back up the steps on the "clean" side of the stairway (Miriam Feinberg Vamosh, Daily Life at the Time of Jesus, Palphot Ltd., PO Box 2, Herzlia, Israel, pp26-27).

This was the symbolism John the Baptist used when he baptized. He was saying to the people of Israel, "You must deeply repent of your rebellion to God and be cleansed. The Messiah is coming soon, and if He finds you in this condition, He will bring upon you God's fiery judgment" (Lk 3:1-18; Ac 13:24; 19:3-4). By being baptized, John's followers were asking God to wash away their sins. Jesus took the meaning of John's baptism even deeper by describing it as a burial (Mk

10:38-39; Lk 12:49-50). To Him the water represented a watery grave. This may well have been what was in His mind when He insisted John baptize Him at the Jordan River (Mt 3:13-17). And this is the meaning that became central to Paul. He taught that a repentant person didn't merely "wash" when they were baptized, they spiritually "died" with Christ and then rose with Him to live a new life of obedience by the power of the Spirit (Ro 6:3-5).

There is one more biblical truth we need to remember in order to properly understand what Jesus means when He speaks of being "baptized with the Holy Spirit." The prophets repeatedly declared that when the Messiah came, He would bring with Him the presence of the Holy Spirit to an extent and intensity never before experienced. The entire planet would be dramatically changed. Five times in the Old Testament it is prophesied that "the earth will be filled with the glory of the Lord" (Nu 14; Ps 72:19; Isa 6:3; 11:9; Hab 2:14), and many other passages describe the coming of the Spirit using different imagery (e.g. Jer 31:34; Eze 36:26-27; 37:9-10, 14; 47:1-12; Joel 2:28-29; 3:18; Zec 14:8-11). Isaiah says "the earth will be full of the knowledge of the Lord <u>as the waters cover the sea</u>," (Isa 11:9). He pictures the planet immersed (baptized) in the glorious presence of the Holy Spirit. This must certainly be the basic idea behind the statements by John the Baptist and Jesus. Both are saying Jesus will bring that promised era of the Spirit, which is exactly why Peter quoted from Joel (Ac 2:14-21; Joel 2:28-32) to explain what had happened on the day of Pentecost.

So at that meeting with His disciples before ascending into heaven, Jesus said this prophesied era of the Spirit was about to begin, but not in the way it had traditionally been expected. Instead of a worldwide outpouring, initially the Spirit would come in this way only upon (and within) Jesus' followers. Peter later defined the category of people able to receive the baptism with the Holy Spirit as those individuals who repent and are baptized in the name of Jesus Christ for the forgiveness of their sins (Ac 2:38-39). The day of Pentecost revealed a mystery. The Messiah must come in two separate events rather than one: first, as our Suffering Servant, dying and rising for our sin, and then, as our glorious returning King. And God's gift of the Spirit also arrives in two distinct outpourings. First, in this season of time which follows Jesus' resurrection and ascension, believing individuals are baptized with the

Holy Spirit to equip them as His witnesses (the "little Pentecost"). Then at His return, Jesus will baptize the whole earth "as the waters cover the sea," (the "big Pentecost") (Asher Intrater, Foursquare Convention, Jerusalem, 2007).

v6: This gathering (vs4-5) probably took place in the upper room (Ac 1:13) of a house owned by John Mark's parents (Ac 12:12). It was likely the same upper room where Jesus celebrated the Last Supper (Lk 22:7-13). After eating with the disciples and teaching from the Scriptures (Mk 16:14; Lk 24:36-48), Jesus led them out of the city along a road which runs eastward over the Mount of Olives toward Bethany, a village two miles east of Jerusalem (Lk 24:50). Somewhere along that road, probably at its crest, which is about 1,000 yards directly east of Jerusalem ("a Sabbath day's journey away," v12), He stopped and had everyone gather around Him.

vs6-8: Someone had the courage to ask the question weighing on everyone's mind. They were confused by His statement about being baptized with the Holy Spirit. Since they were children they had all been taught about the events that would happen when Messiah comes. In their synagogues they had regularly listened to the reading of the Law (Genesis through Deuteronomy) and the Prophets (Ac 13:15, 27), and they knew the prophetic passages which state that when Messiah comes, He will rule the earth from Jerusalem, and the Holy Spirit will be poured out on all flesh (Ac 2:16-17). Yet Jesus had only spoken about the Spirit coming upon them as individuals. Did He mean by this the Spirit would not yet transform the whole earth? Now that He was resurrected from the dead, surely He would set up His throne and the glorious Messianic Age would begin, and the desert would bloom like a rose, and the lion would lay down with the lamb.

To which Jesus answered, "It is not for you to know times [chronos] and seasons [chairos] which the Father placed in His own authority." In other words, "Things will not happen as you expected. There is a divine plan at work you don't understand. But I can tell you this much: the promised outpouring of the Spirit is about to come on those of you who believe in Me to equip you for ministry (Lk 24:49). When that moment arrives, you will receive power to be My witnesses here in the city of Jerusalem, and then to the surrounding regions of Judea and

Samaria, and finally, even out to the gentile nations in the most distant parts of the planet [lit: the end of the earth]."

v8: Jesus was revealing a mystery. He was telling His disciples that their understanding of the timetable for the arrival of the Kingdom of God was incomplete. Yes, someday the Spirit will "baptize" the entire planet, but not yet. Before that day arrives God has ordained a season of sending out Spirit-baptized believers to make disciples (Ac 1:8; Mt 28:19). How long this season will last is something only the Father knows, and He will not share this information with us. He has "placed it in His own authority" (v7). His plan is to pour out the Holy Spirit on Messiah's people so they can effectively win souls. That outpouring is designed to release a rapid expansion of God's kingdom into the nations, and this "harvest" will continue until God determines it is complete.

v9: After giving these instructions Jesus lifted His hands and began to bless His disciples, but while He was speaking, He started to slowly rise up off the ground (Lk 24:50-51). He was lifted upward, as it were, by an unseen hand, higher and higher until He was enveloped by a cloud. Luke literally says, "... and a cloud received Him from their eyes." We're not told whether it was a naturally-formed cloud or a cloud of "glory" like the one that hovered over Mount Sinai (Ex 19:16) and enveloped Jesus on the Mount of Transfiguration (Mt 17:5), but Mark tells us where Jesus went after entering the cloud. He says He was "taken up into heaven and sat down at the right hand of God" (Mk 16:19; Ps 110:1; Ac 2:33-36; Mt 22:43-45).

v10: Luke describes the ascension because he wants his readers to understand that Jesus didn't evaporate into thin air. He didn't disappear suddenly like a ghost; God lifted Him up and took Him to another place. He slowly, physically rose into the air with everyone intently watching, straining their eyes until He entered a cloud and passed out of sight. Then, because their gaze was focused upward, no one saw two men approach the gathering, but it's obvious from their appearance and the way they spoke to the disciples that they were angels. Luke doesn't say their clothing "shone," as was true of the two angels who stood near the empty tomb (Lk 24:2-4), but he does say they wore white garments.

v11: They said, "Men, Galileans, why do you stand looking into heaven? This Jesus who has been taken up from you into heaven will come in the same way as you beheld Him going into heaven." Their question was specifically addressed to the men from Galilee, singling out those who had been accompanying Jesus and listening to Him teach for the past three and a half years. Their question seems to be more of a challenge than an inquiry. They seem frustrated, or maybe shocked, that those who had spent so much time with Him were acting like they hadn't heard anything He said. Surely they weren't standing there waiting for Him to come back down were they? By staring up into an empty sky it looked like they were waiting for Him to reappear. So, in case they hadn't understood, the angels reminded them of what He'd said. Numerous times He had laid out a full scenario of the events that would take place before He returned (Lk 17:20-37; 21:5-36). In fact, one of these very detailed explanations had taken place on that same Mount of Olives (Mt 24:3-31; Mk 13:3-27). Had they forgotten? Indeed, He will come back down "in a cloud with power and great glory" (Lk 21:27), but not yet. First the great harvest of souls must take place.

The fact that Jesus ascended from the Mount of Olives has great prophetic significance. Two hundred years before Jesus was born, the prophet Zechariah saw a future day when Israel's Messiah would rescue Jerusalem by defeating an army made up of combined forces from many different nations (Zec 12:2-14; 14:1-3). The battle he described is the same battle John describes in his Revelation (Rev 19:11-21). John sees the resurrected Christ return to earth with the armies of heaven, and by merely speaking a command He strikes down the Antichrist's forces at Armageddon. This victory ushers in a thousand-year period of world-wide peace under the Messiah's rule (Rev 20:1-6).

What connects Christ's Return with His Ascension is a statement by Zechariah that when the Messiah arrives, He will stand on the Mount of Olives. He says, "In that day His feet will stand on the Mount of Olives which is in front of Jerusalem on the east; and the Mount of Olives will be split in its middle from east to west by a very large valley so that half the mountain will move toward the north and the other half toward the south. You [the inhabitants of Jerusalem], will flee by the valley of My mountains. Then the Lord, my God, will come, and all the holy ones with Him." (Zec 14:2-4; Rev 12:13-17). So when the angels told the disciples that Jesus "...will come in just the same way as you have watched Him go into heaven," they not only meant He will descend from heaven, but it appears He will return to the same spot. The very place from which He ascended may be the place to which He will descend.

v12: When the angels finished speaking, the disciples immediately began to worship Jesus (Lk 24:52). Undoubtedly they must have fallen on their faces and poured out praise declaring Him to be their promised Messiah and now their ascended Lord. Over the past forty days when Jesus met with them, He had reminded them of key passages in the Old Testament which prophetically speak of Him (Lk 24:25-27, 44-47). Now, with His words fresh on their minds, they must have freely quoted from these as they worshiped. Once this burst of amazement and heartfelt thanks subsided, they turned and went back down the mountain into the city filled "with great joy" (Lk 24:52).

The fact that Luke felt the need to tell Theophilus the location of the Mount of Olives gives us some insight into the man for whom Luke wrote this history. It's hard to imagine he was a Jew because even if he grew up in a distant gentile city, a Jewish boy would be taught the basic topography of Jerusalem, the city at the spiritual center of his nation. But it's also hard to imagine Theophilus was a biblically-ignorant Gentile because Luke told him the distance between the city wall and the crest of the mountain was "a Sabbath day's journey away," which would be a concept a Gentile would not be likely to understand. So at first glance, Luke's comment to Theophilus seems confusing. How would a man who doesn't know the location of the Mount of Olives know the distance in a Sabbath day's journey unless Theophilus is what Luke calls a "God-fearing" Gentile (lit: a devout person, a worshiper. Ac 13:43, 50; 16:14; 17:4, 17; 18:7).

As we read the book of Acts we see that there were often Gentiles participating in the synagogues. These gentile men and women were drawn to the holy, monotheistic God of Israel. They recognized that the vulgar polytheism of their own cultures was foolishness, and in some cases they actually converted to Judaism (proselytes), and in others they didn't convert but still worshiped Israel's God and even practiced some of the requirements of the Law (Mt 8:5-13; Lk 7:1-10). As we'll see, this group was very responsive when the gospel was preached (Ac 13:42-52). If indeed Theophilus is one of these, then he would have heard the Torah read each Sabbath and certainly would have been taught Sabbath guidelines along with other aspects of Torah observance. And if that were the case, then he might not know the topography of Jerusalem but would surely know the distance in a Sabbath day's journey.

v13: In his gospel, Luke tells us that after the Ascension the disciples "were continually in the temple blessing God," but here in Acts we're told they entered the city and "went up into the upper room where they were staying." This "upper room" would have been a chamber built on the flat roof of a house. Putting these two pieces of information together, a picture emerges of that ten-day period between the Ascension and Pentecost: The eleven apostles, who Luke lists in this verse, may have been sleeping overnight in that upper chamber. Then during the day others may have joined them there for corporate prayer, but clearly, part of each day was also spent in larger gatherings at the temple. These would have met in the large outer courtyard called the Court of the Gentiles, and undoubtedly they would have taken cover from the sun under the large, colonnaded structure on the south side called the Portico of Solomon or the Royal Stoa. Many groups gathered in this large, covered area, and it also held a bazaar where items for worship were sold.

Luke names the eleven apostles Jesus had chosen (Ac 1:2; Lk 6:12-16). By providing this list he's making it clear to Theophilus that the Lord had designated specific men to lead His church. He names Peter, John, James, Andrew, Philip, Thomas, Bartholomew (probably another name for Nathaniel, Jn 1:45), Matthew, James, the son of Alphaeus, Simon the Zealot and Judas, the son of James (probably another name for Thaddeus, Mt 10:3; Mk 3:18). These men had observed the entire three and a half years of Jesus' ministry (Ac 1:22). They had watched Him heal and deliver people, observed His character, been taught by Him, had seen Him in His resurrected state, and finally, had watched as He ascended into heaven. Luke was telling Theophilus (and us) that because of these men, there is every reason to believe that the gospel is true, and that these men are the ones to whom all believers should listen in matters of sound doctrine. These are the foundation stones of the Lord's church (Eph 2:20; Rev 21:14; Mt 16:18).

v14: Jesus told His disciples to "wait for what the Father had promised…" (v4). He had revealed to them their future assignment, but for now they were not to go anywhere. Not yet. Something had to happen first. Now they were to go back into the city and wait. Thankfully in this verse, Luke gives us a brief, but carefully worded description of what took place during those ten days. He says, "All of these were continually giving their attention to prayer with one mind…" (literal). There are at least four elements to observe here.

The first element to observe is the statement, "all of these." It tells us they waited as a community. They didn't scatter. Both men and women, not just the Eleven, gathered daily. Luke specifically mentions that the group included "…women and Mary the mother of Jesus and …His brothers." This reference to "women" would have undoubtedly included Salome (Mary's sister), Mary, the wife of Clopas (Joseph's brother? See: Alfred Edersheim, The Life and Times of Jesus the Messiah, E.R. Herrick and Co., 1853-1890, Vol. 2, pp602-603), Mary Magdalene, Mary, the mother of James and John (Mt 22:55-56; Jn 19:25), John Mark's mother who was also named Mary (Ac 12:12), very possibly Joanna, the wife of Chuza, Herod Antipas' steward, Susanna, and "many others" (Lk 8:1-3). We often overlook the fact that there was a group of women disciples who traveled with Jesus and the Twelve. Luke also mentions Jesus' mother and His brothers. Though His brothers had been antagonistic toward His ministry, some obviously had a change of heart when they saw their eldest brother resurrected (Mt 12:46-47; 13:55-56; Jn 7:1-10; 1Co 15:7). The word which is translated here as "women" can also mean "wife," and since we know that some, and maybe all, the disciples were married (Mt 8:14; 1Co 9:5), a number of their wives may have been present as well.

The second element to observe in this sentence is the statement, "continually giving their attention to." It means they set aside other things and focused on God. The word Luke uses literally means they "were strong towards." It implies consistent attention and expenditure of energy. In other words, they weren't passive. They actively called on God to do all that He promised. Their goal during this time of waiting was to "prepare the way of the Lord" (Is 40:3-4). Undoubtedly, each one gave attention to his or her own spiritual condition, and would have addressed any unconfessed sin, hidden resentments or wrong attitudes toward God.

The third element to observe in this sentence is the statement, "with one mind." The word Luke uses literally means, "the same mind." He uses it ten times in the book of Acts (1:14; 2:46; 4:24; 5:12; 7:57; 8:6; 12:20; 15:25; 18:12; 19:29). Paul used it in Romans 15:6. It means that a group of people have genuinely agreed as to their purpose and are working together as one to accomplish that purpose. During that time of waiting these disciples refused to withhold themselves from the community of God's people. They loved each other and gathered harmoniously, joyfully pursuing the Lord as a team, not as isolated individuals.

And the fourth element to observe in this sentence is the statement, "in prayer." Those ten days of waiting were largely spent in corporate worship and prayer. In his gospel Luke tells us they went to the temple each day to worship (Lk 24:53); they were "blessing God."

At this point we need to ask an obvious question: How does a group of people pray for ten days? What do they say? One can say all the appropriate things that need to be said in ten minutes, then what? To pray meaningfully for that length of time requires listening to the Spirit, reading the Word (or listening to it being read or recited) and praying specific things as the Spirit leads. When numerous people listen together in unity, and pray out as God guides, a theme emerges and is prayed for in remarkably insightful ways. Then other themes emerge and are prayed for as different people sense God give them something specific. Rather than being chaotic or dull, such Spirit-led prayer becomes very inspiring, and time passes unnoticed. We might suppose that some or all of these elements were present in those meetings.

Undoubtedly, God led them to pray for their city, their families and their nation. Undoubtedly, they declared by faith the great things God would do: that doors would be opened, souls would be saved, the oppressed would be delivered, and the sick would be healed. After all, they had watched Jesus minister, and some had already been sent out by Him to minister in His name, so what they would be doing in the future wasn't a mystery. Jesus had already given them the command, "...as the Father has sent Me, I also send you" (Jn 20:21). So there must have been much faith-filled thanking of God taking place in that upper room and Portico of Solomon. And when over a hundred disciples are doing this together, people take notice. By the time God's appointed day arrived, the Spirit was already mightily at work.

v15: At some point during those days of waiting, Peter "stood up in the midst of the brothers..." and addressed a gathering of about 120 disciples. Apparently, he was already recognized as a leader, and the Eleven put him forward as their spokesman. However, when we use the term "leader," we must remember that Jesus had already profoundly changed their understanding of the purpose of spiritual leadership (Mt 20:20-28; Jn 13:12-17). So Peter should not be thought of as taking control, but rather as someone whom the others considered suitable to serve the need of the moment. Judging from the sensitive, internal nature of their topic, this event almost certainly occurred in the upper room, not in the more public setting of the temple. Replacing Judas Iscariot was not a matter to be discussed in front of unbelievers.

vs16-17: Peter says Judas fulfilled a particular prophecy when he betrayed Jesus. Though he doesn't specifically identify the passage he meant, he says it was one that had been spoken by David. It must have been so familiar to those in the room that he assumed they would all recognize it as soon as he mentioned his subject. Apparently, the purpose of that particular meeting was to choose someone to receive Judas' financial allotment as one of the Twelve. That's why Peter says, "For he was numbered among us and was allotted a portion of this ministry" (literal). If we take this statement very literally, it's possible to conclude that Jesus had customarily shared with each of the Twelve a portion of the financial support given to His ministry (Lk 8:3; Jn 12:4-6, 1Co 9:14). In this way He was providing resources to care for their families since they themselves had stopped working in order to travel with Him.

Ironically, Judas had been the treasurer for the group, and it had, in part, been his frustration over their finances that had made him bitter and finally vulnerable to demonic possession (Lk 22:3-6; Jn 12:4-6).

Having been prayerfully invited to leave his family and livelihood to follow Christ (Lk 6:12-16), it appears that Judas, along with the other eleven, had a "right" to one-twelfth of the revenue designated for family support. But he forfeited that "right" when he betrayed Jesus, so there was now an open share available which could be used to support someone else. That share would allow one more person to go into full-time ministry as an apostle. The Lord had designated twelve positions, and one had been left unused.

It's likely that the passage to which Peter is referring is Psalm 41:6-9. Jesus had quoted from that passage and applied it to His betrayer just before serving the Last Supper in that very room where they were now gathered. Having warned His disciples, "Not all of you are clean" (Jn 13:11), He went on to say, "…I know the ones I have chosen, but it is that the Scripture may be fulfilled, he who eats my bread has lifted up his heel against Me" (Jn 13:18; Ps 41:9; Ps 55:12-14; Mt 26:23-25; Lk 22:21, 23). He quoted this verse while Judas was still in the room.

In Psalm 41:6-9 David laments that he was betrayed by a friend who "ate my bread." Because kings had so much food available to them, they often invited more than their own immediate family to join them. In some cases, certain people were given the "right" to regularly sit at their table (2Sa 9:7, 10, 13; 19:28), and apparently it was one of these who had devised a plot to kill or overthrow David. But Jesus wanted His disciples to understand that David was not merely describing his own betrayal when he spoke these words, he was prophetically describing how the Messiah, the Son of David, would be betrayed as well. Indeed, it could be said that Judas regularly ate at Jesus' table because he received his portion as one of the Twelve, and his "portion" is the matter being attended to in this meeting.

vs18-19: Luke inserts these two verses in order to explain to Theophilus what happened to Judas after he betrayed the Lord. Basically, he ignores the fact that Judas committed suicide (Mt 27:3-10) and tells Theophilus only two things: First, that the money Judas received for betraying Christ, and then returned, was used by the priests to buy a small parcel of ground which came to be considered cursed by the people of the city. They named it the "Field of Blood" since it had been paid for with the money that brought the death of an innocent man

(Ge 4:10). And second, judging from the fact that Luke tells us the grotesque details about Judas' death, it was called the "Field of Blood" because Judas' body may have been dumped on the lot and left there to decompose in the heat of the sun. Luke literally says, "…and having become swollen up he burst asunder and all his bowels poured out." This is the picture of a body rotting in the sun, left unburied in disgrace. The point is that both Judas' body and his field became desolate.

v20: Here Luke returns to Peter's speech. Having pointed out that Judas "was allotted a portion in this ministry" (v17), Peter went on to quote from two more psalms. His first quote seems intended to prove that any claim Judas' family might have on his portion of the financial allotment had been completely forfeited by his actions. Scripture clearly commands that his "camp" become "desolate" (abandoned). In Psalm 69 David laments that he was suffering religious persecution because of his faith in God, and he calls on God to punish those who hated him without cause. One of his requests is, "Let their camp be abandoned, and no one dwell in their tents" (Ps 69:25; Septuagint). In other words, no family members can be allowed to move into that person's empty tent. Not only is the wicked person to be removed, but their family's right to dwell there is removed as well (Job 18:5-6, 14-21).

To this sobering judgment Peter added one more quote from the Psalms. He quoted from Psalm 109 in which David again calls on God to judge his false accusers. One of his requests is, "Let another take his office [his position of authority]" (v8). Peter pointed to this as an expression of righteous judgment on someone who lies about, hates and fights against God's appointed leader. And Judas had done to Jesus what some of David's enemies had done to him, so not just his <u>portion</u> (financial allotment) but his <u>position</u> as one of the Twelve must be given to another. The Lord's original desire to have twelve apostles must be honored (Mt 19:28; Lk 22:30).

vs21-22: Then the process of selecting a replacement began. Peter listed three qualifications for someone to be considered a nominee. First, the nominee must be a man. Second, he must be someone who traveled with Jesus over the entire course of His ministry, beginning the day He arrived at the Jordan River where John was baptizing (Jn 11:29-37) until the day He ascended into heaven (Lk 24:50-51; Ac 1:9-11). And third, he must be an eyewitness of the resurrected Jesus. He must be someone who actually saw Him alive after the crucifixion. What is surprising is that there were numerous people present who fit these criteria. Obviously, there must have been many more than twelve who regularly traveled with Jesus.

v23: Luke doesn't tell us how the two nominees were chosen, but it appears they were selected by the larger gathering after evaluating those among them in order to discover who might meet Peter's qualifications. Joseph Barsabbas (son of the Sabbath), who also had a Roman name, Justus (just, righteous) is the first one mentioned. The other was Matthias whom the church historian Eusebius (A.D. 260-340) said was one of the 70 disciples Jesus sent out, two by two (Lk 10:1) (F.F. Bruce, Acts, Eerdmans, reprint 1974, pp50-51).

vs24-25: After choosing two nominees, the entire gathering prayed, addressing God as the "heart-knower" (Ac 15:8) and asking Him to "lift up" the one whom He had already chosen to take Judas' place in this "ministry and apostleship" because Judas had "turned aside to go into his own place."

This act of replacing one of the Twelve was a unique event. Judas was not being replaced because he died. All but one of the remaining Eleven would die a martyr's death, but no one was nominated to replace them. Jesus left no instructions for there to be a perpetual Twelve. Judas was being replaced by that gathering because he had been disqualified, leaving his position empty and his allotment unused. Yet the Lord had said the Twelve would have a role to play in the future Messianic Age (Millennium) (Lk 22:30; Mt 19:28), so this group intended to restore the Lord's original design, not start a second generation of the Twelve.

v26: After the nominees were selected, and after the Lord was asked to reveal His choice, "they gave lots for them and the lot fell on Matthias..." (literal). A common Jewish way of casting lots was to inscribe a name on a small stone or piece of wood, and these were placed into a jar, or another container of some kind, and shaken. The lot that fell out first was the one chosen (W.E. Vine, Expository Dictionary of the N.T.). Much has been said about their method of selection. Some consider it an immature form of decision-making which showed that the disciples were not yet baptized with the Holy Spirit and therefore unable to discern God's choice in a more mature way. Some have said they should not have nominated any replacement because Paul would become the true Twelfth Apostle (1Co 15:8-11). But the process of casting lots has deep roots in Judaism. This is how the land of Israel was divided among the tribes and families (Jos 7:14-18), and this is how David scheduled the priests for service in the sanctuary (1Ch 24:3-5). The Urim and Thummim were used by the High Priest to determine the Lord's will in certain situations, and though there are still questions about how the process worked, they were very likely a form of casting lots (Ex 28:30; Nu 27:21; 1Sa 14:3, 37:42; 23:6-12). It should also be noted that, if indeed, the person chosen would receive Judas' financial allotment, the process of casting lots, after the entire assembly had nominated the candidates, prevented any accusation of favoritism. It was actually a very wise and righteous way of replacing that position. And based on the criteria Peter gave for being one of the Twelve, Paul didn't qualify. He hadn't observed Jesus during His ministry, but Paul was certainly an apostle. There were many more than twelve who were designated as apostles by the early church. But this group wasn't nominating apostles; they were replacing Judas. And the Holy Spirit had led them to do it before the Day of Pentecost, and in such a way that there could be no doubt that God alone made the final choice. By the way, later tradition says Matthias carried the gospel to Ethiopia (F.F. Bruce, Acts, Eerdmans, reprint 1974, p51).

Acts Chapter 2

v1: Ten days earlier the Lord had commanded His disciples to wait in Jerusalem until they received the promised gift of the Holy Spirit (Ac 1:4). He said when that gift came they would be baptized with the Holy Spirit like John baptized people with water (Ac 1:5). Over the course of those ten days they met continually to prepare themselves and wait. Now Luke will describe in beautiful detail the moment when that gift arrived. It came after the seven weeks which lead up to the Feast of Pentecost (Shavuot) were completed, and the 50th day had arrived. On that day all the disciples had gathered together.

v2: Then Luke says, "…and suddenly out of heaven there came a sound as if being carried along on a strong gust of wind, and that sound filled the whole house where they were sitting" (literal). Luke pictures the disciples gathered in the upper room sometime during the early part of the morning (v15). That gathering could not have taken place in the temple because the temple gates did not open until nine o'clock for the morning sacrifice. Since all were gathered on that special day, we may assume that most or all of the 120 he mentioned earlier (Ac 1:15) were present. They were sitting down at the time. Usually when this verse is translated, it is interpreted to mean that they suddenly heard the sound of a great windstorm, but Luke chooses his words very carefully. He's trying to describe for us a very remarkable spiritual experience. And taking his words literally here's what seems to have happened: As they were sitting in the upper room during a time of morning prayer and praise, suddenly everyone heard a sound that seemed to be coming from heaven. It grew louder and louder until it reached them, and when it did, they felt its impact as if they had been struck by a strong gust of wind. Then this heavenly sound surrounded them, filling the whole room.

We have no way of knowing what they heard, whether it was music or singing or angelic praise or the voice of God Himself (Ex 19:16, 19; Eze 1:24-25; Lk 2:13; 1Co 13:1; Rev 5:8-14; 19:6), but they physically felt it come over them like a wind, and then they were enveloped by it.

v3 Next, they saw a bright light like flames of fire which divided itself into portions, and those portions moved about the room until a fiery light hovered over each person (lit: "it sat on each one"). Luke says, "And there appeared to them tongues of fire dividing themselves, and a portion rested upon each one of them" (literal).

There would have been no mistaking the message: The Holy Spirit had come to dwell in that person. To Jewish believers, no symbol would have been more familiar than the pillar of cloud and fire which led Israel through the wilderness and rested over the tabernacle. The pillar of fire was God's powerful presence manifested in such a way that all could see it. So when tongues like fire were distributed over each head, it made a clear statement that this human body was now a "tabernacle" in which the Spirit of God dwelt. That original pillar of fire had not hovered over the tabernacle or temple for centuries, but it had come to earth from heaven and was now hovering over the disciples of Jesus Christ. When Jesus Himself had been baptized with the Holy Spirit, John saw the Spirit come and rest on Him like a dove (Mt 3:16). Now in the upper room, the Spirit appeared as a fiery light resting over each head.

v4: When that fiery light rested over each one, Luke says, "...they were filled with the Holy Spirit and began to speak in other languages just as the Spirit gave them to speak out" (literal). Jesus had assured His disciples that the Holy Spirit would someday live inside them (Jn 14:17), and this was the moment when that promise was fulfilled for the first time. A new era had begun in the relationship between God's Spirit and His people. Never before had the Holy Spirit inhabited the sin-contaminated bodies of human beings, even though from Adam and Eve onward people had become righteous by faith (Mt 11:11; Heb 11:2, 7, 13, 39-40). In the Old Testament the Holy Spirit was with God's people, sometimes at a remarkably intense level, but never before had He been in them. By responding and putting their faith in God's mercy, the barrier of sin was removed for those who loved God in the Old Testament, but their physical bodies remained "unclean." They were not yet suitable to serve as a place of residence for God's Spirit because those bodies had been used as instruments of sin.

What made it possible for the Spirit to dwell within a person was the death of Christ. On the cross He atoned not only the human spirit (our rebellion, independence, selfishness, pride…), but the human body as well (Ro 8:3-4, 9-11). When God's Son took on our sinful flesh by being born as a man, and when the wrath of God fell on that flesh as He died on the cross, He lifted God's judgment from our bodies so that this inner baptism could take place. Though the full redemption of our bodies will not take place until the resurrection (Ro 8:23; 1Co 15:54), God's judgment against those bodies has been lifted, "cleansing" those bodies so that they are suitable habitations for His Spirit. In other words, Christ's death allows the Spirit to come inside us and to remain in us, even when we sin. So here on the Day of Pentecost we see the Ascended Christ bestow on His people, for the first time, not only the gift of forgiveness but the gift of the indwelling Spirit who, from that moment on, will grant them unlimited power for ministry and personal holiness.

When this infilling took place, a remarkable manifestation occurred. Every one of the disciples began speaking in a language they had never learned. Luke says they spoke words that the Spirit gave them to speak out. There is no record of such a miracle ever taking place before this. There are numerous examples in the Old Testament of God's Spirit coming upon people with the result that they spoke out prophetically in their own native language, but never in a new, unlearned language. Yet, as we read on in the book of Acts, we discover this was not an isolated incident. Luke records the phenomenon, or indirectly refers to it, numerous times. Apparently it occurred again when Peter and John laid hands on Philip's converts in Samaria (Ac 8:12-18). It is reasonable to assume it occurred when Ananias laid hands on Paul (Ac 9:17;

1Co 14:18). Luke specifically states it occurred when Peter preached to the household of a Roman centurion named Cornelius (Ac 10:44-48; 11:15-18), and also when Paul laid his hands on twelve disciples of Apollos in Ephesus 26 years after the Day of Pentecost (Ac 19:1-6). In a letter to the church in Corinth Paul made it clear that he considered every believer to be capable of speaking in an unlearned language and encouraged them to do so (1Co 14:5). However, he cautioned them that they should speak primarily in known languages when they gathered for a church service (1Co 14:1-12).

vs5-8: There was also another miracle which took place on the Day of Pentecost besides speaking in tongues. It was a miracle of hearing. Luke says, "And there were Jews dwelling in Jerusalem, devout men [those who fear God and are careful to obey His Word] from every nation under heaven. And when this 'voice' [sound of many voices] occurred, the multitude came together to listen and were confused because each person heard the entire group of disciples speaking in his or her own dialect" (literal). Luke describes their response: He says they were shocked (beside themselves) (v12) and full of curiosity saying, "Behold aren't all these who are speaking Galileans, then why do we hear them each in our own language in which we were born?" (literal). Please notice Luke's wording. Thousands of Jews were present from all the surrounding regions, people who had undoubtedly learned to speak several different languages in order to function in that multicultural world (Greek, Latin, Hebrew, etc.), but Luke specifically says that each person, regardless of where he or she had been born, was hearing the whole group of disciples speaking <u>one</u> language. And he says each person understood what was being said because he or she heard the entire group of disciples speaking in the language in which he or she had been raised as a child. He literally says they heard the language in which they were born. So on the Day of Pentecost God miraculously caused everyone in the multitude to understand everything that was being said by a group that was speaking multiple languages.

vs9-11: To show us the extent of this miracle Luke lists some of the distant places from which people in that multitude had come. There were Parthians, Medes and Elamites (Iran), Mesopotamians (Iraq), Judeans (Israel), Cappadocians (central Turkey, eastern part), people from Pontus (northern Turkey), Asia (western Turkey), Phrygia (central Turkey, western part), Pamphylia (southern Turkey), Egypt, and as far west along the North African coast as the city of Cyrene in Libya. There were visitors from Rome, both Jews and Gentiles (who had converted to Judaism), people from the island of Crete to the west, and Arabia to the east. Yet everyone understood what the disciples were saying because each one heard the group speaking in his or her native tongue. And what they heard them saying was praise to God. They were declaring the great things God had done. They may have heard prophetic declarations similar to those which Mary (Lk 1:46:55) or Zacharias (Lk 1:68-75) uttered.

vs12-13: Most of them became frightened and confused, saying to one another "What does this mean?" But there were others who mocked what they saw, saying, "They are filled with sweet wine." As is so often the case when God does a miracle, there were people present that day who recognized that God was doing something and honestly wanted to understand it, but there were also others in the crowd, who may have understood that this was a work of God, but who quickly devalued what they saw. They stripped it of spiritual significance, so they could avoid being held accountable by God to repent and participate with this group of believers in Jesus.

v14: On the day before Pentecost tens of thousands of pilgrims entered the city of Jerusalem. When the first stars appeared in that evening sky, priests in the temple sounded silver trumpets to announce that the feast had begun, but the Pentecost offering itself would not take place until the sun rose the next morning. Then, when the gates were opened and the morning sacrifice had been made, the people themselves presented to the Lord a loaf of leavened bread made from wheat flour and two, year-old lambs; one lamb for a sin offering and one for a peace or fellowship offering (Josephus, Antiquities, 3.10.6; 17.10.2). Shortly after midnight the temple gates had been opened so that the sacrificial animals which the people would present the next day could be inspected by lamplight to ensure that each one was without blemish. Many priests worked through the night to carry out these inspections (Edersheim, The Temple, Eerdmans, reprint 1988, p263).

Meanwhile a priest was posted on the pinnacle of the temple to "watch for the morning." When the first ray of sunlight was seen shining on the hills around Hebron (Abraham's ancient home, 19 miles to the southwest), the signal was given to begin the regular, morning sacrifice. This would have taken place around 9:00am. Three blasts on silver trumpets called the people to assemble (Nu 10:2, 10). When that signal was heard, the multitude began to move through the streets toward the temple. And it was while this was taking place that the sound of 120 (or more) voices suddenly could be heard praising God in foreign languages.

It's no surprise that such boisterous worship caught the attention of many pilgrims and drew them toward the large, roof-top shelter from which the sound was coming. The narrow streets around that house were almost certainly not a satisfactory place to address a huge crowd, so at some point the disciples must have moved to a location large enough to permit thousands to assemble and listen to an explanation of what had just taken place. The most likely site was the broad southern steps leading up to the temple. In effect those great, stone steps provided an amphitheater where the crowd could sit and listen while Peter and the Eleven stood at the base of the steps speaking to those arrayed above them, thus allowing their voices to be heard by all.

vs14-16: Luke says, "And standing with the Eleven, Peter lifted up his voice and declared to them, 'Men, Jews, and all those living in Jerusalem, let this be known to you, and listen to my words, for these are not drunk as was mistakenly reported to you, for it is the third hour of the day [9:00am]. But this is that which was spoken through the prophet Joel'" (literal). Peter was answering their question: "What does this mean?" (v12), and what he said was stunning. He announced that the last days had begun. He told the multitude that the miracle they were observing wasn't simply <u>like</u> the miracles which the Bible prophesies will happen at the end of the age, this was the first expression of those miracles.

Most of those listening to him would have been taught since they were children what to expect when the Messiah came. They knew the different ministries He would perform when He came in power to establish His Kingdom. Two of those ministries are described by Joel: First, the Messiah will pour out the Holy Spirit on all Israel, restoring their relationship with God to a far deeper level than it had ever been before. And second, He will rescue those who call on the name of the Lord. He will arrive at a time when Israel will be under attack by gentile armies, and He will destroy those armies in a great battle (Joel 3:1-3, 9-17), the smoke of which will darken the sky until the sun and moon are barely visible through the thick gloom. In the midst of that battle, the sun will grow dark and the moon will glow with an ominous red color. Then He will liberate Jerusalem from under the foot of the Gentiles, and an age of prosperity will begin. The Messiah Himself will rule the earth from Jerusalem.

In effect, Peter told that great congregation: "The Messiah has come, yes, in a way most of us didn't expect because we didn't fully understand the Scriptures, but He has come. And since He is the central feature that makes the "last days" the "last days," just as the prophets promised, He is now pouring out the Holy Spirit. Even though the final battle which will happen at the end of the age has not occurred, the Messiah has, nonetheless, begun to rescue all who will call on His name" (paraphrase). The end of human history had not yet arrived; they all knew that. In fact, Jesus had recently made that chronology very clear to them (Ac 1:6,7). But the most wonderful part of the last days, the arrival of the Messiah Himself, had happened. And now He had begun to pour out the Spirit, not on all Israel, but on all who believed in Him. And He was rescuing all who called on Him.

vs17-21: Here is a literal translation of Peter's words from the Greek: "'And it shall be in the last days,' says God, 'I will pour out from My Spirit upon all flesh, and your sons and daughters will prophesy, and your young [men] will see visions and your old [men] will dream dreams, and upon My male servants and upon my female servants, in those days, I will pour out from My Spirit and they will prophesy. And I will give wonders [miraculous disruptions of nature] in the heavens above [day and night sky]; and signs [miracles that point to a truth about God] on the earth below, blood and fire and vapor [steam] of smoke. The sun will be turned into darkness and the moon into blood before the great and glorious [shining with light] Day of the Lord comes. And it will be that whoever calls on the name of the Lord will be saved'" (Ac 2:17-21; Joel 2:28-32).

v22: Having just quoted from the prophet Joel to explain to the crowd why the disciples spoke with other tongues, and having concluded with the words, "And it shall be that everyone who calls on the name of the Lord will be saved," Peter announced to this great crowd that the name they must call upon is the name "Jesus." But he knew that there was a theological barrier in their minds which would prevent them from calling on that name. That barrier was a confused, or at least incomplete, understanding of what the Bible says will happen when the Messiah arrives. So the next thing he did was to show them prophetic passages they had previously overlooked. He wanted them to see that Jesus' death, resurrection and ascension were clearly prophesied in their Scriptures.

The common assumption held by the vast majority of that crowd would have been that Jesus' crucifixion proved beyond the shadow of a doubt that He could not have been the true Messiah. Since childhood they had only been taught about a Messiah who would come as a powerful warrior to defeat Israel's enemies, and who would be a spiritual leader who turned the entire nation back to God. So in their minds no one who had been disgracefully executed, as Jesus had been, could possibly be the Messiah. Yes, He had done amazing miracles, and some in the crowd undoubtedly still thought of Him as a prophet (Lk 24:19), but they were convinced that His "weakness" in allowing Himself to be executed proved He could not be the Messiah. So Peter turned to the Scriptures to show them that they were wrong.

Though he was about to indict them for executing their Messiah, Peter again (v14) addressed the crowd respectfully. He said, "Men, Israelites, hear these words." Later, he would call them "brethren" (v29), and the crowd responded by calling the disciples "brethren" (v37). In light of all that had taken place in that city just 40 days earlier, the warmth in this exchange is surprising. Obviously, Peter's goal was to win their hearts, not rage against them for crucifying his master. He introduced Jesus by using the title, "Jesus the Nazarene." It was the common practice of the day to identify a man by his place of residence (Jn 11:1; 19:38; Ac 9:11). There were many men in Israel at that time with the name "Jesus" (derived from Joshua), so to distinguish which Jesus someone was talking about, a person's hometown was added, and to distinguish between numerous people with the same name within the same town, the name of the person's father was added (son of…) (Lk 4:22; Jn 6:42).

The title "Jesus of Nazareth" or "Jesus the Nazarene" was the most common way of identifying Him (Mk 1:24; 10:47; 14:67; 16:6; Lk 24:19; Jn 1:45; 18:5; Ac 3:6, 4:10; 6:14; 26:9). It was the title Pilate placed over Him on the cross (Jn 19:19), and the title Jesus used to introduce Himself to Saul on the road to Damascus (Ac 22:8). Peter reminded the crowd of the stunning level of divine confirmation which had accompanied Jesus everywhere He went. God had showed His approval of this man by performing countless numbers of miracles through Him such as healings, deliverances, the multiplication of loaves and fish, and even raising the dead. His ministry had been filled with "wonders" (startling proofs that God was with Him) and "signs" (undeniable miracles that pointed to the truth of who He was). Many of those living in Israel had seen those miracles firsthand, and virtually everyone had heard about them (Lk 24:18-19). So Peter could boldly point to them and declare that they were done "…in your midst, as you yourselves know…" (literal), and no one, not even the nation's religious leaders, could dispute that fact (Jn 3:1-2; 11:45-48; 12:9-11).

v23: Yet in spite of all those signs and wonders, a majority of those present at Jesus' trial had supported the decision to execute Him. Though Roman soldiers actually carried out the crucifixion itself, it was the religious leaders and the crowd who had gathered to watch that bore most of the moral responsibility. The event would not have happened had not Caiaphas, the Sanhedrin and the chanting crowd all pushed for execution. So Peter boldly confronts them with their guilt. He says, "…you nailed Him [to a cross] by the hand of godless men [Roman soldiers] and put Him to death." His boldness at that moment was remarkable. For a man who only days before had fearfully denied to a servant girl he even knew Jesus, Peter now had the courage to stand in front of thousands and tell them, in unmistakable terms, that they were morally responsible for killing their Messiah. Seeing the resurrected Jesus and being baptized with the Holy Spirit had obviously transformed Peter into a fearless and eloquent spokesman for His Lord.

The crucifixion could never have taken place unless God had allowed it. Peter tells the crowd that their failure to recognize their Messiah had been prophesied. A clearly defined plan, and the foreknowledge of God, was behind everything that had happened. Proof of this lay in the fact that Jesus' death, resurrection and ascension were predicted in the writings of the prophets. Notice: Peter isn't simply asking the crowd to believe that a dead man came to life; he's asking them to see that the Scriptures say the Messiah will die and come back to life. Once they realized that these truths were found in their Scriptures, then showing them that Jesus was the One who had fulfilled those prophecies would be relatively easy. Most of the crowd already knew the events that had taken place in Jerusalem (Lk 24:18), and many had probably heard rumors of a resurrection, so the main obstacle that prevented them from believing in Jesus was an incomplete understanding of the Messiah. So Peter reminded them of two key passages in the Psalms.

v24: First, he described the resurrection of Jesus as an escape from the grip of death. Jesus had truly died, but because He was holy (pure, without sin), death was not able to hold Him; it was forced to release Him. He said Jesus was the One "whom God raised up, loosening the cords [birth pangs] of death because it was not possible for Him to be held by it [death]" (literal).

vs25-28: To explain why death couldn't hold Jesus, Peter quoted from Psalm 16:8-11. In that psalm David said he was confident that God would preserve him even after he died, and based that confidence on the spiritual principle that God will not allow someone who is perfectly holy to "see destruction" (meaning decay in the grave), nor abandon His soul (physical life, breath) to the realm of the dead (Sheol, Hades).

v29: But David did die, and by the time Peter quoted this verse, David had been decaying in a tomb for over a thousand years. So David himself was disqualified from being this "Holy One." The psalmist must have been speaking about someone else.

This declaration from Psalm 16 must have been one of the passages Jesus explained to His disciples after He was resurrected (Lk 24:27, 45). As we listen to Peter, it's clear Jesus taught them that David's words were meant to be taken literally. When taken literally, the prophecy says that if a person is perfectly sinless and devoted to serving God, that person's body will not decay after dying but will come back to life. The passage acknowledges that this "Holy One" will experience death, but says, in effect, that the person will not stay dead long enough to decompose. Paul quoted this same verse, and made the same application, in his sermon to the synagogue in Pisidian Antioch on his first missionary journey (Ac 13:34-37).

vs30-31: If David's statement didn't apply to himself since he did decay after he died, then to whom did it apply? Peter answered this question by saying that David never thought of himself as this "Holy One," and we need only remember the events of David's life to realize it's more likely that he thought of himself as a sinner who had received undeserved mercy (Ps 51). Instead, he was prophetically looking into the future and "seeing" the coming Messiah, whom God had promised David would be one of his descendants (2Sa 7:12-13; Ps 132:11). In other words, David was not confident in his own holiness; he was confident that he would not be left in a grave because death would not be able to hold the Messiah in a grave. And by escaping death the Messiah would insure that all believers will someday escape death as well. This means that by raising Jesus from the grave God indisputably confirmed that Jesus is the promised "Holy One," and therefore the Messiah.

v32: At this point Peter, speaking on behalf of the Twelve and many others present, said, "This Jesus God raised up again, to which we are all witnesses." In other words, "We who stand before you testify that we have seen with our own eyes David's prophecy fulfilled. The person you crucified and put in a grave did not decay. Death couldn't hold Him, and by resurrecting Him God declared Jesus to be this "Holy One" of whom David spoke" (paraphrase).

vs33-35: Having proclaimed the resurrection, Peter next proclaimed the ascension. He wanted the crowd to know that not only had Jesus come back to life, but God had physically lifted Him up to heaven and seated Him at His right hand.

This fulfilled another prophecy found in another psalm. As was the case with Psalm 16:8-11, there is a statement made in Psalm 110 which pictures a situation in which David cannot be speaking about himself because this event did not happen to him. In Psalm 110:1 David wrote: "The Lord said to My Lord, sit at My right hand until I make your enemies a footstool for your feet," but as Peter observes, "…it was not David who ascended into heaven…." So this statement must refer to someone greater. During His public ministry Jesus quoted this verse to show that it had been prophesied that the Messiah would be more than David's human descendant; He would also be divine (Mt 22:41-46; Mk 12:35-37; Lk 20:41-44). By the way, Jesus specifically stated that David spoke these words "…in the Spirit" (Mt 22:43), meaning that David was prophesying. He wrote down the words he heard the Spirit speak to him.

This psalm pictures God the Father speaking to the resurrected Messiah, whom David refers to as "my Lord," telling Him to sit at His right hand (the position of greatest honor) until He (the Father) had gone to war against the Messiah's enemies and brought them into total submission to Him ("a footstool for your feet"). In effect Peter is telling the crowd to beware; Jesus is not only the resurrected Messiah who defeated death, He is also the ascended Lord to whom God has given all authority to rule and judge. He was warning his listeners that a day would surely come when they would all stand before Jesus to give an account for their deeds. The disciples had already seen Jesus alive from the dead. At the judgment, all who were listening to Peter would stand before "this Jesus whom you crucified."

The proof that Jesus ascended to the Father's right hand was there in front of them: It was the outpouring of the Holy Spirit which that crowd had observed on that Pentecost morning (v33). One of the main promises concerning the Messiah, which they all knew, was that when He began to rule, He would pour out the Holy Spirit on God's people (Isa 11:9; Jer 31:34; Eze 36:26-27; 37:9-10, 14). So as he preached, Peter must have pointed toward the disciples who had been, and maybe still were, speaking in tongues. There was the evidence. His listeners could not deny that a miracle had taken place because each had been part of that miracle. Each had heard them speaking in his or her native language. They too had been part of that miraculous event.

v36: Peter confronted the crowd with their guilt and called for decision. He said, "Therefore, let all the house of Israel know with certainty [that what I'm telling you is solid, reliable; it won't collapse under your feet; it won't cause you to trip and fall] that God made this Jesus whom you crucified both Lord and Christ" (literal). By calling Jesus "Lord"

Peter pointed to the fact that Jesus was more than David's human descendant, He was also David's king. Peter draws the title from Psalm 110:1 where David calls the Messiah "my Lord." By seating Jesus at His right hand, the Father placed Him in the position of supreme authority and as judge over all creation (Php 2:9-11; 1Co 15:24-28; Heb 1:2-3). There is no ignoring the fact that such power and authority rightfully belong only to God (Dt 6:4). By applying the title "Lord" to Jesus, Peter was declaring His divinity. He was introducing Jesus as the Messiah (David's human descendant), but also as God's divine Son. This is why believers in every generation can call on Jesus' name to be saved. It's why the Father commands the human race to bow our knee to Jesus in full surrender. It's why all humanity and the angels will someday be judged at Jesus' throne.

v37: Thousands of those listening to Peter recognized that what He said about the Messiah was true. They were struck with a deep conviction that they had directly or indirectly participated in the execution of the promised Holy One, and as a result, would someday stand before Him in judgment. Luke says they were "stabbed in the heart," meaning a deep, troubling conviction came over them. They were filled with sorrow for what had happened in the past and with fear for what lay ahead in the future. They called out to Peter and the other apostles who were standing with him, "Brethren, what can we do?" In other words they were asking, "Is there a way for us to escape the wrath which will fall on us for doing such a thing?"

v38: Peter answered using terms with which they were all very familiar. For years John the Baptist had challenged the nation to "Repent, and let each of you be baptized" (Mk 1:4); and many had responded to his call and been baptized in the Jordan River (Mt 3:5-6). But unlike John, Peter didn't warn them about "One who is coming" (Mk 1:7); he announced that the Messiah had already come. Having just quoted a passage from the prophet Joel, which concludes with the words, "And it shall be that everyone who calls on the name of the Lord will be saved" (v21), Peter said the Lord's name is Jesus. And then he explained that the way to "call upon" that name is to repent and be water baptized. He said if they would do this they would receive the same "gift of the Holy Spirit."

English translations of this verse do not normally translate it literally because Peter used a preposition which initially appears to make no sense. He literally instructed his listeners to be baptized upon Jesus' name. Elsewhere in Scripture people are normally described as being baptized "in" or "into" someone or someone's name (Ac 8:16; 10:48; 19:5; Ro 6:3; 1Co 1:13, 15; 10:2; Gal 3:27). So his substitution of the word "upon" is confusing until we recognize that he was deliberately echoing the wording found in Joel's prophecy. Joel said, "... everyone who calls upon the name of the Lord will be saved" (v21, literal). By telling his listeners to be baptized "upon" Jesus' name, Peter was explaining that baptism was a symbolic way of calling upon Jesus to save them. It was a God-ordained way of expressing repentance, of putting faith in the death and resurrection of Jesus, and of calling on God for mercy because of what Jesus had done (Ro 10:13). In effect, the act of baptism was a form of prayer, a cry to God for help, a spiritual language understood by heaven as clearly as words.

v39: Peter referred to this gift of the Holy Spirit as "the promise," echoing the Lord's earlier instruction to "wait for what the Father had promised" (Ac 1:4). Jesus had said when this promise arrive, people would be "baptized with the Holy Spirit" (see Ac 1:4,5), and Peter was explaining that because of Jesus, it was now available to every believer, regardless of age, location or spiritual history (Jew or Gentile). He added that it would continue to be available to all, future generations whenever and wherever people were responding to God's call, and he specifically mentioned that "the promise" was meant to include "your children" (literal). It's very possible that children were fresh on his mind because children had been present in the upper room when the Spirit arrived, and they too may have spoken in tongues.

v40: Luke recorded only part of Peter's sermon, so he informs us that "...with many other words, beyond these, he [Peter] thoroughly testified [concerning Jesus] and exhorted them saying, 'Be saved from this perverse generation which has chosen to walk away from God's true path'" (literal). Peter warns his listeners that they are part of a "perverse" (lit: crooked, bent, winding) generation. The word which is generally translated as "perverse" pictures people wandering away from God's path. They refuse to stay on His straight path of truth choosing instead to walk crooked paths of deception. Even when Jesus Himself did miracles among them, most refused to repent and call on God for mercy. That generation was marked by extremes of lawlessness and legalism. Jesus told them that no matter who God sent they always found a reason to criticize the messenger and reject God's appeal to repent (Mt 11:16-19). They loved to watch miracles but refused to reflect on their own spiritual condition (Mt 11:20-24). Jesus Himself called them an "unbelieving and perverted [lit: distorted, twisted in two] generation," and had asked in exasperation, "...how long shall I be with you? How long shall I put up with you?" (Mt 17:17).

vs41-42: About 3,000 people responded to Peter's message that day and were baptized. If indeed this gathering was held on or near the southern steps of the temple (see notes on Ac 2:14), there were many places near those steps where people could be baptized. Water tanks which contained at least 85 gallons can still be seen in the archeological ruins. These tanks, called "mikvehs" were used for ritual cleansing (Miriam Feinberg Vamosh, Daily Life at the Time of Jesus, Palphot Ltd., PO Box 2, Herzliya, Israel, pp26-27). Under certain circumstances people need to be ceremonially cleansed before entering the temple. That person would walk down one side of the steps, immerse themselves completely, and then walk back out on the other side of the steps. Between the very familiar experience of these ritual baths and the recent ministries of John the Baptist and Jesus (Jn 3:22-23, 26; 4:1-2), that crowd would have easily understood what Peter meant when he called them to be baptized. And as we've noted, there was plenty of water available for 3000 people to line up and be baptized immediately.

From the very first day of its existence, the church numbered in the multiple thousands, and Luke explains how so many new believers were cared for. He says they continually and energetically gathered in two different settings. First there was a large, public assembly held in the temple courtyard in the shade of the Portico of Solomon (Ac 5:12). That daily gathering drew many onlookers, and was the place where the apostles had the opportunity to speak to everyone at once. Undoubtedly their sermons were filled with memories of what Jesus said and did. They must have taught primarily from those passages of Scripture that He had explained to them, and prayed for the sick and cast out demons just as He had done in that same courtyard. In other words, they continued Jesus' ministry. This was the gathering where much evangelism took place (Ac 5:14). But as we read on in the book of Acts, we will see this public gathering come under growing persecution by the temple officials (Ac 4:1-3, 18-20; 5:17-18, 40-42) until Stephen was stoned. After that, open violence, led by Saul of Tarsus, drove believers into hiding and caused many to flee Jerusalem (Ac 8:1-4).

In these early days of the church, Luke says the believers were continually and energetically "pressing into" both the teaching of the apostles and something he calls "koinonia." Koinonia is the word he uses to describe the life they shared together as a community. He pictures those first believers entering into a family-like commitment to each other. People did not get baptized and then return to their former way of life. They immediately became part of a dynamic pattern of communal life: day after day they met in the temple courtyard in large public assemblies, and day after day they met in homes where they ate and prayed together.

v43: Their gatherings at the temple must have drawn many onlookers. There, the apostles preached, taught, prayed for the sick and cast out demons. They followed the same model of ministry as Jesus Himself had used. The continuous flow of miracles that resulted from this kept the whole city profoundly aware that God was powerfully present. No one could think of Jesus as simply one more religious leader or His teachings as one more school of philosophy. A person needed only go to the temple on any given day and watch the sick healed or people being baptized with the Holy Spirit to be reminded that God is real and present and sees everything we do. Luke literally says, "...and fear came to every soul." His meaning is clear: People became very careful in the way they conducted themselves. Hidden sins declined as people grew aware that God was watching everything they did. There was a widespread consciousness in that city being in God's presence. Doubt was at a low level.

v44: In this passage (vs42-47) Luke pictures the depth of their communal life. He says, "...and all who believed upon it [the name of the Lord] had all things common [as common property]." In Acts 4:32 he is even more precise in the way he says this: "...not one said any of his possessions was his own, but all things were common to them."

v45: They were selling real estate (houses, fields, land) and other possessions (livestock, jewelry, heirlooms...) and were giving the revenue into a fund managed by the apostles (Ac 4:34, 35), who then "divided to all as anyone had need." They were living out Isaiah 58:7: Dividing their bread with the hungry, bringing homeless poor into the house, clothing the naked and caring for the impoverished members of their own family. We should emphasize that none of this was planned or required by the church leaders. These were individual acts of generosity in response to genuine need.

v46: One of the main ways this sharing of resources took place was by means of daily, common meals. They must have taken regular offerings to pay for the food. Feeding a houseful of guests each day would have cost way too much for any one family to afford. In this verse Luke reminds us that their communal life was expressed in two gatherings: a large gathering in the temple (for teaching, evangelism and ministry), and many small gatherings in private homes throughout the city where they ate and prayed together in an atmosphere filled with the joy of the Lord and a sincere love for one another.

v47: The conversations between believers which were held in these home meetings were filled with praise to God. There was so much to give thanks for. Jesus had saved them by His death and resurrection, and He was mightily at work doing miracles among them. The more they prayed together, the more they saw God answer their prayers. The more they testified to answered prayer, the more everyone's faith grew. Constant intercession must have been going on for unbelieving family and friends, and then when spiritual breakthrough arrived, delighted announcements would have been shared with everyone. This, combined with praise for all God was doing in their gatherings at the temple, created an atmosphere of celebration and hope.

All those qualities produced a community that was attractive to everyone in the city. Luke says they had "favor with all the people, and day after day the Lord was adding the ones being saved upon it [saved by calling upon the name of the Lord]" (literal). Their reputation was excellent, and their gatherings were open and welcoming, so whether people came to faith at the temple or around a dining table, they were immediately adopted into this growing, spiritual family. By saying, "…the Lord was adding the ones being saved…" Luke is explaining that this remarkable growth was the result of a divine move of God. In no way was it merely the result of human planning or persuasiveness.

Something was happening that cannot be produced by human effort. The growth of the church in that season went far beyond what any human skill or strategy can generate. That does not mean that it is wrong to employ human skill and strategy in the work of evangelism. It's not; those qualities can be very helpful. God is at work every time an individual is converted, whether that conversion comes by a miraculous move of God or by a coordinated program of outreach. He alone is the One who convicts us of sin, reveals the way of salvation and gives us faith to be saved. Without the work of the Holy Spirit no one is able to come to God. But the fundamental truth that God is at work in the salvation of the individual is not what Luke is describing here. What he is describing here is something much bigger. During that season in Jerusalem the ingathering of souls was so enormous that it was evident to all that they were merely helping God. His Spirit, not their efforts, was responsible for all that was taking place.

Acts Chapter 3

v1: During the early days following Pentecost "many signs and wonders were taking place through the apostles" (Ac 2:43), and now Luke describes one of those miracles. The particular event he chose to highlight was so amazing it produced another large ingathering of believers (Ac 4:4) and brought the apostles into direct confrontation with the nation's religious leaders (Ac 4:5-7). He says Peter and John were going up into the temple at the "ninth hour," so it's natural to assume they were headed to the temple to observe the evening sacrifice, which took place every day at the "ninth hour." By that time of year this sacrifice would have been performed at about 4:30 in the afternoon. However, it is also possible that the apostles weren't actually going to the temple to observe the sacrifice but had scheduled their public gatherings during hours when the temple was busy. Crowds flooded in for the morning and evening sacrifices, so these would have been prime opportunities for evangelism. Whatever their plan was for that day, Peter and John did not end up at the evening sacrifice. They ended up in the Portico of Solomon and preached to a large crowd (Ac 3:11).

v2: Peter and John had not yet arrived at the temple complex when they first encountered a man being carried on a stretcher. They were still walking through the city streets on their way there when, at some point, they found themselves walking beside him. The man was on his way to the steps which led up into the inner courts of the temple in order to beg from those pious Jews who would be entering and exiting, before and after, the hour-and-a-half evening prayer service (Edersheim, The Temple, Eerdmans, reprinted 1988, p144). He was a very familiar sight to all who regularly attended the temple. Friends or family brought him there every day and placed him by the eastern gate, which stood between the large outer Court of the Gentiles and the inner courts which surrounded the temple itself. Everyone who went in to worship had to pass by him. He had been born with legs that were "maimed." From the moment he was born it had been obvious they didn't work.

Helping the poor is commanded by the Law of Moses (Dt 15:4-11). God wanted Israel to think of themselves as a family. Jews were to see themselves as brothers and sisters, so a gift to the poor was considered to be a "loan" to a family member with the understanding that it would be repaid, or if not, it would be forgiven at the next Sabbath year (Dt 15:8-9). Every third year their tithe was given locally to the "alien, orphan and widow," so the poor could "eat and be satisfied." Farmers were also instructed to not return to a field, vineyard or grove to collect what they had missed the first time through during the harvest. The grain or fruit left behind was meant for the alien, orphan and widow. Nor was a Jew allowed to take the cloak of a poor person in pledge for a loan because that "brother or sister" would be left with nothing to cover them at night. If a cloak was all they had then that pledged cloak must be returned before sunset (Dt 24:10-13, 17). God wanted His people to "…remember that you were a slave in the land of Egypt, therefore I am commanding you to do this thing" (Dt 24:22). Caring for the poor was to be part of every righteous person's obedience to the Lord. Compassion was an essential virtue.

v3: When the lame man realized that Peter and John were about to enter the temple, he caught their attention and asked to be given a gift. They must have recognized him because they too would have walked through the eastern gate many times over the years. In fact, Jesus Himself must have passed the man.

v4: Luke says Peter and John looked at him and didn't turn away. They kept staring, and then at some point they spoke to him saying, "Look at us!" The man may have diverted his eyes downward out of shame or humility.

vs5-6: When he heard Peter's voice, he looked up thinking he was about to receive a gift, but Peter said, "I don't have silver and gold, but what I have, this I give to you, in the name of Jesus Christ, the Nazarene, walk!" (literal).

vs7-10: Luke says, "And seizing him by the right hand he raised him up, and immediately his feet and ankle bones became firm. And leaping up, he stood and was walking around and entered into the temple with them, walking and leaping and praising God. And all the people saw him walking and praising God. And they recognized him, that this was the one that was sitting at the Beautiful Gate [begging]for alms, and they were filled with amazement (lit: scared stiff) and shock [lit: beside themselves] at what had happened to him" (literal).

v11: Attendance at the evening sacrifice must have been severely reduced that day. The healed man created quite a disturbance in the outer courtyard. Everyone who heard about what had just taken place ran toward the Portico of Solomon where the man was still "holding on" to Peter and John, which probably means he couldn't stop hugging them.

v12: Peter became alarmed when he saw the way people were looking at him. He knew they thought that he and John had the power within themselves to do such things. That idea was blasphemous and he quickly attempted to correct their confusion. As he had on the Day of Pentecost, he addressed the crowd formally and respectfully. He greeted them as, "Men, Israelites…" And then he asked them two questions: First, why were they so surprised that a miracle had happened to this man? And second, why were they staring at the apostles as if the power which had caused this miracle had come forth from them? Did they think that the apostles had such power because they were so zealous in observing the Law of Moses? Did they think Peter and John had attained a level of righteousness where God would perform such miracles whenever they asked Him?

v13: Peter quickly directed them toward the true Source of the miracle. He and John personally possessed no such power, nor had they lived so righteously that they could perform such miracles at will. It was the God of Israel who had done this, and He did it for a very specific reason: To glorify "His servant Jesus" (Mt 12:18-21; Isa 41:1-3). Peter left no room for doubt. It was "the God of Abraham and Isaac and Jacob, the God of our fathers..." who did this. In other words, that miracle had been done by the very God in whose temple they were standing. It had been done by the One whom they had come to call upon for mercy at the evening sacrifice. And He did it to honor Jesus, to prove to the nation how wrong they had been to reject Him as their Messiah. Instead of honoring their Messiah when He walked among them, the nation had handed Jesus over to the Romans to be executed. Loudly and publicly they had rejected Him at His trial before Pilate even when Pilate had tried to release Him.

v14: They had participated in a terrible miscarriage of justice. They had asked Pilate to show grace to a murderer but refused his offer to release God's "Holy and Righteous One" (Mt 27:15-26; Ps 16:10; Isa 53:11; Lk 4:34).

v15: Then Peter confronted them with a terrible irony. He said, "... you killed the Author [the original source] of life." Such a statement is remarkable in its clarity. First, by calling Jesus the "Author of life" (Heb 2:10; 12:2) he declared Him to be the divine One who breathed life into Adam's nostrils (Ge 2:7). And second, by acknowledging that Jesus physically died, he declared Him to be fully human. This statement shows us that Peter grasped the mystery of the incarnation and was not at all hesitant to confront his Jewish audience with it. He told them that God's divine Son, the One who breathed life into all living beings, had become a mortal man, and that they had killed Him. But then he added that God the Father had raised Him from the dead, a miracle to which "we are witnesses."

We shouldn't overlook the fact that when Peter and the disciples stood in front of large crowds like this one boldly declaring that they had seen Jesus alive with their own eyes (Ac 2:32; 4:33; 5:32; 10:39-41); no one laughed or called them liars. Nor was anyone able to produce a dead body to prove them wrong. Luke has already shown us that those crowds contained people capable of mockery (Ac 2:13), but during these early days of the church, the only serious opposition he reports came from senior religious leaders (Ac 4:1-2). The Jewish people themselves seem respectful and interested.

v16: Then Peter began to explain how the miracle had taken place, and in doing so, mentioned that the lame man had not been passive in the process but had participated by responding in faith. Peter said, "...and upon faith in His name this man whom you see and know was made strong [his legs "made firm" so he could stand]." Again Luke places the preposition "upon" (Greek: epi) where the preposition "in" (Greek: en) would be expected (see comments on v38), and again he does this in order to draw our attention back to Joel's promise that "...everyone who calls upon the name of the Lord shall be saved" (Ac 2:21). The point he is making is this: Just as it is possible to call upon the name of the Lord to be saved from our sins, so it is also possible to call upon His name to be saved from sickness (or in this case physical injury or congenital defect). At some moment during that encounter, probably when Peter said, "In the name of Jesus Christ the Nazarene, walk," the man dared to call upon God to heal him and genuinely believed that He would.

Peter added further explanation. He told the crowd that the man's faith had been focused on Jesus. That's what made the difference. The man had called upon God in Jesus' name. It was "that faith which is through Him which gave him this soundness which you see here in front of you." In other words, the man's healing was the result of a combination of two things. First, Peter spoke a command in Jesus' name. The miracle began when Peter obeyed the leading of the Spirit and stepped out in faith. By saying, "In the name of Jesus Christ, the Nazarene, walk!" (v6) he made it clear that he and John were relying upon Jesus' authority, not their own. And second, the lame man had exercised faith by believing that Jesus had such authority. Peter's words presented him with an opportunity, and in that moment he responded.

Peter's use of the phrase "faith which is through Him..." pictures a person passing through Jesus on His way to the Father's throne. That picture fits perfectly with the admonition in Hebrews: "Since... we have confidence to enter the holy place by the blood of Jesus, by a new and living way which He inaugurated for us through the veil, that is, His flesh, let us draw near..." (Heb 10:19-22). That means the lame man dared to believe that God would heal him because of what Jesus had done for him. Remember, the man unquestionably knew some things about Jesus of Nazareth. He had likely seen Him preaching and healing in the temple. And because he lived in Jerusalem, he certainly knew He had been crucified, and it's also likely that he had heard some say that Jesus had come back to life. After all, the apostles were declaring the resurrection in the temple day after day. How could he have missed it? So when Peter spoke Jesus' name and seized his hand, it was with some level of understanding that this man chose to believe that he could come to God through Jesus... and when he did, the power of God shot through him.

v17: Peter bluntly confronted the crowd with their collective guilt (vs13-14). But he also assured them that they were not hopelessly beyond the reach of God's salvation by saying, "And now, brothers, I know your past actions against Jesus were done in ignorance, and your leaders were also ignorant" (paraphrase). What they had done to Jesus was terribly wrong, but they had been deceived at the time rather than being deliberately defiant, and because of that fact, it was likely that their hearts were still capable of repenting when shown the truth (1Ti 1:12-14). Peter very generously included their "rulers" in this statement, which in particular meant the high priest and other members of the Sanhedrin (Ac 4:5-6). While some in the Sanhedrin must have been deceived, others including Annas and Caiaphas (Jn 18:12-14) were not. They did know Jesus was the Messiah, and it was because of that fact that they rejected Him. They did not want to surrender their positions of authority to Him. That is exactly what Jesus told them using a parable about a vineyard (Mt 21:33-41). And Matthew, who recorded the parable, says they fully understood that it was targeted at them (Mt 21:45-46). So the idea that all the rulers were ignorant would have been more than Peter meant to say.

v18: Peter then confronted them with the fact that the nation did just what the prophets said they would do (Act 7:53). He told them that over the course of Israel's history all of its prophets, in one way or another, had declared that God's Messiah would suffer. That statement went directly against the popular belief that when the Messiah came, He would immediately begin to rule in power and glory. The idea of a suffering Messiah was a truth Peter himself had not understood earlier (Mt 16:21-23). This was the central issue being debated here, because once a person acknowledges that the Scriptures do speak of a suffering Messiah, as well as a glorious Messiah, then it becomes quite obvious that the prophets were pointing to Jesus.

The prophetic description of Jesus' suffering and resurrection is stunningly accurate down to the smallest detail, but it requires a major shift in thinking to see it. If all a person had been taught is that Messiah will someday come and overthrow Israel's enemies and set up a glorious kingdom, the passages which describe a suffering and rising "servant" simply make no sense, and are therefore overlooked. So Peter is challenging the crowd to re-think their assumptions, to reflect on the recent events surrounding the crucifixion and to see how they literally fulfilled such passages as Isaiah 52:13-53:12 (v13 "his servant, Jesus"). And even if they were not ready to acknowledge that those passages speak of a suffering Messiah, there was still an undeniable miracle standing right in front of them.

vs19-20: At that point, Peter called for decision. He told the crowd to stop thinking the way they had been thinking and turn instead toward "the wiping away [blotting out with oil] of your sins" (Ps 51:6). He was asking them to admit that they were personally responsible for murdering the Messiah, but he was also encouraging them to trust that the Messiah's death atoned for their sins (Isa 53:4-6). He said if they would do this, then "seasons of refreshing" (lit: to make cool, bring relief) would "come from the presence (lit: face) of the Lord...." In other words, if Israel would undergo a general, nation-wide repentance and turn to Jesus, there would be a wide-spread pouring out of the baptism with the Holy Spirit. By the term "seasons of refreshing" Peter was describing the strong sense of God's presence which had accompanied the disciples since Pentecost. Then he added, "...and He may send the Messiah, who He chose [lit: hand-picked] beforehand for you, namely, Jesus" (literal).

v21: Peter assured them that at some point in the future, the Father would physically send Jesus back to earth to bring to Israel the promised "times of restoration." The word "restoration" is same word is used in Acts 1:6 when the disciples asked Jesus, "Lord, is it at this time you are restoring the kingdom to Israel?" Throughout the prophets there is a recurring theme about the glories of the last-days, Messianic kingdom (Isa 60, 61). Repeatedly we are told that when Messiah comes, He will "restore" a number of things to Israel which had been lost, including a re-gathering of those Jews who had been scattered into other lands, a re-establishing of the security and position of Israel among the nations of the world, and great agricultural abundance. But by far the most important aspect of this restoration will be the return of God's Spirit. In a vision, Ezekiel watched the Holy Spirit depart from the holy of holies, leave the city and finally "stand" over the Mount of Olives (Eze 9:3; 10:4, 18-19; 11:22-24). He later saw a vision in which God's Spirit ("the glory of the God of Israel") would return to a new temple (Eze 43:1-5), one which would exist during the Messianic age (Eze 40-48).

v22: The fact that the Messiah had to first atone for our sin before coming to rule in glory does not in any way alter the many, prophetic promises that He will restore the kingdom to Israel (Ac 1:6). That these "times of restoration" will come is unquestionable. As Peter said, "All the prophets" spoke of it (v24). Peter's next statement was to quote from the book of Deuteronomy. He was telling the crowd that the Messiah, Jesus, will come again, and when He does, it will be as the promised "Second-Moses." Before he died, Moses gave a remarkable promise to Israel. He said, "The Lord God will raise up for you a prophet from among your brothers like me. Him you shall hear according to all things whatsoever he may speak to you" (Dt 18:15, literal). Moses was not simply affirming the general truth that in future generations God would raise up more prophets. His words "like me" are very significant. In effect he was saying, "Another Moses will come. In the future someone will rise up to lead you as powerfully as I have." It takes only a moment's reflection to realize what sort of person this Second-Moses will be. Moses led people out of bondage; he mediated a covenant with God at Sinai; he interceded for the people after they had sinned; he performed amazing miracles including bringing bread from heaven and water from a rock; he spoke directly to God and brought God's word to the people, and he led them to the promised land (R.K. Harrison in <u>The New Bible Commentary</u>, Revised, Eerdmans, 1971, "Deuteronomy," p221). No prophet in history even came close to doing all that which is why the nation was still waiting for that person to arrive (Dt 1:21, 24-25; 6:14; 7:40-41).

Moses exercised supreme human authority in Israel's spiritual, governmental and military matters. The patriarchs had held a similar authority over their households, but after Moses no one in Israel's history, not even their kings, were permitted to do this. Kings could lead in governmental and military matters, but they were never allowed to conduct priestly duties. That privilege was reserved for the tribe of Levi. Saul was severely disciplined by God for crossing over this barrier when he took on the role of a priest and performed a burnt offering (1Sa 13:8-14). So when Moses speaks of a prophet "like me," something very special must happen for this to take place. This is why the author of Hebrews carefully explains that Jesus is a priest "according to the order of Melchizedek" (Heb 5:5-10). He shows us why Jesus, who was born into the tribe of Judah (the tribe of kings), still has the right to be our high priest even though God had given those privileges to the tribe of Levi. He explained that Jesus belongs to an order of priesthood which is superior to the priesthood of Israel. So, like Moses, spiritual and governmental authority can be combined, and the barrier can be crossed. Jesus is also the greatest of all prophets (Heb 1:1-2) and will be a fierce military commander who will lead the armies of heaven against the antichrist's forces (Rev 19:11-16).

v23: When Moses originally made this promise, he reminded the people that forty years earlier when they arrived at Mt. Sinai, they had asked God to communicate with them through a human intermediary (Moses) because they were afraid to encounter Him directly (Ex 20:18-20; Dt 18:16). The Lord had accepted their request and then privately told Moses, "I will raise up a prophet from among their countrymen like you, and I will put My words in his mouth, and he shall speak to them all that I command him. It shall come about that whoever will not listen to My words which he will speak in My name, I Myself will require it of him" (Dt 18:18-19). Peter actually replaced the statement "I Myself will require it of him" with more vivid wording drawn from Leviticus: "…shall be destroyed from among the people" (Lev 23:30), which probably means the person would cease to be a spiritual member of the congregation of Israel. That person would no longer be allowed to take part in the nation's religious activities. By quoting this verse, Peter was warning the crowd that those who reject Jesus would be harming their relationship with God. He was making it plain that believing in Jesus and submitting to Him are not optional.

v24: He said these prophecies about the Messiah must not be questioned. It is certain that they will come to pass. After all, one prophet declaring this truth about Messiah coming with such power would be enough to establish it as a valid promise, but in this case every prophet from Samuel (2Sa 7:12-16) onward declared it. Its scriptural support is overwhelming.

vs25-26: Then Peter began to expand the scope of those whom the Messiah will save. First, he assured the Jews listening to him that they held a privileged position. They were "sons of the prophets" and descendants of the patriarchs with whom God had made a covenant. So it was only natural that God would give them the first opportunity to hear the gospel (Mt 10:5; 15:24; Lk 14:15-24; Ac 13:46; Ro 1:16; 2:9-10). But by quoting the Lord's words to Abraham, "And in your seed all the families of the earth shall be blessed" (Ge 12:3; 22:18), Peter was also telling them that the gospel would soon be carried to the Gentiles (Ac 1:8). Israel was being given the privilege of hearing it first, but God's promise to Abraham included "all the families of the earth."

Acts Chapter 4

v1: While they were still speaking, Peter and John were suddenly interrupted and placed under arrest. A group of priests arrived bringing with them the captain of the Levitical guard. Since the time of David gatekeepers had been assigned to guard Israel's place of worship (1Ch 26:1-19). He undoubtedly brought men with him to make the arrest. Certain families of Levites were scheduled each year to guard the gates and courts of the temple. Ten men were stationed at each of twenty-four locations. It was their duty to see that no "unclean" person entered beyond the Court of the Gentiles and to police any disruptions. Four of the stations were located in the inner courts near the holiest part of the sanctuary, so both priests and Levites were stationed there together.

Two hundred forty Levites and thirty priests were on duty at all times. The night watch served all night, but the day was divided into four watches. The "captain of the guard" oversaw all of these and regularly made rounds to each station to see that the guards were awake and properly performing their duties (Alfred Edersheim, The Temple, Eerdmans, reprinted 1988, pp147, 148). The members of this guard were allowed to carry weapons (Lk 22:52; Mt 27:65).

v2: Luke mentions that among the officials who came to arrest Peter and John were members of a sect called the "Sadducees." One of the main doctrines of that group was that they rejected the idea of a bodily resurrection (Mt 22:23; Ac 5:17; 23:8), so they were furious at what was taking place. Luke describes their emotional condition by saying they were "worn out." In other words, they had grown impatient and angry because day after day these apostles had been preaching in the temple courtyard, and they were especially upset because they were announcing that Jesus Himself had been resurrected, and that He would someday resurrect the dead (Jn 5:25-29).

v3: It was already growing late in the evening (Ac 3:1) when they came to make the arrest, so they took hold of Peter and John and put them in a jail cell overnight, probably somewhere in the temple area.

v4: In spite of the obvious disapproval toward the apostles being shown by the nation's religious leaders, many of those who watched all these things take placed believed. Luke tells us that the number of men who considered themselves to be members of the church grew to a total of 5,000 (Ac 2:41). Since the church had been growing daily following the events of Pentecost (Ac 2:47), the exact number who believed because of the lame man and the message that was preached can't be determined, but it must have been large. It was probably somewhere between 1,000 to 2,000 men, but when we hear that number, we need to remember that the actual number would have been much larger because Luke only reports the number of men. When believing women and children were added, the total must have been two or three times as large.

vs5-6: The next day a very elite group of the nation's religious leaders gathered. The meeting included rulers (mostly Sadducees), elders, scribes (mostly Pharisees), the high priest (Annas), his son-in-law (Caiaphas) and two more of his relatives who are otherwise unknown (John and Alexander). In those years Annas no longer held the title of high priest. He had served in that position from A.D. 6 to A.D. 15 but had been removed from office by the Romans. Yet the people of Israel considered the high priest's office to be one that God gave to someone for life. So even though his title had been taken away, Annas was still thought of as high priest and was really the person in control. Over the years he had arranged for five of his sons and a son-in-law (Caiaphas) to be the high priest at one time or another (D.R. Hall in The New Bible Dictionary, Eerdmans, 1962, "Annas" p39).

v7: Peter and John, along with the lame man who had been healed, were made to stand in the middle of a semi-circle of leaders who remained seated. This was a formal inquiry. The miracle itself couldn't be denied (v16), so their initial question was carefully worded to imply that the apostles may have drawn upon an ungodly source of power such as a false god or witchcraft (Dt 13:1-5). They asked, "By what power or in what name did you do this?" The question itself had two parts to it. The first asked, "What kind of power did you use?" And the second asked, "Who sent you to do this?" To do something in someone's "name" meant that you were acting in another person's authority. Someone sent you. You were there to represent someone else. The obvious answer to their question was: "Who but God <u>could</u> do such a thing?" But they ignored that fact, hoping to find something in the apostles' answer with which to accuse them of a religious crime.

v8: Before Luke tells us how Peter answered them, he wants us to know that the Holy Spirit Himself was the source of the words Peter would speak. He says Peter was "filled with the Holy Spirit," and that term might confuse us if we mistakenly think of this filling with the Spirit as the same miracle that happened to him at Pentecost (Ac 2:4). In the upper room Peter, and those who were with him, "were all filled with the Holy Spirit and began to speak with other tongues…." At Pentecost Peter received what Jesus called the "promise of the Father" (Ac 1:4). The disciples had been told to wait in Jerusalem until they were "baptized with the Holy Spirit" (Ac 1:5). During His ministry Jesus repeatedly spoke to them about a special encounter in which the Holy Spirit would indwell each of them, empowering them for holiness and service.

What happened to Peter in that moment of need was not the arrival of another "baptism," as if the powerful indwelling presence of the Holy Spirit had left him. What happened to Peter in that moment of need was a work of the Spirit to strengthen him for the task at hand. It would soon become apparent to all who were listening that God was speaking through him, and undoubtedly it was apparent to Peter as well. As he was about to speak, he surely felt God's closeness and discovered that he was full of courage rather than fear even though he was standing before Israel's highest court. Then as he began to speak, an inspired flow of words came to his mind far more eloquent and prophetic than anything he might have planned to say.

So by describing Peter as "filled with the Spirit," Luke is telling us that the presence of the Holy Spirit came upon the apostle in that courtroom to strengthen him and give him the words to speak, not repeat his initial baptism with the Holy Spirit. In the Old Testament we read of similar "fillings" which came upon men and women from time to time in order to enable them to perform a special feat or to prophesy (Nu 11:25; Jdg 14:6, 19; 1Sa 10:6; also Lk 1:15, 41, 67). And when Jesus was preparing His disciples to face the persecution that lay ahead of them, He assured them that they too would always be given such help (Mt 10:16-20; Mk 13:9-11; Lk 12:11-12; 21:12-15). So here, we see Peter and John, who had been brought before "rulers and authorities," having the Holy Spirit teach them "in that very hour what… to say" (Lk 12:11-12), just as their Lord had promised.

vs8-10: Peter respectfully addressed the gathering as "rulers and elders of the people." He said if he and John were being accused of doing a good deed for an infirm man, they were guilty, and if they were being questioned to find out the source of power that healed the man, they would gladly explain it to them and the entire nation. They said the miracle was performed "in the name of Jesus Christ the Nazarene whom you crucified whom God raised from the dead," to which Peter added for the sake of emphasis, "in this [name] this man stands before you whole" (literal). By focusing on Jesus' name, Peter directed everyone's attention to the source of the miracle. Yes, he had commanded the man to be healed and then grabbed him by the hand to raise him up, but he and John were merely functioning as the human representatives of Jesus. It was Jesus who directed them to say what they said and do what they did, and it was He who supplied the power that healed the man's feet and ankles. As we noted earlier (Ac 2:22), the title "Jesus of Nazareth" or "Jesus the Nazarene" was the most common way of identifying Him. But Peter doesn't leave Jesus' identity to merely an earthly title. At this point he turns the trial around and put the religious leaders on trial. In case there was any doubt in their minds, the "Jesus" he was talking about was the one they had been personally responsible for crucifying, and the one God had physically raised from the dead.

v11: Then Peter announced God's verdict on this group of judges by quoting from Psalm 118:22. Jesus had already quoted the same verse to warn some of the same people who were now sitting in that room that they were fighting against God's Messiah (Mt 21:23, 42-46). Peter not only quoted the verse but added an explanation so that no one would be able to escape its true meaning. He said, "He is the stone which was rejected," referring to Jesus; and then added, "by you," so they would know that they were the guilty "builders." And finally, he told them that Jesus was Israel's "chief corner stone," meaning that He was their Messiah who would someday rule and judge the nation. What began as a formal inquiry to see if Peter and John had committed a religious crime had now turned into a spiritual trial in which the apostles were pronouncing God's verdict on the leaders of the nation for refusing to acknowledge their Messiah.

v12: Then Peter made a bold announcement. He said, "And there is salvation in no one else; for there is no other name under heaven that has been given among men by which we must be saved." By that statement he was not saying that all those who had died prior to hearing the gospel, those who had never heard Jesus' name so that they could call upon it, were by that fact alone lost. He was telling Israel's leaders, and for that matter the entire human race, that Jesus is God's promised Savior; there will be no other (Jn 3:11-18). His death is the atoning sacrifice to which all of Israel's sacrificial system pointed (Is 53:4-6); He is the resurrected King who has already ascended to the Father's right hand (Ps 2; 110:1-3), and He is the Lord who will come from heaven to judge the living and the dead (Jn 5:24-29; Ac 10:42). He was explaining to them that the Messiah, for whom Israel had been waiting, had come. It was no longer possible to claim ignorance. They must make a decision.

v13: No one on this panel of judges expected a response to their question like that. They had assumed that they would be questioning three frightened men who would be at a loss for words. So the apostles' boldness and eloquence amazed them. Yet at the same time, there was something vaguely familiar about this exchange. It reminded them of the numerous confrontations they'd had with Jesus during His ministry. They had hoped that those frustrating dialogues with Him, in which their positions of authority had been disregarded and their attitudes embarrassingly exposed, would have ended with His death.

But here they were again being confronted by men without formal religious training, who were not intimidated by them and who spoke about the deepest sort of biblical matters with confidence and clarity.

v14: Not only did these apostles talk like Jesus, they had just performed a miracle like one of those that He had done. And the "miracle" was standing in front of them: a man they had all seen seated on the temple steps for decades. It did appear that God was confirming the message about Jesus, but because these judges refused to believe that message, they could not think of anything to say in reply.

vs15-18: The council ordered the three men to leave the room so they could confer together in private. Their only concern was how to restrict the spread of faith in Jesus. There was not a trace of any serious reflection on the implications of such a healing. Instead of being thrilled that a miracle had been done in their midst, or honestly questioning whether or not their hostility toward Jesus was misguided, they only discussed what steps they must take to prevent this new faith from spreading. The plan they decided on was simple: "Let us threaten them to no longer speak upon this name to anyone" (literal). In other words, "Keep preaching, and we'll hurt you!"

v18: Then they called the apostles back into the room to present this decision. They forbade them to teach others to call upon Jesus' name; in fact they forbade them to utter even a single word about Jesus. Before we move on to consider Peter and John's response, we should remember what an intimidating environment this must have been for the apostles. First of all, the men issuing this order were the spiritual elders of Israel, and Peter and John were pious Jews, raised to respect religious authority. So we'd miss some of the internal pressure they must have been experiencing, if we ignore their natural desire to submit. And second, they were being threatened by the same group who, only months earlier, had been responsible for savagely executing Jesus. There could have been no doubt in their minds that this council would carry out their threats. So they also had to overcome the fear of being tortured and possibly put to death.

vs19-20: But Peter and John boldly answered with these words: "Whether or not it is right [righteous] for us to obey God rather than you is a question you must answer for yourselves, but as for us, we believe we have no choice but to speak what we saw and heard" (paraphrase). As much as Peter and John may have desired to submit to Israel's religious leaders and avoid persecution, when forced to choose, they felt a much higher obligation to obey Jesus; and Jesus had commanded them to proclaim Him, beginning in Jerusalem (Lk 24:47).

vs21-22: Hearing this, the council warned them that they would be punished if they continued to preach and then released them because they could not find a sufficient reason to hold them, particularly since the news of the healing had spread rapidly, and the entire city considered it a "sign" from God. The lame man was a highly recognizable figure. He was over forty years old and for decades had begged at a location every pious Jew passed regularly. If they harmed the apostles, they might face an angry backlash.

vs23-24: After being released, the three men reported to the church what the chief priest and elders had said. Their threats had been intended to silence the apostles and stop the growth of the movement they led, but instead of responding with fear, the entire congregation joined together as one in unified prayer and called on God for boldness. They began by declaring God's absolute power to rule over human events. They addressed God as "Lord." The Greek word meaning "lord" is better rendered in English as "Master" (lit: "despot"). They acknowledged God as the rightful owner and powerful master of the universe. With these words they were reminding themselves that the authority of mortal humans is nothing when compared to God's authority. Then they quoted a familiar Scriptural passage which declares God to be the Creator of all things (Ex 20:11; Ne 9:6; Ps 146:6).

vs25-26: Next, they quoted a portion of Psalm 2. This psalm is a very powerful, Messianic psalm which pictures the arrival of the Messiah to rule the earth. Paul says the psalm describes the resurrection of Jesus (Ac 13:33-34), and the author of Hebrews uses it to declare His divinity (Heb 1:5).

v27: The psalm goes on to say that God the Father will give the nations to His Messiah as a gift, along with the authority to "break them with a rod of iron" and "shatter them like earthenware" (Ps2:9). It warns earthly rulers to submit to the Messiah because: "...His wrath may soon be kindled" (Ps2:12). And the psalm ends by saying: "How blessed are all who take refuge in Him" (Ps2:12). So the reason the church quoted this psalm in their prayer is obvious. They recognized that it had already been partially fulfilled when their rulers (Herod and Pilate), along with Roman soldiers and an angry crowd of onlookers, had banded together to oppose Jesus. But they were sure the remainder of the psalm would be fulfilled as well. God's wrath was coming, and in light of that fact, they were not the ones who should be afraid; it was those who opposed His Messiah who should be afraid.

v28: They told God that they understood that the crucifixion hadn't happened because He had been unable to protect His Son. It had happened because the cross and all the events surrounding it were part of God's plan of salvation. His unseen "hand" had actively guided events so that everything that took place was done within the boundary of His will.

v29: The congregation called on God to "look upon" the threats that had been made against them, yet rather than asking Him to protect them from suffering, they only asked Him for the power to be totally free from fear so they could boldly speak His word. By calling themselves His "slaves," they made it absolutely clear who they intended to obey. They would obey God, not the nation's unbelieving leaders.

v30: And finally, they asked God to continue to "stretch forth" His hand to heal and cause signs and wonders to happen through the name of His holy servant ("child"), Jesus. They understood that they were now in a partnership with Him. He would do miracles, and they would proclaim Jesus.

v31: While they were praying these things, God supernaturally confirmed that He heard their prayer. He physically shook the place where they were assembled and filled them with a fresh empowerment of the Spirit to such a degree that they began to speak out prophetically with the freedom they had requested (Lk 1:46-55; 67-79; Ac 2:4, 8, 11).

v32: Instead of being frightened by the threats the religious leaders made against them, the believers in Jerusalem became even bolder in their public ministry and more selfless in their care for one another. Their sacrificial giving, which Luke tells us was part of this church from its first days onward (Ac 2:44-45), didn't die out but grew stronger as the weeks and months passed. Becoming a Christian meant one would be welcomed into a community which shared a common "basket" (Ex 16:15-18). Those who had resources gave to a fund specifically intended to help those in need.

Luke describes that growing church as "the multitude." By now it contained thousands (Ac 4:4), yet he says they were "one heart and soul," which means their unity was both emotional and practical. They not only felt love for one another but expressed that love in selfless deeds, particularly in generously helping believers who were poor. And that level of generosity was not present in merely a few of them but in virtually all of them, for Luke says, "...and not one said any of his possessions was his own, but all things were common (Greek: koina) to them" (literal).

Within a year or two a violent purge led by Saul of Tarsus (Ac 8:1-3) would drive many of these believers out of Jerusalem, but until then the amount of persecution a believer might experience appears to have varied from person to person. We see in the Jerusalem church a puzzling amount of poverty, which continued for decades (Ac 6:1; 11:28-30; Ro 15:26; 1Co 16:1-4; 2Co 8:1-15; 9:1-15; 1Th 2:14-16). I believe this varying amount of persecution was largely caused by the hostility certain individuals suffered at the hands of their own family or community. Some individuals, after believing in Jesus, were able to continue on with their lives relatively untouched, but others appear to have been instantly impoverished. Very likely such poverty was the result of a spouse having divorced them, or parents and siblings ostracizing them, or their businesses being boycotted, or their employment terminated, or synagogues expelling them (Jn 9:22).

To be baptized in the name of Jesus became a very dangerous thing to do. A person could be left suddenly destitute. But impelled by the love of God and led by the Holy Spirit, the church immediately rallied to take care of those who had been abandoned in this way. In effect they said, "Know this: If you're left destitute after receiving Christ, we will step in and care for you as if you were our own flesh and blood. You won't starve or be left alone. We'll be there to help you!" And I believe that the numerical explosion of the church in the midst of that hostile environment is directly related to this spontaneous generosity.

The threat of ostracism is an effective way of stopping most evangelism. It is still used today in many cultures. A person who is "ostracized" is totally cut off from family and/or community leaving them alone and desperate. But the Jerusalem church reduced that threat by drawing its new believers into a close, family-like community. Undoubtedly it was in the "house to house" meetings that people heard one another's "story." They immediately knew the circumstances individuals were facing at home, so they were able to respond right away with real, practical help. Their intense community and selfless generosity helped to remove the terrible obstacles of abandonment and starvation that threatened some if they dared to be baptized. As the years passed it appears the financial resources in Jerusalem gave out, which is why believers in other cities, and in other nations, began to send help as they were able (Ac 11:28-30; 1Co 16:1-4; 2Co 8:1-15; 9:1-15; 1Th 2:14-16).

v33: The early church was founded on the historical fact of the resurrection of Jesus. Different groups within Judaism held varying interpretations of key passages of Scripture, but the followers of Jesus were different. Their faith was focused on a person, Jesus of Nazareth, who had been proven to be God's promised Savior by the fact that He had been physically raised from the dead. No longer could there be any dispute about whether or not the Messiah must suffer an atoning death because He had suffered, but after three days in the grave He rose up in a glorious, new body. The whole church proclaimed this truth, but the apostles were able to personally bear witness to it because they had been with Him throughout His ministry (Ac 1:21-22). And Luke says they testified to that truth "with great power." The term "great power" certainly means the Holy Spirit enabled them to speak persuasively, but those words must also point to the miracles which took place when the apostles ministered. God confirmed their message with healings, signs and wonders (Mk 16:20). That demonstration of power, combined with the church's love for one another, Luke says produced an atmosphere in which "great grace was upon them all." The term "great grace," first of all, means God was pleased with them (Lk 2:40), but it also means that they were held in high esteem by a large percentage of the population of the city (Ac 2:47; 5:13). People were impressed by what they saw and felt drawn to join them.

vs34-35: Those who owned land or houses, beyond those in which they were living, sold them to provide funds to feed the growing number of people who had been impoverished because of their faith. Seeing this "safety net" must have given many in the city the courage to consider being baptized themselves. All donations were brought to the apostles who distributed the funds based on a person's particular need. Some needed more than others.

vs36-37: In order to show us how costly those donations were for some, Luke tells us about a Levitical priest from Cyprus named Joseph. To begin with, for a Levitical priest to be baptized in Jesus' name was a huge sacrifice in itself. Given the hostility toward the church by the high priest and Sanhedrin his decision to follow Jesus must have meant the end of his privileges and service. As a tribe Levites were entitled to receive support from the tithes of the people (Nu 18:21), and because they had that source of income, members of the tribe were not allowed to own land within the borders of Israel. That means the field Joseph sold was probably located near his home on the island of Cyprus. In fact, it may have been his portion of the family estate.

To have a Levite join the church would have been a notable event. Here was a man of high status and education, who had lived a privileged life, yet who was giving up all those things to follow Christ. Not only would he forfeit the financial support he was entitled to receive as a Levite, but then he sold a field he owned which may have severely reduced, if not eliminated, any financial security he had left. And we shouldn't overlook the humility it took for this Levite to place his gift "at the feet of the apostles." Here was an educated priest gladly submitting himself to the leadership of a group of men who were uneducated Galileans.

The apostles nicknamed him "Barnabas," which in Hebrew means "son of prophecy," and when translated into Greek is rendered "son of exhortation or comfort" (Greek: paraklesis). He was a relative of Mary, the woman who owned the upper room in which Jesus had gathered with His disciples (Mk 14:12-16; Ac 12:12). She must have been Barnabas' aunt, either by blood or marriage, because Paul tells us John Mark, her son, was Barnabas' cousin, or possibly his nephew (Col 4:10). In practice Barnabus seemed to take care of his younger cousin as though he were his uncle (Ac 12:25; 15:37, 39). This man named John Mark was the person who later wrote the gospel of Mark. In the future Barnabus would be called a prophet and teacher and would serve as a leader in the rapidly growing church in Antioch (Ac 13:1). He would also serve as Paul's mentor (Ac 11:22-26, 30) and then as his fellow-missionary (Ac 13:2-3). Both Luke (Ac 14:14) and Paul (1Co 9:6) would call him an apostle.

Acts Chapter 5

vs1-2: From the remarkable generosity of Barnabus, Luke now turns to the deceptive selfishness of a couple named Ananias and Sapphira. They too sold a piece of property but agreed to secretly keep a portion of the revenue for themselves. When they laid their gift at the feet of the apostles, they lied saying it was the full amount of the sale. We can only guess at their motives because the church did not require them to give any gift at all. Had they wished to keep the entire amount, they would have been free to do so (v4). They may have been seeking to be admired for their generosity or were possibly positioning themselves so they could be supported by the church's benevolent fund in the future. Regardless of the goal, their action was selfish, but selfishness is a sin which afflicts most of us, yet thankfully God doesn't strike us dead for it. It wasn't their selfishness God chose to discipline; it was their lie.

vs3-4: Peter, who had become very sensitive to the leading of the Holy Spirit, knew by a "word of knowledge" (1Co 12:8) what they had done and confronted Ananias. Ananias came without his wife to present the gift, and no sooner had he given it and said whatever he said that left the impression that this was the total amount, than Peter asked, "Why has Satan filled your heart to lie to the Holy Spirit and steal from the price of the land?" Even the wording of this question was prophetically inspired. Peter identified Satan as the source of the lie. He exposed Ananias' heart and showed that it was "filled" with this lie. And he warned him that the arrogance that had dared speak such a lie before the church offended the Holy Spirit. Peter marveled that Ananias thought he could lie in the midst of that intense spiritual environment and go undetected. Did he think God didn't see what he had done? Did he think God would do nothing? It was as though he was daring God to respond.

vs5-8: Peter did not issue a verdict or announce any form of judgment. He simply asked a question, and then God miraculously stepped in to apply a level of discipline which was shockingly severe. No sooner had Ananias heard Peter's words than he collapsed and died. There has been much speculation on whether or not his death was caused by a heart attack brought on by the trauma of being suddenly exposed. Such reasoning is an attempt to supply a natural, non-miraculous cause for the death. It assumes that he was an unhealthy man, who when publicly embarrassed, had a heart attack and died. But this explanation loses credibility when Ananias' wife, Sapphira, came into the church gathering three hours later. Unaware of her husband's death she was asked by Peter, "Tell me whether for such and such a price you sold the land?" and after answering "yes," indicating she was a knowing accomplice in the deception, she too collapsed and died. To claim that both died of natural causes seems to require a stubborn refusal to admit the obvious, which is that this was a divine act of judgment in which God took their lives.

vs9-10: Peter asked Sapphira, "Why is it that you agreed together to put the Spirit of the Lord to the test?" And once again, functioning in a "word of knowledge," he announced, "Behold, the feet of those who have buried your husband are at the door, and they will carry you out as well." Then immediately she too collapsed and was taken out and buried beside her husband. One final observation we should make about their death is that it seems unusual for two Jewish people to die and be buried without any family reaction or participation. You would have thought the young men would have carried their bodies home, not taken them out and buried them. The apparent absence of a formal burial ceremony or ritualized mourning is odd. Either they were from out of town, and it took time to notify family, or they had been abandoned by their families for becoming Christians, or they simply had no living family members left.

v11: The result of their death was that "great fear came over the whole church and over all who heard these things." Seeing how God reacted to their lie caused everyone who heard about it, whether Christian or non-Christian, to become afraid to try to hide anything from God. The event served to both purify and grow the church. Those who wanted to hide things from God stayed away (v13), while those who were prepared to be totally sincere with Him joined the church, and must have quickly confessed any hidden sins (v14).

v12: Because the church steadfastly refused to allow threats of persecution to silence it (Ac 4:29-30), and because believers gave so generously that the people of Jerusalem could be confident that they would be cared for if ostracized by their families for being baptized (Ac 4:32-35), and because a strong fear of God kept hypocrisy from eroding their faith and lifting the favor of God (4:33), the power of the Spirit continued to work signs and wonders among them drawing many to Christ. And the rhythm of their life together continued unchanged. Each day there were large, public gatherings held in the shade of the Portico of Solomon (a large, covered area on the south side of the Court of the Gentiles) and small gatherings which met in homes throughout the city (Ac 2:42, 46; 5:42).

v13: The crowds at the temple grew larger as many came to listen to the apostles preach and watch them pray for the sick and cast out evil spirits, but others deliberately stayed away from those gatherings because they were frightened by what was taking place. Yet the prevailing attitude in the city was not hostile toward the followers of Jesus, in fact they were viewed with great respect, even admiration. The miracles, the generosity, the joy were all very attractive, but people were also aware that it was dangerous to join them. It was no secret that the high priest disapproved of this movement and had made threats against those preaching Jesus (Ac 4:21; 5:26), and there was also circulating a report about the sudden death of two people who had tried to lie to the apostles (Ac 5:11).

vs14-15: Jerusalem as well as the surrounding region was stirred by what was happening. Luke says multitudes of "believing ones," both men and women, were "added to the Lord," and faith in the healing power of Jesus was widespread. The same circumstances that had surrounded Jesus' ministry (Mk 1:45; 2:2-4; 3:7-10; 6:53-56; 10:46; Lk 12:1; 14:25), people desperately trying to get near Him, were now being repeated with the apostles. The numbers of those being brought for prayer grew so large that it became impossible to pray for each one individually, so people strategically placed their loved ones along the route Peter would walk each day on his way to and from the temple. Some must have waited for hours because they brought with them small beds or cots for their sick to lie on. They lined the streets hoping for a prayer, the touch of a hand or even being close enough for Peter's shadow to pass over them, believing it might to serve as a substitute for his hand being laid on them. Apparently Peter was walking in the Spirit so strongly that power emanated from him. Remember, none of this was new to these apostles. They had often watched Jesus minister under these same conditions (Mk 6:53-56).

The picture Luke gives us of people waiting in the street outside the temple is exciting in that it reveals a growing level of faith, but it also shows us the overwhelming size of the crowds. It can only mean that the gathering in the Court of the Gentiles had swelled to a size where there was no longer any reasonable expectation of waiting in line for prayer. And the fact that Peter couldn't stop to pray for each person placed on the side of the street tells us how many must have lined his path. There were simply too many for him to stop and give personal attention.

v16: Of course the report of these events went out from Jerusalem to the surrounding region which resulted in a "multitude" of people pouring in from other cities. They too brought their sick and those tormented by unclean spirits, which swelled the size of the crowds even further. And then Luke makes a brief statement we must not overlook. He says, concerning this massive amount of needy people, that they were "all healed." In making that statement he carefully selected an unusual word for "all" (Greek: hapas), which is a strengthened form of the normal word for "all" (Greek: pas). Luke is literally saying <u>everyone</u> was healed. No wonder the crowds were huge, and no wonder the religious authorities felt they could wait no longer to stop this mass movement toward Jesus.

v17: The high priest presided over a council of elders called the "Sanhedrin" which governed the nation's spiritual matters (within the bounds permitted by the Romans). Those seated on this council included the acting high priest, those who had been high priest previously (the Romans kept changing high priests), members of their families, tribal elders, certain family heads and scribes (legal experts in biblical matters) (J.A. Thompson in The New Bible Dictionary, J.D. Douglas, ed., Eerdmans, 1962, "Sanhedrin" p143). Some on the council were members of a sect called "Sadducees" and some were "Pharisees" (Ac 23:6), but during the years when the nation was under the control of the Romans, the Sadducees were the largest number present (A. Gelston in The New Bible Dictionary, J.D. Douglas, ed., Eerdmans, 1962, "Sadducees" p1124). The Sadducees were a party of wealth and privilege closely tied to the priestly roles of the temple, and they strongly opposed the idea of a resurrection or the existence of angels and spirits (Ac 23:8).

The high priest and others who held powerful positions within Israel's temple system had the most to lose from this swelling tide of faith in Jesus of Nazareth. Pride, money and control were all at stake, so they rose up in opposition with the kind of emotional fury that ignites when someone feels they must fight to protect their position. They were alarmed and angry that their influence was slipping away.

v18: This time they showed no caution (Ac 4:1-3). They seized all twelve of the apostles, not just Peter and John, and put them in a public jail rather than holding them in a private cell within the temple complex. They wanted the entire city to hear about this arrest. They intended to frighten the church into confusion by removing their leaders and to warn the population at large that this new faith would not be tolerated. Their goal was to stop, or at least slow, the spread of this spiritual awakening. They wanted to drive believers and those coming to their gatherings back into their homes in fear.

vs19-20: The arrest was meant to be a public announcement that their patience with this new faith had come to an end, but God turned it into a public relations disaster. During the night an angel of the Lord opened the prison doors, let the apostles out and then ordered them to return to the temple and continue preaching "all the words of this life."

v21: So instead of a successful demonstration of their power to crush this movement, the event only served to make them look weak and foolish. The next morning at dawn, the apostles walked back into the temple to continue ministering where they'd left off. Thousands of those who had watched the arrest take place now watched as the apostles fearlessly return to the Portico of Solomon. No one would have assumed that the Sanhedrin had met during the night and decided to release them. As the report went out, the whole city would have understood that this was another miraculous "sign and wonder" confirming that God approved this teaching about Jesus.

As the morning wore on, the high priest, and those who had supported his decision to make this arrest, remained unaware of what was happening in the temple courtyard. Sometime later that day, they called a meeting of the Sanhedrin and invited all the tribal elders of Israel to join them (the Senate, literally: "a council of old men"). Their plan was to conduct a formal hearing of the apostles, probably with the goal of getting a consensus which was broad enough to allow them to seek the death penalty (v33). After everyone had gathered, they sent word to the jail for the prisoners to be brought in.

vs22-23: When the council's designated representatives arrived at the prison, they discovered the prisoners were not in their cells. They returned immediately with this report, "We found the prison itself completely locked, with every area secured, and the guards still standing at their posts by the door of each cell. But once the doors were opened, we found no one inside" (paraphrase).

v24: As they listened to these words, the captain of the temple guard and the high priests were completely at a loss as to how to respond. They were stunned, wondering what was going to happen next.

v25: In the midst of this confusion, someone arrived and reported, "Look! The men you put in jail are standing in the temple and teaching the people" (literal).

v26: The captain of the guard, along with those who had originally been sent to retrieve the prisoners, went down to the temple courtyard to summon the apostles to appear before the council. This time they asked them to voluntarily accompany them, taking care to avoid using force because they were afraid of provoking a violent reaction by the huge crowd that had been listening to them preach. The general attitude in the city toward the apostles was by now so favorable they feared they might be stoned if they handled them violently.

vs27-28: Once again the apostles were placed in front of a large semi-circle of seated elders. As they stood there, the high priest took it upon himself to interrogate them. He began by pointing out that they had defied the council's previous command (Ac 4:18, 21). He said, "We specifically ordered you not to teach people to believe upon this name [of Jesus], and now look at what you've done; you've filled Jerusalem with your teaching, and you're trying to convince people that we're criminals, guilty of murdering this man [Jesus]" (paraphrase).

vs29-32: Peter, with the rest of the apostles joining him in support, answered this way, "It's necessary to obey God rather than men. The God of our fathers raised up Jesus whom you took with your own hands, hanging Him on a wooden stake [Ac 10:39; 13:27-29]. He is our Ruler [author, source] and Savior, and God highly exalted Him to His right hand in order to give repentance to Israel and forgiveness of sins. And we are witnesses of these events that we proclaim, as is the Holy Spirit who God gave to those who obey Him" (paraphrase).

vs33-34: Many of the members of the council were cut deeply by these words, and fully intended to kill them. In the midst of the uproar, a certain member of the Sanhedrin, a Pharisee named Gamaliel (Hebrew: Gamliel), who was a teacher of the Law and honored by the entire nation, stood to his feet and ordered that the men be taken out of the room so the council could talk privately about the matter.

vs35-37: He said to them, "Men, Israelites, watch out, you may bring trouble upon yourselves by what you are about to do to these men" (literal). Then he reminded them of two previous insurrections which had died out without the Sanhedrin having to be involved. One had been led by a man named Theudas who gathered to himself a group of 400 men but was killed and his followers dispersed. The other had been led by a man named Judas of Galilee who was outraged by the census Caesar Augustus imposed on them in A.D. 6 (Lk 2:1-3) (F.F. Bruce, Acts, Eerdmans, reprint 1974, p125). That man also perished, and his followers were scattered.

v38: Then Gamaliel's integrity really shone through. He introduced a note of doubt into the room by suggesting that it was possible that this movement was of God. He didn't say that it was, but by simply asking the question, he implied that he, a very prominent teacher of the Law, was not yet sure of the answer. In other words, in his own mind there was still a possibility that God was helping these followers of Jesus.

Any honest observer would have come to the same conclusion that Gamaliel did, yet there was a core of very ungodly people in that council, particularly among the Sadducees, who refused to be moved, even by a resurrection (Mt 28:11-15), an unexplainable healing (Ac 4:14-16, 22) or this miraculous release from prison which had just taken place (Ac 5:22-24). But when Gamaliel stood up and spoke out the way he did, he halted what had become a lynch mob. He ordered everyone to "stand back and leave these men alone" because, he said, if this movement was only the result of human plans or efforts, it would fall apart and collapse because God Himself would oppose it.

v39: But if it came from God, if He were the One who had willed these things to happen, if it were His power that was at work among them, then, warned Gamaliel, "You will never be able to destroy them, and you might be found fighting against God" (literal). And thankfully, they were persuaded by him.

v40: The apostles were called back into the room and flogged for disobeying the Sanhedrin's previous command (Ac 4:18, 21), which means the high priest made them lie down on the ground and had them whipped on their bare backs, up to 40 times, while he oversaw the process (Dt 25:2-3; 2Co 11:24). When the punishment was finished, they were once again commanded "not to speak upon the name of Jesus" (literal) and then released. Gamaliel's advice to the council had been to leave the men alone because God would stop the movement if it were not from Him. But the high priest and Sadducees who supported him refused to entertain even the slightest possibility that Jesus might have been raised from the dead. Nor were they willing to let these men go unpunished. Gamaliel had intervened and prevented the high priest from getting the consensus he needed to stone them, but he refused to let them go without beating them and commanding them to stop preaching Jesus. And undoubtedly the high priest threatened them with further harm, though Luke doesn't mention this.

v41: The apostles left the council chamber rejoicing that they had been considered worthy to be dishonored for the name of Jesus. They were experiencing exactly what their Master had said would happen to them (Mt 10:17; Mk 13:9; Lk 12:11; 21:12-19; Jn 15:20-21; 16:2-4). Undoubtedly they remembered His words that when people insulted, persecuted and lied about them, they should "rejoice and be glad, for your reward in heaven is great; for in the same way they persecuted the prophets who were before you" (Mt 5:11-12). So as painful and humiliating as that experience must have been, it confirmed to them that they were on the right track. It meant there was enough "salt" in their words (Mt 5:13) and "light" in their deeds to provoke a response.

v42: After they had been released, they picked up where they had left off, preaching and teaching Jesus as the Messiah, with possibly a slight adjustment in their routine. In Acts 2:42-46 the pattern seems to be that the apostles would teach at the temple gatherings but not in homes. But here, Luke's wording shifts slightly to say that the apostles were teaching and preaching in the temple but also in the homes. They may have begun circulating through the home meetings because they recognized that the conflict developing at the temple might mean that in the near future it would no longer be safe to gather there. In fact, that day would arrive quite soon (Ac 6:7-9; 8:1)

Acts Chapter 6

v1: The enormous growth of the church brought with it practical problems which needed to be solved. Luke describes this season in Jerusalem as "days when large crowds of people were becoming disciples." With huge numbers pouring in, it's not surprising that conflict arose. In this case, there was grumbling among the "Hellenists" toward the "Hebrews" because they felt their widows were not receiving their fair share of the resources being distributed. The "Hellenists" were basically Jews who spoke Greek, dressed like Greeks and often had Greek names. They were usually Jews who had moved to Israel from other nations. When Luke says "Hebrews," he means those born and raised in Israel and whose native tongue was Hebrew. Actually in those years most of the people in Israel didn't speak Hebrew, but rather a language from Syria which was very similar to Hebrew called "Aramaic."

The Hellenists' claim that their widows had been "looked past" is highly unlikely since it appears that the apostles themselves were still running the benevolent ministry (Ac 4:34-35; 6:2). But a language barrier did exist between the two groups, so mistakes may have been made. At any rate, the perception of unfairness was enough to send the apostles to the Lord for guidance.

v2: The Twelve convened a formal meeting of the entire church, probably at the southern steps of the temple, or some similar place, where a large number could gather and hear what was said. Here is a literal translation of what they said: "Us, leaving the Word of God to serve tables, is not pleasing." By this they certainly meant it was not pleasing to the Lord. Apparently, the Twelve were still personally overseeing the daily distribution of benevolence funds. Financial gifts had been coming in since the first days of the church (Ac 2:44-45; 4:32-37), but as time passed, the number of people needing aid grew rapidly until their participation in other areas of ministry was being reduced. The most serious result was that the apostles were preaching less. Others may have attempted to preach in their place, but their voices were irreplaceable. No one else had been personally taught by Jesus to the same degree or appointed by Him to lead His church.

v3: It's evident that the Twelve had prayed and sought the Lord's guidance before convening this meeting because they presented the congregation with a well-conceived plan. They told them to prayerfully reflect on those who were in the church, and identify seven men whose lives gave testimony to the fact that they were "full of the Spirit and wisdom." These seven should be individuals in whom the congregation had already seen the Holy Spirit at work. And they should also be "full of wisdom," which probably meant in this case that each had a history of honestly and successfully managing people and money. Once these candidates were duly nominated, the apostles said they would "set [them] down over this need" (literal), meaning they would publicly appoint them to oversee the distribution of funds. No explanation is given as to why exactly seven should be chosen. The number might have been borrowed from a pattern used in Jewish business practices (J. Rawson Lumby, Acts, J.J.S. Perowne, ed., Cambridge Greek Testament for Schools and Colleges (21 vols.), Cambridge Univ. Press, 1904, p153). But another possibility might be the fact that there are seven days in a week, and each man would be assigned to handle the duties for an entire day. If so, this would not have been a full-time responsibility that pulled these seven men away from everything else. Each man may have simply needed to reschedule one day each week to manage the benevolence ministry.

It does not appear that the apostles intended to create a formal "office" that would become a permanent part of all church government, yet they did leave an example by which they showed us how to respond when such needs arise. They showed us that it's wise for the congregation to be involved in the process of nominating these ministers. Yet in doing so, they did not abandon their own authority. They were the ones who finally put the nominees in place and to whom those ministers undoubtedly reported. So a structure involving "elders" and "deacons" did emerge. And later on when Paul planted churches, he used this same model (Ac 20:17; 1Ti 3:1-13; 5:17-19; Titus 1:5).

v4: The apostles announced what they considered to be their most important responsibility. They said they had to continue to "press into" corporate prayer (Ac 1:13-14) and the "ministry of the Word" (Ac 2:42). They considered those two activities to be foundational to everything else that was happening and were soon proven correct by Luke's observation in verse seven, "...and the Word of God grew, and the number of disciples in Jerusalem multiplied greatly (literal)."

v5: After hearing the apostles' proposal, the entire congregation indicated their approval. How this was done is not mentioned. Then they set to work selecting seven candidates. Luke lists their names partly to introduce Stephen and Philip, who will both soon make significant contributions of their own, but also to show the wisdom of the congregation in picking seven Hellenists to oversee the distribution of funds. If it was the widows among the Hellenists who had been overlooked in the past, then the congregation would select men who were Hellenists themselves and spoke fluent Greek, so that mistake would not happen again. Each of the seven men who were chosen had a Greek name.

v6: Luke says the congregation "set" the men before the apostles whose first response was to pray (Ac 13:1-3). He probably didn't intend to describe the whole process they went through, so they may have interviewed the men and withdrawn for a season of prayer in order to confirm in their own hearts that the congregation had made the right choices. But when they finally laid their hands on these men, they were publicly bestowing on them the authority to do the ministry they were being asked to do.

v7: Luke concludes this passage by noting that the church continued to grow. What had started out as a problem (v1) had ended up being used by God to make the church even more effective. Now the Word of God was being preached to more people, even to the point of persuading a "great crowd of priests" to "obey the faith." The number of people becoming "disciples" was surging at a rate that became overwhelming. It's interesting that Luke chose not to use the title "disciple" in the first five chapters of Acts, but now in the sixth chapter he uses it three times in the first seven verses (vs1-2, 7). He previously chose such terms as "multitude" (Ac 4:32), "church" (Ac 5:11) and "believers" (Ac 5:14), but here he begins to employ this familiar term which is found so often in the gospels. Over the remainder of the book of Acts he will go on to use it a total of 28 times. By using the word "disciple," Luke assures us that even though massive numbers were pouring in, the quality of what was taking place within each individual was not diminished. People were becoming true disciples of Jesus Christ.

v8: Luke now focuses on Stephen, one of the seven men chosen to manage the church's benevolence fund. Earlier he mentioned that Stephen was a "man full of faith and the Holy Spirit" (v5). Here he describes him as someone who was "full of grace and power," and we learn that, beyond his duties to care for the poor, Stephen was regularly ministering healing and deliverance like the apostles themselves (Ac 2:43; 5:12, 16).

v9: Stephen was also an exceptional preacher. He seems to have understood better than most the radical impact faith in Jesus Christ would have on Jewish legalism. In no way was he disloyal to Judaism any more than Jesus was disloyal to Judaism (Mt 5:17-20), but he did recognize that the Messiah's coming had initiated a new era in God's dealings with the human race. In particular he recognized that the temple and the Law of Moses had found their fulfillment in Christ, and it was his preaching on these two topics which formed the basis for the formal charges made against him (vs13-14). His accusers claimed he had spoken against the temple and Moses, but undoubtedly his only crime was that he proclaimed the same truths Jesus had taught on these subjects.

Jesus reinterpreted what it meant to truly fulfill the Law. He repeatedly said the attitudes of a person's heart must become obedient, that it is not enough to simply change our outward behavior (Mt 5:17-48). He declared that He was superior to the Sabbath (Mt 12:8) and the temple (Mt 12:6), and that "everyone who beholds the Son and believes in Him will have eternal life..." (Jn 6:40). He taught that faith in Him was the way to salvation and sanctification, not zealously trying to keep all the ritual requirements of the Law. To those who did not believe He was the Messiah, such words would have, indeed, sounded like blasphemy.

Jesus also said things about the temple which were misunderstood when He originally spoke them. It was those statements that were central to the charges made against Him at His trial (Mt 26:59-61; Mk 14:58). In speaking about the resurrection of His body, He had said, "Destroy this temple, and in three days I will raise it up" (Jn 2:19). By "temple" He meant His physical body (Jn 2:21), but those who didn't understand His statement thought He meant Herod's temple (Jn 2:20). His words were distorted and used as evidence at His trial (Mk 14:57-58), and then mockingly quoted back at Him while He hung on the cross (Mk 15:29). Indeed, Jesus did prophesy that the temple would be destroyed saying "... not one stone here will be left upon another, which will not be torn down" (Mt 24:2), and those words were horribly fulfilled in A.D. 70. Jesus had made many statements that if Stephen quoted any one of them, would have brought him trouble. All he had to do was to accurately quote His Lord, and there would have been people who accused him of blasphemy.

At some location where Stephen was ministering (it may have been the court of the Gentiles), a group of Hellenistic Jews decided to debate him hoping to discredit him in front of the crowd. That group included men from a synagogue of "freedmen," which was a title that could be applied to any slave who had gained freedom. But this synagogue was particularly populated by people from cities in northern Africa (Cyrene and Alexandria), and southern and western Asia Minor (Cilicia and Asia). Of particular interest is the mention of "some from Cilicia," since Cilicia is the province in which the city of Tarsus is located, and Tarsus was the childhood home of Saul of Tarsus (Ac 22:3).

It's seems likely that Saul attended this synagogue made up of people from his hometown, and we know from Luke's account that he became personally involved in this event (Ac 7:58). If so, it also seems likely that they recruited him to be their spokesman since he was one of the best, young minds of his day (Gal 1:14). We don't know if he was personally present at the initial debate with Stephen, but if so, it might help explain some of his fury toward him (Ac 8:1). It would have been hard for a proud man to be defeated publicly in this way (Ac 6:10). And it does seem odd that Saul became so violent toward Christians (Ac 8:1-3) when his mentor, Gamaliel, counseled restraint toward them (Ac 22:3; 5:34-39).

v10: Luke says that those who "stood up" and "argued" with Stephen "… were not able to stand against the wisdom and the Spirit with which he was speaking" (literal) (see: Lk 12:11-12; 21:12-15).

v11: Up to this point there had simply been an open debate in front of a listening crowd, but Luke now tells us that an evil element was introduced. Unable to argue against Stephen successfully, these men began to work their way back through the crowd planting suspicion in people's minds. They told them, "We have heard him speaking blasphemous words against Moses and God" (literal). It's uncertain as to whether they were so rigid in their legalism that they actually believed those accusations or whether they were so desperate to silence him that they were willing to violate the ninth commandment by bearing "false witness" (Ex 20:16). Since Paul later claimed that in his early years as a Pharisee he had been blameless with respect to the righteousness required by the Law (Php 3:6), we can be confident that even if he was involved in that public debate, he did not take part in the dishonest slander. Yes, he was passionately hostile toward Stephen, but he was not a perjurer (1Ti 1:13).

v12: The campaign against Stephen worked. The slander stirred the crowd to anger, including the elders and scribes who by now had joined the gathering. They all rushed toward Stephen, seized him and then led him to the council chamber for trial. There was no doubt as to their intentions. He was going to be found guilty of blasphemy and then stoned.

vs13-14: When the council assembled, "false witnesses" stood to testify against Stephen. They said, "This man does not cease speaking against this holy place and the Law, for we have heard him saying that Jesus the Nazarene will destroy this place and will change the ritual ceremonies which Moses delivered to us" (literal). As we noted earlier (v9), Jesus did indeed say that the temple would be destroyed, but He didn't say He would be the one who destroyed it. And He did de-emphasize the ceremonial requirements found in the Law, and judging from the astute way Stephen handled Scripture (Ac 7:2-50), we can be certain that he presented Jesus' teachings on those subjects accurately. So the charges the council made against him were based on the same distortions and half-truths that had been used against Jesus.

The first charge, concerning the destruction of the temple, contained a blatant lie. Stephen's accusers distorted the meaning of Jesus' words. They turned words meant as a prophetic warning on one occasion (Mt 24:1-3), and as a parable describing His resurrection on another (Jn 2:18-22), into a ridiculous claim that Jesus had threatened to personally destroy the temple (Mt 26:61). And their second charge, concerning the "ritual ceremonies which Moses handed down to us" (literal), ripped Jesus' words out of their original context to make it sound as if He disrespected those ritual ceremonies. But when His words are put back into their original context, it becomes clear that Jesus did not disrespect the Law but was announcing that a new era in God's salvation had arrived. He was explaining that the rituals required by the Law were not intended by God to be an end in themselves. They were intended to be symbols pointing toward the coming Messiah, and now that He, the Messiah, had arrived, the focus of a person's devotion should be on Him rather than on the symbols which pointed to Him. That same truth must have been what Stephen was preaching in one form or another, and any honest listener would have recognized his intent. But whoever was orchestrating these charges was not trying to be honest; they were trying to get a conviction.

v15: This is the sort of statement only an eyewitness makes: "And staring at him, all those sitting in the Sanhedrin saw his face as a face of an angel" (literal). Luke wasn't personally present at that event, so he had to gather that information from someone who saw and heard what happened; someone who was in the room when the Sanhedrin gathered to try Stephen; someone who saw that angelic look on his face; someone who listened to his defense and could remember it point by point (Ac 7:2-53); someone who watched and may also have felt the anger that surged through the council after Stephen accused them of murdering the Messiah (Ac 7:54); someone who observed the council cover their ears and rush forward to drag him out of the city to stone him (Ac 7:57-58); someone who stood close enough to hear Stephen speak as he was dying (Ac 7:55-56); someone who heard him cry out, "Lord, do not hold this sin against them" (Ac 7:60). I believe that person was Paul. I believe that he was the eyewitness who reported these things to Luke nearly 30 years later while the two men waited for Paul's trial before Caesar Nero (Ac 28:16, 30-31). It's very likely Acts was written during the two years they spent together in Rome (see comments on Ac 1:1).

If indeed Paul was the source of this information, it must have been very painful for him to recall the martyrdom of Stephen. Obviously, he could still picture in his mind Stephen's face. He said it was like the "face of an angel." In other words, it was not filled with fear as you would expect, but unnaturally peaceful; not full of hate as you would expect, but unnaturally full of love for his accusers; not full of confusion as you would expect, even though he was standing before the elders of Israel. And it seemed in that moment that he was looking directly into the spiritual realm. Who but an eyewitness could have seen that face, and who but Paul would have told Luke? We know Paul oversaw the execution (Ac 7:58; 8:1), so it's not hard to imagine that he watched the trial as well.

Acts Chapter 7

v1: The high priest started the interrogation process by asking, "Are these things so?" When Luke uses the title "high priest," we can't be certain whether he means Annas or Caiaphas (Ac 4:6). As we noted earlier (Ac 4:5-6), Annas was the high priest as far as the nation of Israel was concerned, but by this time the Romans had placed his son-in-law, Caiaphas, in the office. Regardless of which man was running the council at the time, both had been involved in Jesus' trial, so both had heard these charges before because they were the same charges that had been brought against Jesus (Mk 26:59-61; Mk 14:58).

v2: Instead of trying to defend himself, Stephen put his accusers on trial. He confronted the Sanhedrin with their own guilt. Using a concise history of Israel, he showed them that in situation after situation they, and their ancestors, had failed to recognize what God was doing and had repeatedly opposed those God had sent to deliver them. Surely Stephen knew that no defense, unless he was willing to renounce Christ, would succeed anyway, but to preach such a sermon at a moment like that would have required a strong inner conviction that God was directing him to say such things. What he did took amazing courage.

He opened his sermon with the words, "Men, brothers and fathers hear!" (literal) and then used a very unusual title for God. He called Him "the God of glory." The only other place in the Bible where this title is used is in Psalm 29:3. A similar term, "King of glory," is used in Psalm 24:7-10. Of course there could be many reasons why he used the term, but coming as it does right after the description of him with a "face like the face of an angel" (v15), and combined with the fact that at the end of that sermon he would stare into heaven and see "the glory of God" (the Father) with Jesus standing beside Him (Ac 7:55), it's possible that he may have started looking into heaven before he began to preach. If so, that may help explain the beautiful radiance on his face and why God's "glory" was fresh on his mind.

vs2-8: Rather than examining Stephen's sermon (Ac 7:2-50) verse by verse and revisiting each historical event, we will simply review his main points and observe how he used each to expose the nation's pattern of resisting God. Verses 2-4: Of course Stephen began with Abraham. The point to note here is that in order for God to work in Abraham, he had to leave his family and homeland. God had to isolate him because his family and culture were so deeply involved in idolatry. Verses 5-7: Only after his father died did God allow Abraham to see the promised land. After he arrived, he was given several important promises, one of which said his descendants would be enslaved for 400 years in a foreign land. Verse 8: Stephen mentions the covenant of circumcision and then the expansion of Abraham's family, moving quickly from Isaac to Jacob's sons, who became the patriarchs of the twelve tribes.

vs9-16: Verse nine makes a very significant point. Here was another example of Israel's persistent blindness. Instead of recognizing God's hand on Joseph, or accepting the prophetic dreams that God had given to him, his brothers became jealous and sold him into slavery. Yet Joseph was the one God had appointed to be their deliverer. It was through him that their family would be preserved from starvation.

vs17-29: Then Stephen moved forward in his telling of Israel's history to the time of Moses. He reminded the council that God had given Abraham a prophetic revelation that told him precisely how long Israel would remain in Egypt (Ge 15:13-16; Ac 7:6-7). But as he recounted the story of Moses, it became obvious that by the time they were slaves in Egypt, the people of Israel had completely forgotten that promise. Had they remembered it and trusted God's faithfulness to fulfill it, they would have been watching expectantly for a deliverer to arise.

Instead they rejected Moses when he first appeared. Verse 25 is a key verse in this section. Stephen said of Moses: "...he supposed that his brethren understood that God was granting deliverance through him, but they did not understand" (Ac 7:25). Stephen's point in saying that was to show them that they had sinned like their fathers. They rejected Jesus just like their fathers rejected Moses.

vs30-36: To drive that point home Stephen reminded his listeners of the divine nature of Moses' call. God personally spoke to him from the burning bush. He was indisputably called by God, yet when he arrived in Egypt to deliver God's people from slavery, they disowned him. The charges the council made against Stephen claimed that he had blasphemed Moses, but in reply Stephen reminded the council how their ancestors had treated Moses. He said, "This Moses whom they disowned, saying, 'Who made you a ruler and a judge?' is the one whom God sent to be both a ruler and a deliverer with the help of the angel who appeared to him in the thorn bush" (v35). Stephen was telling the council that they were the blasphemers, not him. They had disowned the Messiah.

v37: He said the problem was that their fathers had forgotten a very important promise that God had made to Abraham 400 years earlier (Ge 15:13). God told him that in the future his descendants would become slaves in Egypt, but He also promised him that He would deliver them from that slavery. But because Israel had forgotten the promise, they weren't watching for a deliverer and rejected Him when He arrived (v17). And Stephen was telling this council that was putting him on trial, that they, along with most of the nation, had forgotten a much more important promise. Moses had told Israel to watch for "a prophet like me" (Dt 18:15). He said God would send another leader like himself: Someone who would perform signs and wonders (v36); someone who would speak directly with God just as he had (v38); someone sent by God to deliver and rule Israel (v35). But just as their fathers forgot Abraham's promise, the council and the nation had forgotten Moses' promise. And as a result, they weren't expecting the Second-Moses and rejected Him when He arrived.

vs38-43: Stephen described Moses as a man who spoke directly with God and received "living oracles" which he wrote down in the Law.

If a person really honored Moses and believed that the written Law came from God, then that person would obey it. And above all else, obedience to that Law produces single-hearted worship to God. Yet in the wilderness, their fathers had continued to worship idols. Stephen said they worshiped "the works of their hands" (v41), and then, taking that idea of people worshiping the works of their hands, he turned to the subject of the tabernacle and the temple.

vs44-50: He basically said the tabernacle was something God ordained, but the temple was something which was conceived in the human mind and built by "human hands." He was telling his listeners that their reverence for the temple had crossed over a line and that they were worshiping it as an idol. They were no longer focused on the God for whom they had built it (vs48-50). In that council meeting there were two charges being made against Stephen. One was that he disrespected Moses, and the other was that he disrespected the temple. He answered the second charge by reminding them that God never asked the nation to build a temple. The divine directive was only to construct a tabernacle. It had been David, not God, who wanted a temple; and it was Solomon, not God, who built it. Then, using a passage from Isaiah to support his argument (Isa 66:1-2), Stephen made the point that God is too big to live in the little buildings humans build. He was confronting an attitude in the council which nearly deified the temple itself. He was telling them to get their eyes off the building and look at the greatness of God.

v51: Stephen then came to the end of his sermon. He had begun that sermon in a warm, respectful tone, calling the Sanhedrin, "Men, brothers and fathers…" (v2), but he ended it with a blunt confrontation. Revisiting the sad realities of Israel's history, combined with the realization that many of those sitting in front of him had been personally responsible for condemning Jesus (Mt 26:57, 59; 27:1-2), may have produced in him this righteous outburst. He boldly announced God's verdict. He said they were "stiff-necked" (stubborn, uncorrectable; Ex 32:9), "uncircumcised in heart and ears" (they didn't love or obey God any more than unbelieving Gentiles did; Dt 10:16; 30:6; Jer 4:4; 9:25), and they were consistently opposing the Holy Spirit (which probably meant they refused to listen to the Spirit speaking within their conscience). In these ways, he said, they were just like their rebellious ancestors.

v52: But in one very important way they were far worse than their fathers. Their fathers had grievously sinned by murdering the prophets who spoke of the coming Messiah, but those listening to Stephen were the generation who actually killed the Messiah. It is surely no accident that in that moment Stephen called the Messiah "the Righteous One." That title exposed the hypocrisy of the council even further. These men who claimed to be so loyal to the Law of Moses had condemned the most righteous person in human history. Speaking through the prophet Jeremiah, the Lord had said concerning the Messiah, "...I shall raise up for David a righteous Branch; and He will reign as king and act wisely and do justice and righteousness in the land... And this is His name by which He will be called, 'The Lord our righteousness'" (Jer 23:5-6). Stephen was telling them that this was the Person they had handed over to the Romans to be murdered.

v53: He ended with a statement which essentially asked this question, "If you really believe that God gave us the Law of Moses, why don't you obey it?" He was announcing his verdict: guilty. The council had disobeyed the Law of Moses in two areas. First, they had rejected and arranged the execution of the Deliverer promised by Moses, and second, they had turned the temple into an idol.

Stephen's reference to "angels" in this verse can be confusing. Anyone who's read the Exodus account knows it was God, not angels, who gave the Law to Moses on Mt. Sinai. So why did Stephen insert the word "angels" here? The likely answer is that he is practicing a form of Jewish piety in which a direct reference to God is avoided by replacing it with the word "angel" or "angels." This same type of respect is shown when the word "Lord" is substituted for the name of God (YHWH). Such substitutions are done out of respect based on the conviction that we humans aren't worthy to use God's name directly. Examples of this can even be found in Moses' own writings (Ex 14:19; 23:20) as well as the prophets (Isa 63:9). Earlier in his sermon when Stephen was relating his history of Israel, he said concerning Moses, "The angel of the Lord appeared to him in a blazing fire from the midst of a bush," but during that encounter that "angel" actually revealed His name to Moses calling Himself "I Am Whom I Am" (Ex 3:14). There is simply no doubt that the person speaking to Moses was God Himself, yet Stephen reverently used the term "angel." We see this same form of respectful substitution used elsewhere in the New Testament by Paul (Ga 3:19) and the author of Hebrews (He 2:2, 9).

v54: Luke says, "And hearing these things they were cut to their hearts..." (literal). Stephen's words slipped past their mental defenses and brought a momentary realization that his charges were true; that indeed, they may be in trouble with God. However, no one was willing to repent, and Gamaliel was not present to counsel restraint (Ac 5:33-41), so their moment of contemplation was quickly replaced by outrage. The entire Sanhedrin began to function as one man. They were seized with anger, and many ground their teeth so violently an audible sound could be heard (Ps 35:16).

v55: Even in the midst of that storm, Stephen did not recoil in fear. In fact, it appears he was not fully aware of what was taking place around him because he had already been caught up in a vision of heaven. God was sustaining his faithful witness in that terrible moment. The Holy Spirit filled him with a fresh baptism of power, and the Father, in His mercy, drew back the spiritual veil to allow him to see the heavenly throne room with the resurrected Jesus standing at His side. Luke's reference here to the "glory of God" may mean there was a lot of bright light in the scene, but I think those words may be the term by which Stephen referred to the Father Himself. If so, in the vision there may have been a special concentration of light indicating the Father's presence, with Jesus standing to the left of that beautiful brilliance at His "right hand."

v56: Stephen announced what he was seeing. He said, "Behold I see the heavens having been opened up and the Son of Man standing at the right hand of God" (literal), and his choice of words would have incited the council to even greater anger. The term "Son of Man," when used in this context, refers to a well-known vision of heaven given to the prophet Daniel. In that vision Daniel saw "One like a Son of Man" stand before "the Ancient of Days" and be given authority to rule the human race forever (Da 7:13, 14). And Stephen's reference to Jesus standing at God's right hand points to another very important Messianic promise. Psalm 110:1 states, "The Lord said to my Lord, sit at My right hand until I make your enemies a footstool for your feet." By locating Jesus at the Father's right hand, Stephen declared Him to be that exalted Lord, seated in the place of divine power and authority. No one in that council missed his meaning. During His ministry Jesus had applied these same scriptures to Himself. He had used Psalm 110 to reveal His divinity in a debate with the Pharisees (Mt 22:41-46), and He had outraged the high priest during His trial by claiming to be the heavenly Son of Man (Mt 26:64-65).

v57: Everyone on the council began yelling at once, which created a loud uproar, and covered their ears with their hands to protect themselves from hearing Stephen's "blasphemies" any longer. Then they rushed forward as a mob and seized him, dragging him out of the room and taking him to a place outside the gates where they would execute him (Lev 24:14; Nu 15:35).

v58: Normally, a set of orderly procedures guided the process of stoning, but few rules appear to have been followed in this case. Luke says Stephen was "thrown" out of the city and stoned. His words picture the fury of a lynch-mob, and it's probable that the execution was performed as quickly as possible because no permission for an execution had been sought for or received from the Roman government which alone held the final authority over the death penalty (Jn 18:31).

One procedure they did appear to follow was the requirement that those who testify against a victim must cast the first stone (Dt 17:7). Those men who swore they heard Stephen blaspheme (Ac 6:11, 13-14) started the execution by ceremoniously laying their outer garments at the feet of a Pharisee named Saul of Tarsus. This indicates that he held some sort of special role in what was happening. As we noted earlier (Ac 6:9-10), it is almost certain that Saul would have attended the synagogue in Jerusalem that was made up of people from Cilicia, his home region; and it was young men from that particular synagogue who had stepped forward to debate Stephen. The fact that the accusers placed their coats at Saul's feet also suggests that those "key" witnesses were from Saul's synagogue.

v59: After the accusers threw their stones, the crowd was permitted to participate. But Stephen didn't die immediately. While still conscious he had called out, "Lord Jesus receive my spirit." His prayer was very similar to the one Jesus prayed when he died (Lk 23:46), only Jesus' prayer had been addressed to the Father. It's very significant that when Stephen prayed, he asked Jesus to receive his spirit. This is clear evidence that he considered Jesus to be divine. Having just seen a vision of Jesus standing waiting to receive him, Stephen in effect said, "Lord, here I come!"

v60: The proper procedure in Judaism for stoning someone was that the victim's hands and feet were bound, and then the person was pushed off of a high ledge (F. F. Bruce, The New Int'l Commentary on the N.T., "Acts," Eerdmans, reprint 1974, pp170-171). But judging from Luke's account it's very unlikely that these procedures were followed in this case because Luke specifically tells us that Stephen "placed his knees" before dying, which means he was able to kneel down to pray (Mk 15:19; Lk 22:41; Ac 9:40; 20:36; 21:5). Either he dropped to his knees from a standing position or pulled himself up from the ground to a kneeling position. This is a small detail, but it is another indication of the hastiness of that execution. Then Stephen cried out, "Lord, do not hold this sin against them!" His prayer to grant mercy to his murderers, just like his previous prayer to give his spirit to Jesus (v59), was addressed to Jesus which, again, confirms the fact that he believed Jesus to be divine. Luke described Stephen's death by saying, "…he fell asleep." He chose the image of sleep because he understood that those stones did not put an end to Stephen. When his body collapsed, his conscious spirit stepped through whatever barrier separates this world from the next and went directly into the presence of God. And then, just as the body of a sleeping person awakens in the morning, Stephen's dead body will awaken forever at the resurrection.

Acts Chapter 8

v1: Luke says Saul of Tarsus "was consenting to the killing of [Stephen]." The Greek word which is translated as "consenting" (Greek: suneudokeo) carries the sense of formal or legal approval of a matter (Lk 11:48; Ro 1:32; 1Co 7:12-13), and 25 years later Paul chose that same word to describe his role in Stephen's death (Ac 22:20). Clearly, he was not just a bystander. In some significant way he contributed to the verdict or helped organize the execution. That means he bore some of the moral responsibility for that innocent man's death.

Before the execution of Stephen, the temple authorities had been forced to restrain their persecution of the church because it enjoyed widespread approval among the people in the city. But now that the entire Sanhedrin had been enraged by Stephen's sermon, the temple authorities felt confident that they had enough political support to rid the city of what they considered to be a dangerous, religious movement.

The ugly process of neighbors reporting the addresses of believing neighbors would have been the first step; then soldiers would have been sent from house to house to arrest and imprison the men and women they were able to capture; and then those prisoners would have been beaten and executed if they refused to blaspheme Christ (Ac 22:4-5, 19-20; 26:9-11). The effect of that violence was to scatter the church far and wide. Believers fled for their lives. Luke says, "And there was in that day a great hunt upon the church in Jerusalem, and all were sown out into the rural country areas of Judea and Samaria except the apostles" (literal). He pictures believers being "sown" like a farmer sows seed. People fled into the rural areas of Judea and neighboring Samaria to hide. The southern boundary of the region called "Samaria" lays about 25 miles north of Jerusalem, and because Samaritans were culturally and spiritually hostile to both Judaism and the temple, Samaria would have provided a measure of refuge for those able to reach its borders.

Luke notes that the apostles themselves did not flee but remained in the city. In the future all of them would travel widely, but in the midst of this crisis it appears they did not feel they could abandon their flock (Jn 10:11-13). Many believers, because of age or ill health or family responsibilities, would have been physically unable to flee, and therefore, would have been forced to hide in the city. As the persecution raged on, more and more of those left behind would have ended up suffering in jail. So the apostles believed that their assignment from the Lord was to remain steadfast and pastor the remnant of the persecuted church.

v2: This verse should not be overlooked. Burying Stephen and loudly lamenting his death in the midst of that dangerous atmosphere was a very brave and defiant act. Stephen had been executed as a blasphemer, and in such cases public lamentation was forbidden (F. F. Bruce, Acts, Eerdmans, reprint 1974, p174). Aaron was forced to model this type of silence after two of his sons were executed by God because they presented incense using coals from a common fire. God's divine fire burst out of the holy of holies and consumed them. Then after their dead bodies were carried out of the camp, Moses sternly ordered Aaron and his two remaining sons, to show no grief (Lev 10:1-11). In this way they were to teach the nation to be grateful, not sad, that those who had treated God as unholy had been removed from among them. The death of the guilty ones had spared the rest of the nation from God's wrath. So when "devout men" (men who carefully obeyed God's law) loudly lamented Stephen's death in the midst of Jerusalem and gave him a proper burial, those men, by that action, were openly rejecting the Sanhedrin's verdict. They were publicly proclaiming that Stephen had been the victim of a terrible miscarriage of justice. They were fearlessly declaring that their consciences would not allow them to watch his corpse treated shamefully. For them to have been silent would have meant that they agreed with the charges against him.

v3: Most of the temple authorities were Sadducees, but Saul was a Pharisee, raised from his youth to reject many of their beliefs (Ac 23:6-8), yet they happily employed him to lead the work of persecuting the church. His zeal was unmatched. Luke uses a word which pictures Saul tearing the church apart like a wild animal. The anger that produced this persecution didn't come from the people of the city. What we're seeing here was not an explosion of mob violence against the church. This was a police action orchestrated by the high priest (Ac 9:21; 26:12) with Saul apparently managing the day-to-day operation. To hunt people down and make so many arrests, he must have been supplied with soldiers from the Levitical guard (Ac 4:1; 1Ch 9:22-23; Mt 27:65; 28:11-12). Luke tells us Saul entered houses and forcefully dragged men and women off to prison. Later, after becoming an apostle and calling himself Paul, he confessed that during that season of time, he flogged believers in synagogues in an attempt to force them to blaspheme Christ (Ac 22:19; 26:11). But he also said those experiences left him "furiously enraged," likely because few, if any, of the believers renounced their faith (Ac 26:11). When trials were conducted to determine whether or not to execute one of them, Paul said, "I cast my vote against them" (Ac 26:10).

v4: As we read Luke's brief but chilling account of this vicious persecution, we might assume that God's work was quickly brought to an end, but thankfully Luke added this statement: "Therefore the ones being sown passed through these regions preaching the word [about Jesus]" (literal). This remarkable sentence explains that not only did persecution fail to stop the expansion of the church, it accelerated its growth. It turned ordinary believers into missionaries. It scattered them like seed into Judea, Samaria and even the remotest parts of the earth. It drove them into the very places to which Jesus had commanded them to go after they were "clothed with power from on high" (Lk 24:49; Ac 1:8).

Beginning with Philip, Luke now shows us how the church expanded into Samaria and Judea (Ac 8:4-11:18). Later on he will describe how the gospel reached the "remotest parts of the earth" (Ac 11:19-28:31).

v5: Luke introduced Philip earlier as one of the seven men chosen to administrate the church's benevolence fund (Ac 6:5). Like Stephen, Philip was a Hellenistic Jew (6:1). To escape arrest in Jerusalem, he fled to the city of Samaria, which by that time had been renamed "Sebaste" by Herod the Great in honor of the Roman emperor Augustus (D. J. Wiseman, The New Bible Dictionary. J.D. Douglas, ed., Eerdmans, 1971, pp1130-1131). When Philip arrived there, he began to preach.

vs6-8: The people in the city were very responsive. Crowds gathered, and everyone listened intently because when Philip ministered, God performed amazing miracles. Luke says God did things people could see and hear. For example, many who had been in bondage to "unclean spirits" were set free, and as the demons departed, that person might cry out with a loud voice. Philip also prayed for the sick, and many of those who had been weak or crippled in some way were dramatically healed. We can only imagine the joy that must have filled the city when those who had been healed ran into the arms of their loved ones or arrived home well.

vs9-11: Before Philip came to Samaria, a man named Simon had been spiritually dominating the people in that region for a long time. Luke says he achieved that level of influence by practicing magic, meaning he was what is commonly called a "shaman" or a "witch-doctor." Such people use magical arts (sacrifices, incantations, special ceremonies, etc.) to curse or protect, prosper or impoverish, cast spells or break spells, and Simon's magic had an observable effect. When he cursed someone, trouble came. When he invoked protection on someone, things got better. So people paid him to do this kind of spiritual work. And he was good at what he did so his reputation grew. Young and old, rich and poor called him "the great power of God" (v10). He was able to convince them that he was God's representative, so if they wanted help from God, they had to come to him. For any human being to allow himself to be revered to that degree shows that the person has no fear of the true God.

v12: Philip baptized both men and women who believed his message, and Luke says his preaching focused on two important topics: the "kingdom of God" and "the name of Jesus Christ." In this case, by the term "kingdom of God" Luke means Philip showed them God's plan of salvation as it is revealed in the Old Testament. His sermons were almost certainly based on the Law of Moses because the Samaritans believed that only those five books were sacred. They did not accept the writings of the prophets. Then Philip must have explained how Jesus of Nazareth fulfilled God's plan through His cross and resurrection. And finally he would have urged them to call on the "name of Jesus Christ" to be saved (Ac 2:21-24).

The Samaritans were the remnant of the ten, northern tribes of Israel which had been conquered by the Assyrians in 721 B.C. Over the course of the seven centuries that followed that conquest their culture and religion had been subjected to many outside influences. Yet a sizable portion of the population still worshiped the God of the Bible during the years when the New Testament was written (Jn 4:12, 20, 25, 29, 42). They believed in one God; they considered Moses to be His prophet and the five books which he wrote (the Law of Moses) to be Scripture. They believed that a day of judgment was coming in the future; and they believed that Moses would someday return as a powerful Restorer, meaning he would lead people to repent and obey God (Dt 18:15, 18, Ac 3:22; 7:37) (A. Gelston, The New Bible Dictionary, J.D. Douglas, ed., Eerdmans, 1971, pp1130-1131). When we read this account about Philip, we should keep in mind that Jesus Himself had spent two days preaching in a city called Sychar which was only seven miles to the southeast of the city of Samaria. John says that when Jesus preached there, "…many of the Samaritans believed in Him…" (Jn 4:39). So as the crowds listened to Philip, it may not have been the first time that many of them had heard about Jesus. Some may even have had neighbors who already believed that Jesus was the Messiah (Jn 4:25-26).

v13: When Philip began to minister, it immediately became obvious that he had much more power than Simon. The signs and powerful miracles that took place through him made Simon look weak by comparison. Amazed by what he saw, Simon announced that he too believed in Jesus and was baptized, but as we will soon see, his response was not sincere (vs 18-24).

v14: When the report about Philip's ministry reached the apostles in Jerusalem, they sent Peter and John as their representatives to greet these new believers. They wanted to ensure that a good foundation was being laid for their faith. It appears they knew that Philip was a zealous evangelist but that he was someone who was not yet able to minister the baptism with the Holy Spirit effectively. And that was indeed the condition of Phillip's converts when they arrived.

vs15-17: Luke says the first thing Peter and John did was to pray that these believers "might receive the Holy Spirit, for He was not yet fallen upon any one of them, but they had only been baptized in the name of the Lord Jesus" (literal). In other words these new converts had been baptized with water but not baptized with the Holy Spirit (Ac 1:5). We should note that at that point in time there was no doubt in the apostles' minds that God desired to give these Gentiles "the same gift as He gave to us after believing in the Lord Jesus Christ" (Ac 11:17). Peter himself was the one who proclaimed on the day of Pentecost that "the promise is… for all who are far off, as many as the Lord our God shall call to Himself" (Ac 2:39). Yet as more and more people with legalistic backgrounds joined the church in Jerusalem, a controversy later arose as to whether or not Gentiles could be saved without first becoming Jews, let alone that they could be baptized with the Holy Spirit (Ac 11:1-3, 17-18; 15:1, 4-9). Thankfully that confusion had not yet affected the apostles, and when Peter and John arrived in Samaria, they were confident that it was God's will to give this gift to these new believers. They humbly asked God to pour out His blessing and undoubtedly spent time spiritually preparing themselves to minister effectively. We should also note that there does not appear to be a moment's thought given to the idea that since the Holy Spirit had not yet come upon the Samaritan believers in power, maybe it was not God's will. They simply assessed the situation as an unfinished work and began to wait on God. The next thing they did was to place their hands on them and "they were receiving the Holy Spirit." Luke does not tell us what manifestations occurred, but he does indicate by Simon's reaction that whatever they were, they could be observed or heard, and everyone upon whom they laid their hands received the Holy Spirit that way (vs18-19).

There are two verbs in this passage that need to be defined as carefully as possible: "receive" and "fall upon." The verb "fall upon" will later be used twice to describe the Spirit coming upon Cornelius' household

(Ac 10:44-11:18). Luke describes that moment by saying, "…the Holy Spirit fell upon all those who were listening…" (Ac 10:44), and then he later quotes Peter's explanation of that same event in which Peter said, "…the Holy Spirit fell upon them just as He did upon us, as at the beginning" (Ac 11:15). When we read the entire account of what happened in Cornelius' home, it becomes clear that we are to understand the term "fall upon" to mean that a person is given the same gift as that which the apostles received at Pentecost. Luke explains that Peter and those who were with him knew that the Spirit had "fallen upon" the household of Cornelius because "…they were hearing them speaking in tongues and exalting God" (Ac 10:46). In the next verse Peter will say they "received the Holy Spirit just as we did…" again referring to the day of Pentecost (Ac 10:47). And later on, when Peter reported to the leaders in Jerusalem, he left no doubt what the term "falling upon" meant. He said, "The Holy Spirit fell upon them just as He did upon us at the beginning. And I remembered the word of the Lord, how He used to say, 'John baptized with water, but you will be baptized with the Holy Spirit'" (Ac 11:15-16). In other words, the Roman believers in Caesarea were also baptized with the Holy Spirit.

vs18-19: This helps us understand what Luke means when he tells us that the Spirit "... had not yet fallen upon any of them" (v16). He means the Samaritans were not yet baptized with the Holy Spirit. But when Peter and John laid their hands on them, the Spirit "fell upon" them, and supernatural manifestations took place. And it was Simon's response to those manifestations that exposed his unchanged heart. He was thrilled to see such genuine power in action, and he knew that if he too could control that power and administer it to people at will, he would become richer and gain even greater honor. Basically from his point of view he was asking Peter to teach him how to operate this new kind of magic. He offered money saying, "Give me also this authority so that upon whomever I lay my hands, he may receive the Holy Spirit" (literal). Basically he was trying to purchase a new skill to enhance his business. That response was amazingly hard-hearted. To be standing nearby as God's love was moving so powerfully on people, yet not be drawn into worship by the holiness of the moment, meant Simon was still spiritually blind. His confession and baptism (v13) must have been insincere. His heart still lusted after power and money.

vs20-24: Peter instantly recognized Simon's spiritual condition. He said, "May your silver go with you into eternal destruction because you thought you could buy the gift of God with money" (literal). He told Simon that he was not saved. He said, "You have no part or lot in this matter because your heart is not straight before God." Then he warned Simon to repent and ask God to forgive his wicked attitudes. But the way Peter worded this warning, "...<u>if indeed</u> you will be forgiven the thought of your heart," (literal) shows that he perceived Simon's heart to be so hard that it would be very difficult for him to sincerely repent. Finally, Peter spoke prophetically, telling Simon that he saw him being full of bitterness and enslaved to sin. Sadly, Simon responded like a magician, not a believer. Instead of repenting, he merely asked Peter to pray that such a curse would not come upon him.

v25: There was now a vital church in Samaria full of believers who had been water-baptized and baptized with the Holy Spirit. So before returning to Jerusalem Peter and John spent time with them laying a solid foundation of teaching. Luke says they "solemnly bore witness" to that young church. He used a word which describes someone testifying in a courtroom. In other words he is telling us these two apostles stood in front of this new church and carefully reported the things they had seen Jesus do and the words they had heard Him say. Few of these Samaritans would have had firsthand information about Jesus. They had to trust Peter and John to tell them the truth. Their eternal destinies depended on the accuracy of the information they received. Then, after "...having spoken the word of the Lord," the two apostles began walking back toward Jerusalem stopping along the way to preach in the villages they passed. Undoubtedly they would have tried to connect those that came to Christ in each village with the new church in the city of Samaria.

v26: Angels play a significant role in the book of Acts. Peter was twice released from prison by an angel (Ac 5:19; 12:5-10); he saw an angel in a vision who directed him to the household of Cornelius (Ac 10:3-8); it was an angel who struck down Herod Agrippa (Herod the Great's grandson) in Caesarea (Ac 12:23), and an angel appeared to Paul during a storm at sea (Ac 27:23-25). On some occasions the angel appeared in a vision, but at others the angel took on what looked like a physical body and spoke directly to the person. Here we read that an angel spoke to Philip, but Luke doesn't tell us which method this angel used to communicate with him, only that he gave Philip definite instructions. He was to "Rise up and go south down along the road that descends from Jerusalem to Gaza Deserta [a city built on the ruins of the old Philistine city that had been destroyed in 96 B.C.]" (J. Rawson Lumby, Acts of the Apostles, Cambridge Greek Testament, University Press, 1904, p184).

Philip may have traveled back to Jerusalem with Peter and John, or he may have remained in Samaria and received this instruction from the angel after the apostles left. But whether he traveled alone or with the apostles, in order to obey the angel, it would have been necessary for him to pass through Jerusalem. He had been told to walk south along the road which connected Jerusalem with the coastal highway called the Via Maris. The Via Maris was the main road that ran between Egypt and Asia. The road Philip was told to take intersected the Via Maris at Gaza Deserta.

v27: Philip did as the angel commanded, and somewhere along that stretch of road, which was about 50 to 60 miles long, he overtook a man sitting in a carriage reading a passage from the prophet Isaiah. The man was the treasurer of the royal court of Ethiopia, and he was on his way home after worshiping in Jerusalem. Luke mentions that this man served under a queen named Candace. At the time the Ethiopians believed the sun-god was the father of each of their kings, so the king himself was considered to be too holy to be involved with secular matters. So in Ethiopia, the queen-mother was designated to manage the government, and each one was given the title "Candace," much like Egypt's kings were called "Pharaoh" (F.F. Bruce, Acts, Eerdmans, reprint 1974, p186).

Luke says the man was a "eunuch," but it is not at all certain that he was actually a eunuch in the physical sense of the word because the term could also be used as a general title applied to any trusted court official. If indeed he was a eunuch physically, his mutilation would have made him ceremonially unclean according to the Law of Moses (Dt 23:1). So even though he had traveled all the way to Jerusalem to worship, he would never have been permitted to enter the inner courts of the temple or take part in any of its worship services even if he had formally become a Jew. Yet if he was physically a eunuch, that fact would make his encounter with Philip all the more remarkable. As we read about the miraculous process by which God guided Philip to find this man, we realize we are seeing the fulfillment of an ancient prophecy. Now, because the Messiah had come, ritual uncleanness was no longer a barrier that prevented people from coming to God. Everyone, regardless of their condition or history, was welcome. In fact, as we observe Philip being sent to find this court official, we are watching God aggressively pursue a man who was both a Gentile and possibly ceremonially unclean. This profound lifting of the restrictions concerning who could enter God's presence fulfilled a promise spoken by the prophet Isaiah. Isaiah specifically stated that when the Messiah came, foreigners and "eunuchs" would be given a greater place of honor in God's presence than a parent honors a son or a daughter (Isa 56:3-8). He said, "To them I will give in My house and within My walls a memorial, and a name better than that of sons and daughters; I will give them an everlasting name which will not be cut off" (Is 56:5).

vs28-31: The angel told Philip to walk down that particular road but apparently gave him no further instructions. So as he walked along Philip must have continually listened for further guidance from the Holy Spirit. When he passed someone he may have asked if that was the one to whom he had been sent. Anyone as powerful as the treasurer of Ethiopia must have had an armed guard escorting him, yet the pace of the man's carriage was slow enough for Philip to overtake him on foot. When Philip saw the carriage, the Spirit spoke to him and said, "Go up and keep pace beside that carriage" (paraphrase). Apparently, judging by the Greek words Luke used here, he had to run to catch up, and then when he reached the carriage, he walked or jogged alongside it. He was able to draw close enough to hear the man reading out loud, and what he heard must have instantly confirmed that here indeed was his assignment. At that very moment the man was reading from the fifty-third chapter of Isaiah. Nowhere in the Bible is there a clearer explanation of the meaning of the cross of Jesus Christ. Philip must have been absolutely amazed at God's ability to arrange such a divine appointment. He only listened to two verses before asking the man a question which would have sounded something like this, "So then, do you know what those words really mean?" (paraphrase). The response that came out of the official's mouth immediately indicated why God had sent Philip on that mission. The man was neither offended nor annoyed to have this stranger challenge his comprehension of Scripture. We hear in his response a person who was humble and teachable. He said, "Well, how could I unless someone guides me?" Then he invited Philip to come up and sit with him in the carriage.

vs32-33: The verses Philip heard him read aloud were Isaiah 53:7-8. Luke quotes them from the Septuagint which is a Greek translation of the Hebrew Bible. It's possible that the man was reading from the original Hebrew, but as a court official, particularly one who worked in the area of finance, it's very likely that he spoke fluent Greek. Greek was the language in which business dealings at that time were carried out between nations. So it is more likely that he was reading from the Septuagint. This passage in Isaiah vividly describes the Messiah dying for the sins of the human race. He's pictured as a sacrificial lamb who did not resist being executed. The original Hebrew literally prophesies that this suffering Messiah would be taken out of prison and denied justice. It also says that the people of Israel who were alive when this took place would not understand that He was dying for them.

v34: The court official must have re-read or pointed to that passage when he said, "I ask you, of whom does the prophet say this? About himself or about someone else?" (literal). He was asking Philip a very important question. The identity of the one who is suffering in this passage of Isaiah is still debated today. Some choose to believe the prophet was speaking about his own sufferings. Others believe he was describing the sufferings of the nation of Israel. But when this passage (Isa 52:13-53:12) is read in context (Isa 49-53), and when its grammar is taken literally, it clearly describes a righteous individual who would be despised by the nation, upon whom God would place the sins of humanity, and who by his sacrifice would make possible the salvation of Gentiles as well as Jews. It vividly pictures a substitutionary death. When the passage is read in context, the "Servant" whom Isaiah describes is unmistakably the Messiah. What makes this passage so problematic for some is that it pictures a Messiah who suffers and dies. It says, "But the Lord caused the iniquity of us all to fall on Him" (Isa 53:6). It says He would become a "guilt offering" (Isa 53:10) and that He would "justify the many" (Isa 53:11). And it says, "He Himself bore the sin of many and interceded for transgressions" (Isa 53:12).

The passage teaches that at some appointed time in the future God would transfer human guilt to the Messiah, and that He would then die as our substitute.

vs35-37: It's hard to imagine that Philip didn't smile when he heard the man's question. Had he ever been given an easier opportunity to preach the gospel than this? Luke simply says: "And opening his mouth, and beginning from this Scripture he preached Jesus to him" (literal).

v36: As the carriage rolled along they passed by either a pond or a stream, and the official, who by now had surely been told that he must "repent and be baptized in the name of Jesus Christ for the forgiveness of your sins…" (Ac 2:38), saw the water and said, "Look! Water! What prevents me from being baptized?" He was ready to be joined by faith to the death and resurrection of Jesus Christ.

v37: The words recorded in this verse as Philip's reply: "If you believe with all your heart, you may," are not found in some ancient manuscripts of the book of Acts, but the substance of what is said here is certainly accurate. Whether or not Philip used those exact words, one way or another, he would have told this man to believe with all his heart. And the Ethiopian official's heartfelt response, "I believe that Jesus Christ is the Son of God!" would have been the substance of what he confessed. So we would do well to accept this verse and let it bear its beautiful witness.

v38: The official commanded his driver to stop the carriage, and then both he and Philip waded into a nearby creek or pond. Philip must have prayed for him and listened as he prayed a prayer of surrender and faith. Then Philip baptized him.

v39: Both men walked out of the water together, but as soon as they reached the shore, Philip suddenly disappeared. The word Luke uses to describe what happened to Philip means to "seize forcefully" (Jn 6:15; 10:12, 28-29; Ac 23:10; Jude 23) or "snatch away," and is used elsewhere in the Bible when God lays hold of someone and lifts that person up to heaven (2Co 12:2, 4; 1Th 4:17; Rev 12:5) (W.E. Vine, Expository Dictionary of New Testament Words, Fleming H. Revell,

1966, p174). Luke literally says here, "the Spirit seized Philip and the eunuch did not see him anymore." Apparently Philip was miraculously transported to another location (Jn 6:21), and his sudden departure must have confirmed to the official that God had sent him "...for he went on his way rejoicing."

v40: Philip then found himself in the middle of a city called Azotus (ancient Ashdod) which is also located on the Via Maris about 25 miles north of Gaza Deserta (read comments on v26). Starting in Azotus Philip slowly walked north on the Via Maris (coastal trade highway) evangelizing each city he passed until he arrived at Caesarea, 75 miles up the coast. There in that port-city he settled down and raised a family (Ac 21:8-9).

Acts Chapter 9

Intro: As we read through the book of Acts, we can often guess the names of those who were Luke's likely sources of information. In the prologue to his gospel he said he gathered information from "… those who from the beginning were eye witnesses and servants of the word…" (Lk 1:2). In other words he compiled his gospel by using written records and verbal testimony from those who had been with Jesus. It seems he did the same with this history of the early church. The first chapters (Ac 1-5) appear to have Peter and John as their source. One or both are present at nearly every event and preached the sermons that are quoted. Philip must have narrated much of the account of the evangelization of Samaria (Ac 8:4-40), and Paul is almost certainly Luke's source for the description of the stoning of Stephen, and now in this chapter, to his account of Paul's conversion. All we need to do is substitute first person pronouns into many of these sentences and we can almost "listen" to Paul give his testimony.

v1: With Philip settled in Caesarea (Ac 8:40), Luke returns to the horrible persecution taking place in Jerusalem (Ac 8:1-3). While Philip had been evangelizing in Samaria, Saul had continued to attack the church. By the time Luke returns to his description of Saul, it appears that Saul had arrested every believer he could find because his attention had turned to pursuing those who had fled the city. Somehow he discovered that many of the followers of Jesus had sought refuge in Damascus, and they were spreading this new faith in its synagogues.

Damascus is located about 140 miles northeast of Jerusalem, and since he was in a hurry, Saul may have taken the most direct route, which was to walk up the Jordan River valley to the Yarmuk River and then up that valley to the ancient "King's Highway" which ran north to Damascus (Y. Aharoni and M. Avi-Yonah, The Macmillan Bible Atlas, New York, 1968, p17). That city had a sizeable Jewish population and many synagogues (J. D. Douglas, ed., The New Bible Dictionary, Eerdmans, 1971, p289). Some of those Saul had been persecuting in Jerusalem must have fled there and found shelter with relatives, friends or fellow believers (Ac 9:19, 21).

Luke uses an odd word to describe Saul's state of mind. He pictures him literally "breathing in boastful threats and murder against the disciples of the Lord." It would seem more logical for Saul to "breath" out such things. And indeed, there is a Greek word built on the same verb (pneo) which means exactly that. Had Luke used that word, it would mean Saul was constantly speaking threats, and undoubtedly he was. But for him to breathe in "boastful threats and murder against the disciples of the Lord" may indicate that he had fallen prey to demonic influence. It appears he was being infused with rage. This insight would never excuse him for the violence he was committing, but it may help explain his extraordinary zeal (Eph 2:1-3).

v2: Many years later Paul looked back and described himself during that season as "raging like a madman" (Ac 26:11). When he captured someone, he would try to force his victim to blaspheme Christ by flogging the person as he or she lay face down on the floor of a synagogue (Mt 10:17; Ac 5:40; 22:19; 26:11; Dt 25:2-3; 2Co 11:24). In order to conduct an inquisition in a foreign city like Damascus, Paul needed a letter of introduction from the high priest as well as a letter explaining who was to be arrested and why. Hopefully these letters would convince local leaders to cooperate. He needed them to be willing to betray family and friends. The group that traveled with him very likely included temple police to help him do the dirty work of arresting, questioning, flogging and, when necessary, transporting prisoners back to Jerusalem to be tried before the Sanhedrin. Then if the person were found guilty, the Sanhedrin would have the authority, if given permission by the Roman governor, to execute those unwilling to renounce Christ (Ac 22:4-5, 19; 26:10).

Luke says Saul was searching for people who belonged to "The Way." It was a title used by the early church to describe itself. A person who believed in Jesus was said to be worshiping God "according to The Way" (Ac 24:14). In other words they believed and worshiped according to the way Jesus of Nazareth taught people to believe and worship. The term "Christian" was coined later (Ac 11:26). The Bible often pictures life as a path to be walked. A person can walk through life on God's path, or turn and wander off His path, so it's easy to see why Jewish believers would have used this metaphor to describe themselves. They were a people who were following their Shepherd, their Lord; they were walking toward heaven on the "way of Jesus of Nazareth."

vs3-5: In the first two verses of this chapter we see the heart of Saul before he met Jesus, and then beginning at verse 3 and continuing down through verse 18, Luke describes Saul's transformation from a violent persecutor of the church to a passionate disciple of Jesus. As he and those traveling with him drew near to Damascus, a brilliant light from out of heaven suddenly shone round him, and falling to the ground he heard a voice saying, "Saul, Saul, why are you pursuing [hunting, chasing] me?" (literal). And Saul said, "Who are you, Lord?" And He answered, "I am Jesus whom you are pursuing." In the original language Jesus does not say, "Why are you persecuting Me?" He says, "Why are you pursuing Me?" And there is a subtle difference. It's true that Saul's goal was to persecute the church, but there is a double meaning in Jesus' question. In spite of all his fury, Saul was a God-seeker, and though he didn't know it yet, his heart was pursuing Jesus.

The Lord had compassion on Saul because He knew he was genuinely deceived (1Ti 1:12-13). Saul thought that in this horrible way he was serving God (Jn 16:2-3). Years later when retelling this event, he mentioned that Jesus had also said, "It's hard for you to kick against the goads" (Ac 26:14). In other words Jesus told him he was like a stubborn ox or mule that tries to kick its master rather than move forward when prodded with a sharp stick. This suggests that Saul's conscience may have been troubling him while he was carrying out this vicious campaign. But instead of repenting when he felt such twinges of compassion or shame, Saul angrily silenced his conscience and continued on with even greater zeal.

vs3-6: It was midday when Jesus appeared to Saul, yet the glorious light radiating from Him shone brighter than the light of the sun (Ac 26:13). And this was not a vision; Saul directly encountered the resurrected Jesus. Twenty-two years later when writing to the Corinthian church, he included himself among those who had physically seen Jesus after He had risen from the dead. He said, "…and last of all, as to one untimely born, He appeared to me also" (1Co 15:8). The Lord was merciful to Saul because he had been deceived. He knew Saul would serve Him with all his heart once he knew the truth. There was no need to threaten him but to simply confront him and then command him to wait in the city for further instructions. Jesus said, "Now stand up and go into the city, and it will be told you what you are bound to do" (v6, literal).

v7: It is possible to assume that Paul's statement in Acts 22:9 conflicts with the report made here in this verse. Here Luke reports that the men traveling with Saul heard Jesus' voice but did not see Him. The statement made in Acts 22:9 can give the impression that the men saw a brilliant light but did not hear a voice. Any confusion disappears when the original Greek words are examined carefully. Acts 9:7 reports that they heard the sound of a voice but does not say they understood what they heard. Acts 22:9 says they did not understand the meaning of what they heard. This lack of comprehension may have to do with the fact that Jesus spoke to Saul in the Hebrew dialect (Ac 26:14) rather than the everyday language of Aramaic. Saul, of course, as a biblical scholar spoke fluent Hebrew.

vs8-9: The men traveling with Saul lifted him up from the ground, but they soon found that even though his eyes were open, he had become blind. So they led him by the hand into Damascus to a house located on "Straight Street." Straight Street was a colonnaded boulevard running through the center of the city past the theater and royal palace (Yohanan Aharoni and Michael Avi-Yonah, The Macmillan Bible Atlas, Macmillan Pub., 1968, pp152-153). Judas, his host (v11), must have been a prominent, synagogue leader, and his home, given its address, was likely an estate. He had been expecting to host a distinguished guest, the high priest's representative. And Saul had planned to stay there while conducting his inquisition of the Jewish community. So what a surprise it must have been when the high priest's representative was led into Judas' house blind and in shock. Saul remained there for three days neither eating nor drinking. Those must have been days of deep mourning for Saul. At times he may have wondered if that encounter with Jesus had only been a dream, but it couldn't have been a dream. He was blind. His eyes were physically damaged. As he waited there in the darkness, he may have remembered the faces of those he'd beaten or watched die because they had refused to deny Jesus, the same Jesus whom he now knew to be the resurrected Son of God. His own evil must have overwhelmed him. Yet Jesus hadn't killed him, instead He'd said something about serving Him. How could that be?

vs10-12: The Lord brought Saul's days of darkness to an end by sending to him one of the leaders of the church in Damascus. The man's name was Ananias, and Paul would later describe him as someone who carefully obeyed God's Word and was highly regarded by the Jewish community (Ac 22:12). In that case it is almost certain that Judas, Saul's host, would have known Ananias, and he may have known that he was a follower of Jesus. If not, he soon would. Luke says, "There was a certain disciple in Damascus named Ananias, and the Lord said to him in a vision, 'Ananias!' And he said, 'Behold, I, Lord.' And the Lord [said] to him, 'Rise up and go to the street called 'Straight' and seek in the house of Judas a man from Tarsus named Saul, for behold he is praying, and in a vision he saw a man named Ananias coming in and putting hands on him so that he may see again" (literal).

vs13-14: Given Saul's reputation, who can blame Ananias for gently questioning Jesus to see if he realized how dangerous this mission would be. "And Ananias answered, 'Lord, I have heard from many about this man, what things he did to Your saints [holy ones] in Jerusalem. And here he has authority from the chief priests to find all the ones who are calling upon Your name'" (literal). Based on Saul's past actions, Ananias was worried he would be walking into a trap.

vs15-16: But Jesus' response to Ananias completely ignored Saul's past. Instead He focused entirely on Saul's future. He said, "Go, because this man is a chosen vessel to pick up and carry My name before nations and kings and sons of Israel; for I will give him a glimpse of how many things he will be bound to suffer on behalf of My name" (literal). Jesus is able to see the human heart and know a person's future. He saw beyond Saul's present condition to the great apostle he would become. In other words, He saw Paul.

He called Saul a "chosen vessel." This isn't favoritism. It isn't that He loved Saul more than other people, and therefore, went to great effort to save him. Indeed the Lord did love Saul of Tarsus and knew he would say "yes" when he saw the truth, but that's not the only reason Saul was a "chosen vessel." His encounter with Jesus on the road to Damascus is an example of God's loving heart strategically targeting certain people. There are individuals, who after becoming saved, will lead a great number of people to faith. And God knew that this man would preach and write in such a way that multitudes would believe in Jesus Christ. Being "chosen" went beyond Saul's personal salvation to include his fruitfulness as a minister.

vs17-19: Ananias needed no further prodding. Luke says, "Ananias went away and entered into the house and putting hands on him said, 'Brother Saul, the Lord Jesus, who appeared to you along the road by which you were coming, has sent me so that you may see again and be filled with the Holy Spirit.' And immediately there fell away from his eyes something like scales, and he saw again, and rising up was baptized, and taking food was strengthened" (literal). Ananias not only prayed for Saul's healing, but he also prayed for him to receive the baptism with the Holy Spirit. This is notable because, as we recall, Philip did not minister the baptism with the Holy Spirit to those he led to Christ. Peter and John had to come to Samaria to perform this ministry (Ac 8:14-17). But Ananias did, and he also prophesied. Later on when Paul related what Ananias had said to him during that encounter, he added more than is recorded here. We learn that Ananias also said, "Brother Saul… the God of our fathers hand-picked you beforehand to know His will and see the Righteous One and hear an utterance out of His mouth because you will be a witness to Him to all men of the things which you have seen and heard" (Ac 22:14-15, literal). Then he told Saul to rise up and "be baptized and wash away your sins, calling upon His [Jesus'] name" (Ac 22:16). In that one encounter Saul was healed, baptized with the Holy Spirit, water baptized and called into ministry. Then he was given food, after which Luke says, his strength was greatly restored.

vs19-21: Saul spent several days with the disciples in Damascus probably listening and asking questions while they pointed out passages in the Bible that speak of Jesus (Lk 24:44-47). It's likely there were people present who had heard Jesus use some of these passages to explain Himself. If so, Saul would have listened attentively, and he was so theologically astute he would have processed what he was hearing very quickly.

Apparently Saul began visiting the city's synagogues as soon as the next Sabbath arrived. Since he was a respected Jewish scholar, it would have been customary to invite him to greet the congregation, and when given the opportunity, Saul then boldly proclaimed Jesus to be the "Son of God." Luke says those who heard him were stunned (beside themselves) and were saying, "Is not this man the one who captured and slaughtered those who call upon this name in Jerusalem and who had come here for this, in order that after binding them, he might bring them before the chief priests?" (literal).

v22: During those early days following his conversion, Saul was extremely full of the power of the Holy Spirit, and like Stephen before him (Ac 6:10), he was able to effectively prove from the Scriptures that Jesus is the promised Messiah (Christ). Some of the leaders in the Jewish community rose up and tried to disprove his logic, but they were not able to do so. The debate between them became confused and full of noisy disorder.

vs23-25: After enough days had passed to allow Saul to preach Christ to those willing to listen, a group of Jewish leaders met secretly to form a plan to kill him. They posted people at the city gates, day and night, so they could follow him to a secluded location and murder him. But someone warned him about the plot, and though he had only recently become a believer, he had already gathered around himself a group of disciples who loved him. They knew the location of a hole or window in the city wall through which he could escape. So in the dark of night he climbed into a large woven basket, the kind of basket normally used for hay or bales of wool (Rienecker/Rogers, Linguistic Key to the Greek New Testament, Zondervan, 1980, p282), and then a rope was attached to the basket, and he was lowered down undetected. He immediately headed back to Jerusalem.

vs25-26: At this point we will try to put the events that took place during this season of Saul's life into a chronological order. By drawing on statements made elsewhere, we discover that between verses 25 and 26 Luke chose to skip over three years of Saul's history. Saul did indeed return to Jerusalem immediately after escaping from Damascus, but that first visit to Jerusalem was very brief, and it is not the same as the visit he describes in verses 26-30. Those verses describe events which took place three years later. That first, brief visit is mentioned in Acts 22:17-21. It seems he arrived alone and faced a very dangerous environment. It was necessary to avoid being seen by the high priest or members of the Sanhedrin. The Lord appeared to him and warned him to quickly leave the city. A report of his activities in Damascus had surely reached them by that time.

Meanwhile believers in Jerusalem were still terrified of him. Here was the man who had led the persecution against them and may have been directly responsible for the death of family members or friends. When retelling these events years later, Paul said that he went to the temple to pray, and as he was praying, "I fell into a trance and I saw Him saying to me, 'Make haste, and get out of Jerusalem quickly, because they will not accept your testimony about Me.' And I said, 'Lord, they themselves understand that in one synagogue after another I used to imprison and beat those who believe in you…' And He said to me, 'Go! For I will send you far away to the Gentiles'" (Ac 22:18-21). This was not a missionary call to evangelize non-Jews; it was an urgent warning to flee to a foreign nation for asylum.

We learn from his letter to the Galatians that he fled to "Arabia" (Gal 1:17). Traditionally it has been assumed he went there for a time of reflection and prayer, and undoubtedly those activities took place, but the Lord's purpose in sending him out of Jerusalem was for his safety. He was protecting Saul's life. At that time the term "Arabia" included not only the deserts of the Arabian Peninsula but also the areas east and south of Israel. The Negev (southern deserts of Israel), the regions to the east (ancient Bashan, Gilead, Moab, Edom and Midian) and even much of the Sinai Peninsula had come under the control of an Arab people called the Nabateans (Nelson Glueck, Rivers in the Desert, Farrar, Straus and Cudahy, New York 1959, p194).

To escape Jerusalem Saul probably fled south. If so, he would have passed through the Negev and into the region that had once been Edom. It's possible he went all the way down to Midian. Centuries earlier Elijah took that same route to escape Jezebel (1Ki 19:1-18). We have no way of knowing whether Saul, like Elijah, traveled all the way to Mt. Sinai, but it is interesting that in the same letter in which he mentions he went to Arabia he notes that Mt. Sinai is in "Arabia" (Gal 4:25). In his letter to the Galatians he says that he returned to Damascus after an unspecified amount of time in Arabia (Gal 1:17). An ancient highway (the King's Highway), which is still in use today, runs north from the tip of the Red Sea (Gulf of Aqaba) and passes through Damascus on its way to Mesopotamia. It's likely that he took that road.

In his letter to the Galatians Paul says he returned to Jerusalem three years later (Gal 1:18). We don't know how that time was divided between Arabia and Damascus, but he was in Damascus long enough to create a crisis. Once again he had to be lowered down in a basket through a window in the wall (2Co 11:32-33), but this time he was escaping the anger of the Nabateans, Arabians who controlled Damascus for a few years during the reign of King Aretas IV (9 B.C.-A.D. 40). The chief officer in charge of the city (Greek: ethnarch) posted a guard in order to capture Saul, but he escaped using the same method he had used before.

v26: Now, having tried to reconstruct the sequence of events between Saul's first escape from Damascus and his second, we return to Luke's narrative in Acts 9. Three years after briefly visiting Jerusalem (Ac 22:17-21), Saul returned to the city, only this time he came with one specific purpose in mind. He wanted to meet Peter (Gal 1:18). But when he arrived, the believers were still afraid of him and refused to associate with him. Undoubtedly they assumed he wanted to infiltrate their community as a spy and would then betray them.

v27: For some reason Barnabas, whom Luke introduced earlier (Ac 4:36), trusted Saul and aggressively stepped in as his sponsor. Barnabas may have had friends in Damascus who gave him firsthand accounts of Saul's ministry there, or God may have given him a revelation concerning Saul, but whatever the cause, Luke says he "...took hold of him and led him to the disciples" (literal).

Barnabas led Saul to a gathering where Peter and possibly James were present (Gal 1:18-20) and then personally introduced him. He described for them how Saul had met the Lord on the road to Damascus. He told them that Jesus spoke to him, and he noted that Saul had boldly preached about Jesus in that city.

v28: Considering all that Saul had done to them, it's amazing the church welcomed him into its fellowship. Not only were they risking their lives, but many would find themselves face-to-face with the man who had cruelly abused their loved ones. Forgiving him would require the deepest level of obedience. In order to describe their acceptance of Saul, Luke simply says, "…he was with them going in and going out in Jerusalem speaking boldly in the name of the Lord" (literal). In other words they invited Saul to join them in their daily public ministry. He became one of their preachers, fearlessly proclaiming Christ in a city where he had previously been a rising religious scholar and a vicious persecutor of the church. One can only imagine the tension and controversy that surrounded him every time he stood to speak.

The phrase, "…going in and going out" also means Saul was invited to stay in their homes. It pictures the daily rhythm of someone going into a house in the evening and then out into the city during the day. Luke chose that phrase to show us that Saul went out each day with the church as they conducted their public ministry and then returned with them to their homes at night where he was provided room and board. In Galatians Paul says he stayed with Peter for fifteen of those days (Ga 1:18). Peter was undoubtedly very busy, yet he took Saul with him during the day so Saul could observe the ministry the disciples were doing and to give Saul the opportunity to minister as well.

We can be sure that Saul would have questioned Peter during their time together. He likely asked him to describe what Jesus looked like and how He ministered. He surely wanted to hear the very words Jesus had spoken. Since Saul was a highly educated man and since this information was of supreme importance to him, we can safely assume that he took notes on those conversations. Might some of these notes be the parchments he valued so highly later on (2Ti 4:13)?

v29: When the church went out into the city to preach and pray, Saul went with them and was invited to be one of the speakers. When given the opportunity, he preached boldly. Afterward he would talk with individuals and get into heated scriptural discussions. Because he himself was a Hellenistic Jew, it's no surprise that Luke mentions he got into intense debates with other Hellenistic Jews. Many of them may have been old friends because Saul had grown up in that city (Ac 22:3). One can only imagine the intensity of those debates between Jewish scholars who had memorized huge portions of Scripture arguing back and forth about prophetic passages. Some of their discussions ended bitterly, and as had already taken place twice in Damascus, a plot was formed to physically attack Saul and kill him.

v30: Somehow the church discovered the plot and quickly escorted him to the seaport of Caesarea. There they helped him find a ship headed north. The plan was for him to escape to his childhood home of Tarsus, but Luke uses a verb here which possibly hints that they had another purpose as well. He says, "they sent him away to Tarsus." Saul's presence in the city, combined with his confrontational style of ministry, had once again stirred up the fires of persecution. Prior to his arrival they had begun to die down.

v31: Saul's departure marked a turning point for the church in Israel. With their chief persecutor converted, and his aggressive style of preaching and debate gone, the church entered into a peaceful season. They continued winning souls and growing in numbers, but the way they did ministry was more in line with Peter than with Paul.

Beginning at the next verse (v32) and continuing on through most of the following three chapters, Luke turns his focus back to Peter. As we watch Peter, we discover that his approach to ministry seems to be centered on divine guidance and healing. Then the miracles that resulted would open a door for him to preach the gospel. That approach stands in stark contrast to Saul's style of ministry. Saul used bold proclamation followed by scriptural debate. But as we noted, Saul tended to provoke anger and stir persecution. He was repeatedly forced to flee for his life. But as we'll soon see, Peter repeatedly gained great favor and led whole communities to Christ.

v32: Luke's first example of Peter's ministry, during that more peaceful season after Saul's departure, is the healing of a man named Aeneas. Peter was systematically visiting churches in all the regions of Israel (Judea, Galilee and Samaria), and in the course of those travels he went to a town called Lydda located on Israel's coastal plain.

vs33-34: When he first arrived, he met with the "saints" (believers), but at some point during his stay he encountered a man lying on a mattress who had been paralyzed for eight years. In a manner very similar to the healing of the lame man in the temple (Ac 3:6), Peter spoke authoritatively to the paralyzed man and commanded healing. He said, "Aeneas, Jesus Christ heals you; stand up and make your bed! And immediately Aeneas stood up" (literal).

v35: Luke says everyone in that town saw Aeneas after he was healed. It was a good-sized town with a very conservative Jewish culture (R.J. Knowling in The Expositor's Greek Testament, W. Robertson Nicoll, ed., Eerdmans, 1983 reprint, Vol. 2, p245). He says even those living in the surrounding region, which was called the Plain of Sharon, saw him. Judging by the widespread response to his healing, many of them must have known Aeneas. If so, they probably knew why he was paralyzed, and whether his paralysis had been caused by a disease or an injury. So when they saw him walking normally, there would have been no question in their minds about the validity of the healing. They knew a profound miracle had taken place which is why Luke says everyone who saw Aeneas began to call on the name of the Lord Jesus.

v36: Joppa is the only natural harbor between Haifa, near the northern border of Israel, and Egypt. It's located 35 miles from Jerusalem and historically served as its seaport (D.F. Payne, The New Bible Dictionary, J. D. Douglas, ed., Eerdmans, 1971, p654). Lydda was located about 12 miles southeast of Joppa on the road that connected Jerusalem to Joppa. While Peter was ministering in Lydda, a beloved member of the church in Joppa died, and the believers there immediately sent two men to ask Peter to come and pray for her. Even if those messengers were young enough to walk rapidly or jog those intervening miles, it was at least a three to four hour journey each way.

That response shows a high level of faith. The church in Joppa sent for Peter after one of their members had already died. So they must have believed that it was genuinely possible for her to be raised to life even though Peter would not be able to arrive for at least six to eight hours. Their confidence in him also reveals the remarkable degree of power at work in Peter's ministry during those days. Jesus had promised His disciples that they would be able to do the same type of miracles that He had done (Jn 14:12), and indeed here we see Peter doing exactly what we might have expected Jesus to do in that same situation. The passage reads like one of the events in the gospels.

Luke says the deceased woman's name was "Tabitha," an Aramaic word for "gazelle" (Greek: Dorcas), and he specifically identifies her as a disciple by using a feminine form of the word. This shows that women as well as men were referred to as "disciples." He says she was "full of good works and merciful deeds," and many examples of her compassion were displayed when Peter arrived at Joppa. She must have been a skilled seamstress because "all the widows" showed Peter the clothes she had made for them. She had lovingly provided for women who had been left in poverty (v39).

v37: We have no idea how old she was, nor is there any indication of what may have caused her death. Luke simply says, "And it happened in those days, being weakened, she died…" (literal). His reference to "those days" seems to point to the days during which Peter was in the area, meaning something sudden and unexpected may have happened to her. Her loss was deeply felt, and the response by the church shows that they did not think that her assignment from God had been completed. This was not the anticipated passing of an elderly member, but rather the abrupt removal of a vital member of their community. To prevent speculation about whether or not she truly died, Luke mentions the fact that they washed her corpse and placed it in an upper room. In other words, no one should look for a natural explanation for her resuscitation. The normal things that happen when people die had happened to her.

vs38-39: When the two messengers reached Peter, they implored him not to remain in Lydda any longer but to return with them to Joppa. Peter immediately stood up and went with them. As soon as he arrived, he was led to an upper room where the body had been laid. It was full of widows weeping for her. It's not hard to imagine the excitement that arose when Peter entered. The women gathered around to show him the clothes they were wearing because Tabitha had made them. Obviously, they were trying to persuade him to do a miracle by convincing him that she was a wonderful person, but they were also communicating to him how desperately they still needed her. None of this, of course, was necessary. The Spirit had directed Peter to respond to their request, or he would have stayed in Lydda.

vs40-41: Peter asked everyone to wait outside, and once the room was quiet, he knelt down to pray. We're not told how long he remained there, but he surely took enough time to prepare himself spiritually and receive the Lord's instructions as to how to proceed. He had watched Jesus minister in a very similar situation. He had been present when Jesus raised Jairus' daughter from the dead in Capernaum (Mk 5:21-24, 35-43). Then while still on his knees, Peter turned and spoke to the body. He said, "Tabitha, stand up!" She opened her eyes, looked at him and then sat up. At that point he must have stood to his feet because he reached out and took her hand, undoubtedly to steady her as she rose up, because the miracle itself had already happened. After that Luke says, Peter called "the saints and widows" back into the room so they could see their friend standing alive beside him. By distinguishing between "saints" and "widows" he may be indicating that this group of widows included unbelievers. Tabitha's generosity may have extended far beyond the boundaries of the church.

v42: The report of that miracle swept through the city. As had been the case in Lydda, so many credible witnesses testified to this miracle that its validity simply could not be contested. Tabitha had come back to life. The result was that "…it became known throughout all Joppa, and many believed upon the Lord" (literal).

v43: The spiritual awakening ignited by this event lasted long enough to require Peter to make arrangements for his own housing. There must have been a steady flow of people desiring for him to pray for their healing or needing to be water baptized or to receive the baptism with the Holy Spirit. And of course, they all needed to be taught how to become disciples of Jesus Christ, so Peter remained in Joppa until they were strong enough to carry on without him. During that time he stayed in the house of a tanner named Simon. That Peter chose to stay with a tanner is surprising. Not only does tanning leather produce terrible odors, which is why Simon's house was by the sea (Ac 10:6), but Simon and his house would have been considered ceremonially unclean by the Jewish community, because that type of work required constant contact with the bodies of dead animals (Lev 11:39-40). So for Peter to stay in such a place indicates that he was already moving away from the constraints of the ceremonial laws.

Acts Chapter 10

vs1-2: While Peter was ministering in Joppa, an angel of the Lord appeared to a Roman soldier in a nearby city. What the angel said to that soldier set in motion a series of events which would become a major turning point in church history. The soldier's name was Cornelius. He was a centurion, a captain in charge of a hundred men. The unit he led belonged to a larger company of soldiers called the "Italian Cohort." It was an auxiliary unit made up of Roman citizens with the very special assignment of protecting the representative of the Roman government. When these events took place, King Herod Agrippa was Rome's official representative (J. Rawson Lumby, The Acts of the Apostles, Cambridge Greek Testament, J.J.S. Perowne, ed., Univ. Press, 1904, p208).

Luke says Cornelius was "devout," meaning that he worshiped the God of the Bible but had not become a Jew. He also says he was "God-fearing," meaning that he lived his life aware that God saw all that he did and would hold him accountable for his sin or reward him for his obedience. And Cornelius was not alone in those qualities. The members of his household shared his faith. He did many acts of kindness; he gave gifts to help the poor, and he prayed continually asking God to help him in everything he did.

v3: Around three o'clock in the afternoon on that particular day, he saw a vision so vivid it was as if he were seeing it with his physical eyes.

He saw an angel enter the room, come up to him and address him by name, "Cornelius!"

v4: For a moment he was so terrified he could only stare at the angel. Finally he asked, "What is it Lord?" The angel explained that his prayers and gifts to the poor had risen up before God like the smoke of the memorial portion of a grain offering when it is placed on the altar of sacrifice (Lev 2:2,9,16; 5:12; 6:15). He described them as a "soothing aroma to the Lord," meaning that God viewed them as sincere acts of worship. He was not implying that Cornelius had earned a reward, but by calling his prayers and gifts a "soothing aroma," he was assuring him that God received them as though he were a Jew who had gone into the temple to offer heart-felt worship.

v5: It appears that while he was stationed in Israel, Cornelius recognized that the God of the Bible is the true God. Because he was a man of integrity, he responded to this revelation by forsaking the gods of Rome. This was a remarkably humble step given the fact that most Jews hated the soldiers of the occupying army, and it was a remarkably bold step given the fact that the Roman government would view any disloyalty to their gods, particularly a lack of reverence for Caesar, as treasonous. Yet when he saw the truth, he stepped toward it. So now we see God about to give him more truth through Peter. (Mt 13:12). The angel told Cornelius that a man named Peter was staying in Joppa, and that he was to send men to ask him to come back with them to Caesarea. He was told that Peter had a message for him from God (v22).

v6: Peter was staying as a guest in the home of a man whose name was also Simon. His host made his living tanning leather which was probably why his house was located outside of town near the seashore where sea breezes could carry away the unpleasant odors produced by his trade.

vs7-8: As soon as the angel went away, Cornelius summoned two of his household servants as well as a trusted soldier who shared his faith. He knew this soldier well because the man had been assigned to him as his aide. When he gave them their orders, he explained everything that had happened to him and then sent them to Joppa.

v9: It's approximately 32 miles from Caesarea to Joppa along the main road which would have required about 16 hours of steady walking. The angel appeared to Cornelius at 3:00pm in the afternoon, and immediately afterward he sent his messengers out. So they reached Joppa a little after noon on the next day. But before they arrived, Peter had gone up onto the roof of the home in which he was staying to pray. Noon is a prayer time for observant Jews.

vs10-11: Apparently someone was cooking lunch down below, and the smell of the food drifted upward and surrounded Peter because Luke says he became "starved" and was longing to "taste" what they were cooking. While waiting for them to finish preparing the food he was suddenly overwhelmed by the power of the Holy Spirit, and a vision began to unfold in front of him. Heaven "opened up," meaning the sky must have appeared to pull back to allow the brilliant light of heaven to shine through. Then a huge, cloth sheet came down through that opening. It was made of fine, white linen, and it was lowered down by its four corners until it rested on the earth.

v12: When it reached the ground, it flattened out, and Peter was able to see what was in it. It contained a great variety of creatures which were considered to be unclean by the Law of Moses (Lev 11). Luke says it was filled with representatives from "all the four-footed animals and reptiles of the earth and birds of the air." The eleventh chapter of Leviticus probably gives us an itemized list of the "unclean" creatures Peter saw: animals, fish, birds, rodents, lizards, insects and "whatever crawls on its belly… whatever has many feet."

vs13-16: So when Peter heard a voice command him to "Rise up, Peter, butcher and eat!", he responded with shock and revulsion, "Not even one, Lord, because at no time have I ever eaten from all those things that are common and unclean!" (literal). Then a voice spoke a second time saying, "What God made clean, you do not make common." Three times this dialogue between God and Peter took place, and then the sheet full of animals was taken back up into heaven.

v17-18: After the vision passed, Peter remained on the roof reflecting on all that he had just seen trying to understand what it meant. While he was still in this condition, the messengers from Caesarea arrived. They had asked for directions to Simon's house in Joppa and now stood on his porch calling to those inside asking if a man named Simon Peter was staying there.

vs19-20: Peter didn't hear them, but the Holy Spirit interrupted his thoughts telling him, "Behold, two men are searching for you. Stand up, go downstairs and go with them. Don't hesitate [even though they are Gentiles, and one is a Roman soldier] because I have sent them" (literal).

v21: Peter went down and said to the men, "Behold, I am he whom you seek. What charge has been made against me which brought you here?" (literal). In this statement Luke uses a word which implies that when Peter saw the Roman soldier, he assumed he was being officially summoned or possibly arrested.

v22: The messengers quickly assured him they were bringing an invitation, not an arrest-warrant. They had been sent on this mission by a very godly man: "Cornelius, a centurion, a man who observes the Jewish law and whose faith in God actively governs the way he lives [v2], a man whose reputation for giving gifts to the poor and prayer has spread beyond the Jewish community in Caesarea to include the nation's spiritual leaders in Jerusalem" (paraphrase). They explained that Cornelius had sent them because he had received a revelation from God. They said, "A holy angel instructed him to summon you to his house to hear a statement from you."

v23: Peter must have been standing in the doorway of the house while the three men remained outside because when he heard their words, he invited them to come in, and then Luke says he provided for their room and board. Though they were staying in the home of Simon the Tanner, Peter treated them as though they were his guests. Very likely it would have been a financial challenge for his host to feed three more people. The next morning they began their journey to Caesarea, but the church in Joppa was still concerned for his safety, so they sent six men (Ac 11:12) to accompany him.

v24: The group arrived in Caesarea at about three o'clock in the afternoon on the next day (v30), and Cornelius, along with a large gathering of relatives and close friends, was waiting expectantly for them.

v25: When Peter finally met Cornelius, the Roman centurion prostrated himself on the ground in front of him. Probably nothing in this story proves the sincerity of Cornelius' vision more than this amazing act. For a Roman officer to prostrate himself before a Jew with family and friends nearby would have been absolutely unthinkable unless, of course, an angel really did instruct him to send for Peter and assured him that Peter would tell him and his loved ones how to receive eternal life (Ac 11:14). In that case Cornelius' zeal makes perfect sense. By the way, the word Luke uses to describe Cornelius' response does not mean he tried to "worship" Peter; it means only that he prostrated himself flat on the ground. A person takes that position to express total submission. Only when someone takes that position before God, or a god, does it become an expression of worship.

v26: Still what Cornelius did look too much like worship for Peter, so he stooped down and helped him get back on his feet saying, "Stand up. I myself am also a man" (literal).

v27: Then to put to rest any thought that he viewed himself as superior to Cornelius, Peter apparently took him by the arm, and the two men walked into the meeting room side-by-side as friends.

v28: There Peter discovered a large group waiting to hear him speak. As he stood in front of this gathering, he was very conscious of the fact that this was an awkward situation given the cultural boundaries that existed between Jews and Romans.

vs28-29: He began by explaining why he, a Jew, had been so willing to enter a Gentile's home. He said, "You are familiar with the fact that we Jews have customs that forbid us to associate with, or even physically get close to, a foreigner, and [yet] God showed me that I am not to call any man common [unwelcome among God's people] or unclean [unwelcome in God's presence]. Indeed that's why I came without asking questions or raising objections when I was summoned. And it's because I didn't ask these questions that I need to ask you now, 'For what reason did you summon me?'" (paraphrase).

vs30-33: Cornelius answered him this way: "Four days ago at this very hour of the day, I was praying in my house at three o'clock in the afternoon, and behold, a man stood in front of me wearing a robe which shone with a brilliant light. And he said to me, 'Cornelius, your prayer was heard, and your gifts to the poor were remembered before God. So send [messengers] to Joppa and summon Simon who is also called Peter. This man is lodged in the house of Simon the Tanner by the sea.' So I sent [messengers] to you at once, and you promptly responded to my request and came right away. So now we are all here, present before God, to hear everything the Lord commanded you to tell us" (literal).

vs34-36: "And opening his mouth [stepping out into anointed speech, Mt 13:35] Peter said, 'I now truly understand that God is completely just. He does not distinguish between people based on their outward circumstances such as nationality, physical appearance, wealth or social standing. But in every nation anyone who has genuine faith in the true God and who sincerely tries to obey Him is accepted by Him. This is the message He was trying to tell our nation through the preaching of Jesus Christ. Jesus told us that He came to bring peace between Jew and Gentile and said that He is the Lord over all the peoples of the earth, not just Israel'" (paraphrase).

vs37-39: Having declared to them the meaning of the vision, Peter began to preach. He said, "You know the proclamation which took place throughout all Judea, beginning from Galilee, after the baptism which John announced. [You know] that God anointed Jesus of Nazareth with the Holy Spirit and power, [that it was] He who went from place to place doing good works and healing all those being oppressed by the devil because God was with Him. And we are witnesses of all the things which He did both among the Jews who live in the countryside and in Jerusalem. Indeed they killed Him by hanging Him on a wooden stake" (literal, see Ac 5:30; 13:27-29).

vs40-43: "This is the one God raised on the third day and caused Him to become visible, not to all the people, but to witnesses who had been selected [hand-picked] by God beforehand, to us who ate and drank with Him after His resurrection from among the dead. And He commanded us to proclaim to the people and to thoroughly testify that this is the One who has been designated by God as judge of the living and the dead. To this One all the prophets bear witness that through His name every one believing in Him receives forgiveness of sins" (literal).

v44: Then Luke says, "Yet, while Peter was still speaking these words, the Holy Spirit fell upon all the ones who were listening to the message" (literal). That statement would later play a critical role in a debate that took place in Jerusalem about what had happened that day (Ac 11:1-18). The fact is Peter did nothing more than present a few, basic statements about Christ, and then while he was still talking, God acted unilaterally. This divine involvement proved that Peter could not be held responsible for what happened. He had not at that point laid his hands on anyone, nor had he coached any sort of behavior.

v45-48: In this statement Luke uses a term which gives us an important insight into the six men who accompanied Peter from Joppa to Caesarea. He calls them "the faithful of the circumcision," and he would soon use a similar term, "those from the circumcision" (Ac 11:2). By the time Luke wrote the book of Acts, that term, "the circumcision," had become a title which was used to refer to a particular group of Jewish Christians who believed that a Gentile must first become a Jew before becoming a Christian (Ro 4:9-12; Ga 2:12; 5:6; Eph 2:11; Php 3:2,3; Col 4;11; Titus 1:10) (J. Rawson Lumby, The Acts of the Apostles, Cambridge Greek Testament, J.J.S. Peroune, ed. Cambridge Univ. Press, 1904, p222). So Luke is using a term his readers would have understood to identify a very early form of that false teaching. In time this debate would swell into the crisis we see being resolved at the Jerusalem Council (Ac 15). This helps us understand why Luke says, "And as many as had come with Peter were [so shocked that they were] beside themselves because the gift of the Holy Spirit had also been poured out upon the nations [Gentiles], for they were hearing them speaking in tongues and magnifying God. Then Peter answered, 'Can anyone prevent these who have received the Holy Spirit, just as we also received Him, from entering into the water to be baptized?' And he commanded them to be baptized in the name of Jesus Christ. Then they asked him to remain with them for a while" (paraphrase).

Acts Chapter 11

vs1-3: The report of what had happened at Caesarea spread rapidly. Luke says, "And the apostles and the brothers who were throughout Judea heard that the Gentiles [nations] received the word of God." Many must have rejoiced, but those who considered Gentiles to be ceremonially unclean and felt that they must first become Jews before being admitted into the church were alarmed by the report. Luke says, "And when Peter went up to Jerusalem, those from the circumcision [the ones loyal to circumcision] judged him saying, 'You went inside the homes of men who are not circumcised and you ate with them!'" (literal).

vs4-14: The meeting with these elders had quickly turned into a trial. And Peter's defense of himself was to carefully retell everything that happened. He wanted to prove to them that God had revealed His will in the matter. So starting with his encounter on the roof of Simon's house, he rehearsed the entire sequence of events. He told them about the vision (vs5-10), the arrival of messengers from Cornelius (v11), the Spirit's command to accompany them to Caesarea (v12) and Cornelius' encounter with the angel (vs13-14). And in this retelling he became so specific that he even quoted the very words that the angel spoke to Cornelius. We learn that the angel told him that Peter would bring "words by which you may be saved, you and all your household" (literal).

vs15-17: As he continued his account, it became increasingly obvious that Peter could not be held responsible for what had happened. God had sovereignly stepped in and indicated His will by performing a miracle. Peter described that dramatic moment this way: "And as I began to speak, the Holy Spirit fell upon them just as also upon us in the beginning" (literal). By using the words, "…as also upon us in the beginning," he was saying that the same gift which had been given to the apostles at Pentecost had been given to these Romans. That, he explained, was why he had ordered them to be baptized with water: "And I remembered the Lord's statement, how he used to say, 'John indeed baptized into water, but you will be baptized with the Holy Spirit.' Therefore, if God gave the same [equal] gift to them as to us, having believed upon the Lord Jesus Christ, who was I to be able to hinder God?" (literal).

v18: Thankfully their respect for Peter's apostolic authority and their reverence for the undeniable miracle which had taken place caused "those from the circumcision" to submit, at least for the moment (Ac 15). Luke says, "And hearing these things they became silent and glorified God saying, 'Then God also gave to the nations the repentance [that leads] to life'" (literal).

v19: At this verse Luke turns his attention from Caesarea to Antioch, a Syrian city 250 miles to the north, because it was in that Syrian city that the church began to expand rapidly among the Gentiles. Even though Jesus had commanded His disciples to take the gospel to the Gentiles before He ascended into heaven (Mt 28:19; Mk 16:15; Lk 24:44; Ac 1:8), even though Philip had already gone to Samaria (Ac 8:4-8, 14-17, 25) and had been divinely guided to evangelize an Ethiopian official (Ac 8:26-39), even though Peter had been given a vision and then watched a house full of Romans be baptized with the Holy Spirit (Ac 10:1-48), the cultural barriers between Jew and Gentile were so deep that the leadership in Jerusalem had made no effort to evangelize those who were not Jews. The fact that most of the twelve apostles are not mentioned in Acts after the first chapter (Ac 1:13, 26) probably indicates that they soon left Jerusalem to travel to other lands. Christian tradition says they did. So when we encounter this harsh attitude toward the Gentiles in Jerusalem, we need to be very careful not to assume that the apostles themselves disobeyed their Lord. But as far as the church they left behind was concerned, their response to Jesus' command to go to the Gentiles was to remain passive. That's why the remarkable move of God that Luke shows us beginning at this verse is so significant. We are seeing how the gospel broke through those barriers. From this point on the Gentile church will actually become larger than the Jewish church, and the gospel will rapidly spread into other nations.

The violent persecution which arose after the stoning of Stephen drove many Jewish believers out of Israel, but it did not change their pattern of preaching only to Jews. Luke says, "However, those who had been scattered by the persecution which occurred after the stoning of Stephen left the country and went to Phoenicia, Cyprus and Antioch, but they were not preaching the gospel to anyone except Jews" (literal). Many escaped northward to what is now Lebanon, some to the island of Cyprus and others to the Syrian city of Antioch. Antioch was the third largest city in the Roman Empire with over half a million people. Its main street ran four miles from gate to gate (G. Campbell Morgan, The Acts of the Apostles, Fleming Revell, 1924, p285), and it had a large Jewish community which had been in existence since its founding by Alexander the Great's general, Seleucus Nicator, in 300 B.C. (Jamieson, Fausset, Brown, A Commentary, Eerdmans reprint, 1982, Vol. 3, Part Two, p75).

v20: Luke gives us a very important insight: At some point Jewish believers from Cyprus and Cyrene broke through that religious barrier and "preached the Lord Jesus" to Gentiles. The gospel probably arrived in Cyprus and Cyrene (Libya) shortly after Pentecost (Ac 2:10, 41; 4:36), and though Luke doesn't name the men who first took that brave step, it seems likely that Lucius the Cyrenian was one of them, and Simeon, who was called Niger, was another (Ac 13:1).

v21: By saying that the "hand of the Lord was with them…" Luke is telling us that God entered into that situation and worked powerfully through those men which is why "…a great number of people believed their message and turned to the Lord." Their ministry probably looked very much like Philip's ministry in Samaria (Ac 8:5-8) where God had used signs and wonders to confirm the truth of his words. We should not overlook the fact that by helping these men to evangelize Gentiles,

God was indicating His approval. Had He disapproved, His hand would not have been with them.

vs22-23: Someone reported to the leaders in Jerusalem that a large number of Gentiles were pouring into the church in Antioch, and it appears that report was met with concern (Gal 2:11-14; Ac 14:26-15:1). Barnabas was sent to investigate. Since he himself had ties to Cyprus (Ac 4:36), he likely knew the men who were doing this or at least knew the families of those who were from Cyprus. And being a Levite he would also be very aware whether or not the laws concerning "cleanness" were being violated. It's interesting that Peter wasn't sent on this mission. He may have had obligations which prevented him from going, but he may also have been disqualified in the minds of "the brethren" because of his role at Caesarea (Ac 11:1-18). He did go to Antioch later on only to have some "men from James" follow him there and cause controversy (Gal 2:11-14).

vs23-24: If anyone in Jerusalem expected Barnabas to hinder the evangelism of Gentiles, they were soon disappointed. He was a very discerning man, and when he arrived and saw the "grace of God at work among them," instead of discouraging the evangelization of Gentiles, he "rejoiced and encouraged all of them to resolve in their hearts that they would remain committed to the Lord" (literal). Luke then explains to us that Barnabas responded this way because "he was a good man, full of the Holy Spirit and faith…" As a result, a "sizable multitude was added to the Lord…"

v24: The reference to Barnabas as being "a good man" in particular points to the fact that he was generous, and we certainly have evidence of his generosity. He was a model of sacrificial giving in the early church (Ac 4:36-37). But when he came to Antioch, his generosity became evident again as he gladly gave the gospel to the Gentiles. Luke also says he was "full of the Holy Spirit," certainly meaning that he had been baptized with the Holy Spirit, but here he notes it because he wants us to understand that Barnabas was still moving strongly in the supernatural gifts of the Spirit. And finally Luke describes him as "full of faith," meaning he deeply believed the gospel. Luke says when Barnabas came to Antioch he "witnessed the grace of God," and clearly based on that assessment, he decided that if God was blessing these

Gentiles, then so would he. And instead of returning to Jerusalem to report on what he had seen, he stayed to help.

vs25-26: It did not take Barnabas long to realize that if this church, filled with Gentiles, was to keep growing, it must have more teachers. Yet the cultural resistance in the Jerusalem church made it difficult to recruit help from there. So when he sought for guidance, the Lord must have reminded him of Saul of Tarsus and of the call to ministry he had received on the road to Damascus (Ac 9:15-16; 26:15-18). After all, Barnabas was the one who had carefully listened when Saul described his encounter with the risen Jesus, and who had then taken him and presented him to the apostles (Ac 9:27). Luke says he left Antioch and went to Tarsus determined to search for Saul until he found him. When he found him, he brought him back to the city, and the church provided room and board for both of them for a whole year so they could devote themselves to gathering with the church and teaching the growing crowd. Luke also notes that it was in Antioch that the title "Christians" was first applied to believers, and the way he words that statement implies that Barnabas and Saul were the ones who named them that.

vs27-28: Sometime during that year prophets traveled from Jerusalem to Antioch. One of them, named Agabus, stood up and warned the church that a great famine was about to come upon all who were living on the earth. Judging from the word Luke uses to describe how Agabus communicated this warning, he probably pictured that famine using very symbolic language (Ac 21:10-11). Luke notes that it arrived during the reign of the Roman emperor named Claudius (A.D. 41-54). According to ancient historians there was a famine during the fifth, sixth and seventh years of Claudius' reign which means it began in A.D. 45 and lasted three years (Josephus, Antiquities, 20:2.5. see footnote in Josephus, The Complete Works. translated by William Whiston, Thomas Nelson, 1998, p634).

v29: This largely Gentile church did not respond by hoarding resources for themselves even though the prophecy stated they too would experience famine along with everyone else. Instead they took up an offering for impoverished believers in Judea. Those who had sufficient resources sent help to those who would be most vulnerable during a time of famine.

v30: And Luke observes that the believers in Antioch followed through on that commitment. Their financial gift was sent to the elders in Jerusalem by means of Barnabas and Saul. Paul (Saul) later described that visit in his letter to the Galatians (Gal 2:1-14). There he tells us that the trip took place 14 years after he met Christ (Gal 2:14), and he says that while he was in Jerusalem, he seized upon the opportunity to present the gospel, as he preached it, to James (the Lord's brother), Peter and John and invited them to correct him if he had erred in any way. On that trip he and Barnabas had taken with them a young believer named Titus, who was Greek, and his very presence served as a test case: Would the leaders of the Jerusalem church require this young Gentile to be circumcised before welcoming him into their fellowship? When Titus was presented to them, they did not require him to be circumcised but welcomed him just as he was. And Paul points out, that by doing so they endorsed the righteousness that comes by faith alone. Those "pillars" of the church (James, Peter and John) gave Saul and Barnabas the "right hand of fellowship," meaning they formally acknowledged that what was happening in Antioch was a valid ministry of God (Ga 2:9). And finally they encouraged them to keep preaching to Gentiles but stated that they themselves would continue preaching only to Jews.

In the midst of his account of this meeting in his letter to the Galatians (Gal 2:1-14), Paul mentions that "false brethren" slipped into those meetings. He says they pretended to be friendly but actually came as spies. They were there to "examine" his gospel, hoping to find a way to discredit him so they could demand that the converts in Antioch observe the ceremonial laws of Moses. Paul says their real motive was to "enslave us" (Gal 2:4). Apparently, they tried pulling rank on him, positioning themselves as his elders, but he says, "Not for an hour did we yield in subjection to them" (Gal 2:5). We can only imagine the intensity of those debates. When the dialogue was finished, Paul says those Jerusalem leaders "added nothing to me," meaning that he had learned no new truths from that confrontation, nor were those elders able to find fault with anything he preached. When that difficult confrontation was over, the leaders in Jerusalem still asked Paul and Barnabas to remember their poor, and Paul's amazing response was, "...the very thing I was eager to do" (Gal 2:10).

Acts Chapter 12

vs1-2: While Barnabas and Saul were in Jerusalem (v25), the church in that city experienced violent persecution. Herod Agrippa I, Herod the Great's grandson, seized some of the believers to "harm" them, and in the process he executed the apostle James "with a sword," which most likely means he had him beheaded. Herod Agrippa I reigned from about A.D. 37-44 (46?) and managed to hold onto power by being fiercely loyal to Rome in order to please the Roman government, but also by conducting himself as a devout, Pharisaic Jew to please the religious leaders in Israel. Persecuting the church became a way to show the nation how zealous he was for the Law of Moses. It was politically advantageous for him to demonstrate that he too was outraged by these followers of Jesus, in particular anyone who dared to cross the cultural barriers that separated Jew and Gentile (Ac 10, 11). If by that time word had reached Jerusalem that there were Jewish believers in Antioch who were fellowshipping with Gentiles, that news alone would have been enough to reawaken a general hostility toward the church (Ac 22:21-22; 28:28-29).

v3: Herod apparently carried out his attack shortly before the days of Unleavened Bread. Passover and the week which follows it, called the Feast of Unleavened Bread, form one of the three festivals held each year during which Jews from all over the nation and around the world gather in Jerusalem. He selected James because he was a highly visible leader of the church, and by executing him during such a busy season, he ensured that the greatest number of people possible would see or hear about his display of religious zeal. His plan worked, and when he saw how much James' execution pleased the religious leaders, he decided to execute Peter as well.

v4: Since Peter had already escaped from prison once before (Ac 5:18-25), Herod had him placed under maximum security. Luke says he "put him in jail, delivering him to four squads [four soldiers per squad] to guard him...," and then adds that he planned to "bring him up to the people after Passover." Apparently Herod wanted to conduct a public trial and execute Peter as soon as the festival concluded before the crowds went home.

v5: But by delaying the execution, he unintentionally gave the church time to pray, and they used those days to pray fervently. Luke describes their prayer this way: "... prayer concerning him was continually being stretched out by the church toward God" (literal). And their prayer had a powerful effect beyond anything they expected.

v6: Peter was manacled with a chain attached to each arm. These two chains were attached to two soldiers who were rotated every three hours so they would stay awake. Two different sets of guards were also posted outside his cell, and finally, there was an iron gate at the outer wall of the prison. In other words, everything humanly possible was done to prevent him from escaping.

v6 (continued): The fact that Peter was asleep in the midst of such a dangerous situation shouldn't be overlooked. On the night before a man is sentenced to be beheaded we might expect that man to be wide awake, tormented with fear, but he was sound asleep. And he had not collapsed into sleep out of exhaustion because, as was the custom for men in those days, he had loosed the belt around his waist, taken off his sandals and laid his outer coat aside or put it over himself as a blanket. In other words he was sleeping comfortably, which is profound evidence of his faith. Like Jesus asleep in the boat during a storm (Mk 4:35-40), Peter was not afraid.

vs7-10: The arrival of an angel to rescue him is told in delightful detail: "And behold, an angel of the Lord stood beside him, and a light illuminated the cell. Patting Peter's side, he awakened him saying, 'Stand up quickly,' and the chains fell off his hands. The angel said to him, 'Tighten your belt and put on your sandals,' and he did. Then he said to him, 'Wrap your outer cloak around you and follow me.' So he followed him out, but he didn't know that what was happening through the angel was true but supposed he was seeing a vision. And going past the first and second guard posts they came up to the iron gate leading into the city which opened to them by itself, and going out they went forward one street, and immediately the angel left him" (literal).

v11: The angel led Peter out the gate and down one block to the first intersection and then disappeared. At that moment Peter finally awoke to the fact that he was out of jail. He realized he was not dreaming but had been delivered from Herod's plan to execute him and "from all the Jewish people expected." His death, which had seemed unavoidably certain just minutes earlier, had been miraculously prevented by God.

v12: Before anyone could recognize him standing there on that street corner in the middle of the night, Peter hurried to a house which had become the gathering place for the church in Jerusalem. It was probably the same house in which Jesus had celebrated the last supper (Mk 4:12-16; Lk 22:7-13) and where the Holy Spirit had been poured out on the day of Pentecost (Ac 1:12-15; 2:1-2). It belonged to a woman named Mary. She was the mother of a young man named John, who people also called Mark, and she was either Barnabas' sister or cousin because later on Paul described the relationship between John Mark and Barnabas using a word for John Mark that means either nephew or cousin. Barnabas and Saul (Paul) took him with them on their first missionary journey (Ac 13:5), and he served with Barnabas in Cyprus (Ac 15:39) and later on with Paul and Peter in Rome (2Ti 4:11; Phm 24; 1Pe 5:13). He is also the author of the gospel of Mark. Luke says many believers were "crowded together" in that house praying for Peter.

vs13-14: When he arrived, he knocked on the outer courtyard door, and a servant girl named Rhoda came up "to listen." She may have asked, "Who is it?" and when he answered, she recognized his voice, but instead of opening the door, she became overwhelmed with joy and left him standing outside while she ran to announce his arrival.

v15: The response by everyone in the house to Rhoda's announcement was disbelief. They replied, "You're talking like a crazy person!" (literal). When she continued to emphatically insist that Peter was at the door, they concluded she must have encountered "his angel," which most likely meant they assumed he had been executed and his disembodied spirit was visiting the house before it departed for heaven. Surely the purpose of this gathering of believers was to pray for Peter's rescue, but when told that he was at the courtyard door, no one believed it.

vs16-17: Yet Peter kept knocking, and when they finally opened the door and saw him, they were "beside themselves" (literal) with amazement and joy. Everyone began saying something, probably shouting his name and giving thanks to God, but he motioned to them with his hand to be silent and then gave them a thorough, step-by-step account of how the Lord had led him out of prison. When he finished, he said, "Report these things to James and to the brothers," and then leaving the house, "he went to another place" presumably to hide from Herod.

vs18-19: Luke now turns his attention back to the prison and Herod. He says, "When it became day, there was not a little confusion among the soldiers as to what had become of Peter. And Herod, searching for him but not finding him, after questioning the guards ordered them to be led away [to execution]. And going down from Judea to Caesarea he remained there." (literal)

v20: While in Caesarea, Herod Agrippa I collapsed during a speech to delegates from Phoenicia and later died. For some reason he had become "bitterly angry toward the people of Tyre and Sidon, so they came to him united in purpose" (literal). They befriended Blastus, his trusted servant, a man who watched over him as he slept, and Blastus helped them arrange an audience so they could plead for peace. Their country depended on trade with Israel in order to maintain a sufficient supply of food, but apparently Herod had suspended those imports by issuing a royal decree.

vs21-23: On a day designated for a special festival to honor the emperor (Rienecker/Rogers, <u>Linguistic Key to the Greek New Testament,</u> Zondervan, 1980, p.290), Herod, dressed in his royal clothing and sitting on the platform of the city's great amphitheater, delivered a public speech in which he apparently ended up haranguing the delegates from Phoenicia, but they responded by crying out, "The voice of a god, not a man." And Luke says, right after that an angel of the Lord struck him because he did not give the glory to God. Later on after being "eaten by worms, he breathed out his last breath and died" (literal).

v24: This event was seen by many as divine punishment for the death of James, and as a result Luke says the Word of the Lord (the gospel of Jesus Christ) continued to increase in influence and reputation and to bring more and more people to salvation.

v25: Then Barnabas and Saul left Jerusalem and returned to Antioch having completed the ministry which they had been sent there to perform (Ac 11:29-30), and they took John Mark along with them.

Acts Chapter 13

In the first twelve chapters of the book of Acts Luke showed us the early church fulfilling the Lord's command to carry the gospel to Jerusalem, Judea and Samaria (Ac 1:8). But when He spoke that command, Jesus had also told them to carry the gospel to "...the remotest part of the earth" (Ac1:8), yet a decade and a half after Pentecost the Jerusalem church was still struggling with the question of whether or not to welcome Gentile believers into its fellowship. In spite of Jesus' command, other than the apostles themselves, who tradition tells us went on missionary journeys all over the world, the leaders in Jerusalem chose to remain passive toward the evangelization of Gentiles. Thankfully the church in the city of Antioch, 320 miles north of Jerusalem, obeyed the prompting of the Holy Spirit and began to send missionaries to Greek and Roman communities. From the 13th chapter onward Luke focuses on the missionaries who were sent out by the Antioch church to the "remotest part of the earth," and in particular on a missionary named Saul of Tarsus.

vs1-3: God called the Antioch church to send out missionaries during a small gathering of its church leaders. Five men, all of whom functioned as prophets and teachers, had set aside time to fast and worship. It appears from the casual way Luke describes it that this sort of gathering was a normal part of life. He names the men: "Now among the church in Antioch there were both prophets and teachers, Barnabas, Simeon, who was called Niger, and Lucius the Cyrenian [Ac 11:20], and also Manaen, the foster-brother of Herod the tetrarch [Herod Antipas, the tetrarch of Galilee and Perea, 4 B.C.-A.D. 39] and Saul" (literal). Then Luke tells us what happened: "And while ministering to the Lord and fasting, the Holy Spirit said, 'Set apart to Me now Barnabas and Saul for the work to which I have called them.'" And finally, he tells us how they responded: "Then having fasted and prayed to prepare themselves, and having laid hands on them, they released them" (literal).

vs4-5: The city of Antioch was located beside the Orontes River about 16 miles inland from the Mediterranean coast. Seleucia, its port, was five miles north of the mouth of the river. Luke says, "Therefore, truly sent out by the Holy Spirit, they went down to Seleucia, and from there sailed to Cyprus" (literal). It's about a 130-mile journey from Seleucia to Salamis, the easternmost harbor on the island of Cyprus. "And upon arriving in Salamis they proclaimed the Word of God in the synagogues of the Jews, and they also had John as an assistant" (literal). As a young man John Mark lived in the home with an upper room in which Jesus and His disciples likely gathered (Lk 22:12; Ac 1:13; 12:12). Aside from running errands and carrying luggage, he would have made a very valuable contribution to this team because he had seen and heard Jesus in person.

vs6-7: After landing on the island Barnabas, who had been born there (Ac 4:36), would have been able to guide them to the various synagogues. Most likely they moved from east to west across the island until they came to Paphos which is on the southwest coast. There "they found a certain magician, a Jewish false prophet whose name was Bar-Jesus [son of Jesus]." He served as a spiritual counselor to Sergius Paulus, the Roman proconsul (governor) for the province of Cyprus. Luke calls him an "intelligent man," and uses a word which means he was able to comprehend things very quickly. A report must have come to Bar-Jesus about the preaching of Barnabas and Saul because he summoned them so he could hear their message for himself.

vs8-10: Bar-Jesus' actual name was "Elymas," which is not a normal Hebrew name, so Luke merely wrote out the Greek letters which when pronounced would sound like his name. Luke identifies him as a sorcerer (magi). When this man learned that his master had summoned

Barnabas and Saul, he grew alarmed. Undoubtedly he was afraid they would replace him, so he opposed them by "seeking to turn the proconsul away from the faith."

vs9-11: Here Luke introduces Saul's Roman name, "Paul," which would have been given to him as part of his Roman citizenship (Ac 21:39; 22:25-29). Then Luke says Paul, "being filled with the Holy Spirit, stared at Elymus and said, 'You're a person who is completely filled with deceit and laziness. You're a son of the devil, an enemy of all righteousness. When will you cease twisting the straight ways of the Lord? And now behold, the hand of the Lord is upon you, and you will be blind, not seeing the sun for a season.' And immediately a mist and darkness fell upon him, and going about he sought for someone to lead him by the hand" (literal).

vs12-13: After watching this display of spiritual authority Sergius Paulus believed, being "frightened out of his senses at the teaching of the Lord" (literal). Luke does not tell us anything more about Sergius Paulus, so we are left to wonder about the depth of his faith; however, the destination to which Paul and Barnabas went after leaving Cyprus may give us some clue. They took what appears to be an illogical turn northwest to the southern coast of Asia Minor (Turkey), and then went twelve miles inland to Perga. At that point John Mark left them and returned home (Ac 15:36-39).

v14: From there they travelled 100 miles due north, crossing over the range of the Taurus Mountains into the province of Galatia, to a city called Pisidian Antioch which served as the civil and military center in that region for the Roman government. The question this raises is why did they make such an effort to reach this remote city? The answer may be found in the fact that archeologists have uncovered there an inscription which honors a man named "L. Sergius Paullus" (D. H. Wheaton, on Paulus Sergius, in The New Bible Dictionary, Eerdmans, reprint 1971, p955). It is possible that this man is the son of the Sergius Paulus they met on Cyprus. If so, the Roman proconsul may have asked Paul and Barnabas to go to that city in order to carry the gospel to members of his own family. That would indicate that he was not merely impressed by the miracle Paul performed but converted to the point that he was concerned for the salvation of his loved ones.

Perga was the first city Paul and Barnabas encountered when they reached the southern coast of Asia Minor. It was the main city for the region of Pamphylia located seven miles inland along the Cestrus River, yet Paul and Barnabas passed through it without stopping to preach. Apparently they were in a hurry to reach Pisidian Antioch. The weather may have played a part in their decision. Depending on the time of year the mountain passes through which they must walk could be blocked by snow. We do know they considered Perga to be a city worthy of an evangelistic effort because they stopped to preach there on their return trip home (Ac 14:24-26).

The journey from Perga to Pisidian Antioch was both difficult and dangerous. Here's how one commentator described it: "It was a long and rugged journey; and lying as it did almost through entirely rugged mountain passes, while rivers burst out at the bases of huge cliffs, or dash wildly down through narrow ravines, it must have been a perilous one. The whole region was, and to this day is, infested by robbers, as ancient history and modern travels abundantly attest (Howson, as quoted by David Brown (1803-1897) in A Commentary, Jamieson, Fausset, Brown, Eerdmans, reprint March 1982, "Acts," Vol. 3, p90). In his comments on this passage, David Brown went on to note that when Paul later referred to "dangers from rivers" and "dangers from robbers" that he had experienced in the course of his ministry (2Co 11:26), it's likely he was thinking of this journey. The prospect of these dangers may have influenced Mark's decision to get on a boat and sail home.

v15: But Paul and Barnabas arrived safely in Pisidian Antioch and began their outreach by going to the local synagogue on the Sabbath (Saturday). There they sat down among the congregation and listened as the prescribed passages were read from the Law and the Prophets. A typical synagogue service at that time would have consisted of reciting the Shema ("Hear, O Israel…," Dt 6:4), a prayer by the synagogue leader, reading passages of Scripture and a sermon by a member of the congregation (Rienecker/Rogers, Linguistic Key to the Greek New Testament, Zondervan, 1980, p292). As strangers to that city and distinguished visitors to the synagogue, they were courteously invited by the synagogue leaders to preach a sermon. They said to them, "Men, brothers, if there is among you any word of exhortation to the people, say it."

v16: When the invitation came, Paul stood to his feet and signaled to everyone to be quiet by waving his hand up and down (Ac 12:17; 19:33; 21:40). He opened his message by acknowledging not only the Jews who were present, but also the God-fearing Gentiles. He said, "Men, Israelites and those who fear God, hear me!" (literal).

v17: Beginning at verse 17 and continuing down through verse 41 Luke records the text of the sermon Paul gave that day. Paul may have provided Luke with a summary of that message when he was writing Acts years later. This passage probably preserves a sermon outline that Paul used on numerous occasions.

vs17-19: To begin with he briefly rehearsed some of the key elements in Israel's history in order to establish the fact that Israel was a chosen people. He wanted everyone to see that they had a unique role among all the nations of the earth because God had chosen to send His Son into the world through them (Jn 4:22). He said, "The God of this people Israel chose our fathers and lifted the people up during the sojourn in the land of Egypt, and with an uplifted arm [Dt 5:15] He led them out from it" (literal). Then he mentioned the 40 years they spent in the wilderness and used a word drawn from Deuteronomy 1:31 that pictures God carrying Israel "just as a man carries his son." Next he mentioned the conquering of seven Gentile nations that resulted in Israel's possession of the promised land and noted that the period of time between Jacob's family first entering Egypt and the conquest of Canaan was about 450 years.

vs20-23: He used only one short sentence to refer to the period of the judges, explaining that it ended when the prophet Samuel anointed Saul as the first king. He reminded his listeners that Saul was from the tribe of Benjamin, which as we know was his own tribe (Php 3:5), and then after simply stating that God removed Saul, he arrived at David, a central figure in his sermon. Unlike Saul, David was someone whom God testified to be "…a man after My heart, who will do all My will" (v22, literal). And that quote is a very important part of this sermon. The godly character of David is a key point. Paul wanted his listeners to understand that David was a very good man, good enough for God to promise him that He would bring a Savior to Israel from one of his physical descendants. Yet as Paul will soon point out, as good as

David was, he was not good enough to escape death (v36). Without directly quoting the passage where David was given the promise that his descendant would be the Messiah (2Sa 7:12-16), Paul reminded his listeners that "From the seed of this man, according to promise, God brought a Savior to Israel, Jesus" (literal). His point is that Jesus of Nazareth is the promised Son of David, the Messiah, and then he set about to prove it.

vs24-25: He began with John the Baptist. Obviously, John was still highly respected among Jews. Even in a synagogue in central Asia Minor Paul could assume that the congregation had heard about John and knew that he had called Israel to repent in preparation for the soon-coming Messiah. Paul reminded them that John had emphatically refused any suggestion that he himself might be the Messiah. John said his assignment was to prepare Israel because the appointed time for the Messiah had arrived.

v26: Again, addressing both Jews and Gentiles, he announced that their Savior had come, "Men, brothers, sons of the race of Abraham, and those among you who fear God, to us the word of this salvation was sent forth" (literal).

vs27-29: He had come but Jerusalem didn't recognize Him because they did not understand the meaning of the prophetic passages which describe His sufferings. They had only focused on His glories. So instead of welcoming Jesus and sending out messengers to announce His arrival, they ended up fulfilling the negative parts of the Messianic prophecies by condemning Him in their religious courts, asking Pilate to crucify Him and burying Him in a tomb.

vs30-31: Yet, declared Paul, God proved that Jesus is the Savior by raising Him from the dead. And he emphasized that it was a literal, physical resurrection which had been confirmed by many witnesses. Paul said Jesus "appeared over many days to the ones who came up with Him from Galilee to Jerusalem…." His disciples were now "His witnesses to the people."

v32: Then Paul declared that Jesus was "the promise made to the fathers." Since God made numerous promises to the fathers, we have to ask ourselves which one does He mean. Which promise, above all others, fulfills the highest desire in their heart and grants the greatest blessing? Later on in Acts when Paul makes his defense before Felix, the Roman procurator of Judea (A.D. 52-59), he said he had "a hope in God… that there shall certainly be a resurrection of both the righteous and the wicked" (Ac 24:15). Soon afterward while making a similar defense before the great grandson of Herod the Great, he said, "And now I am standing trial for the hope of the promise made by God to our fathers, the promise to which our twelve tribes hope to attain as they earnestly serve God night and day" (Ac 26:6, 7). And then he quickly added, "Why is it considered incredible among you… if God does raise the dead?" (Ac 26:8). In effect he seems to be saying that all other promises lead to this one: that believers will rise from the dead and live with God forever. By raising Jesus from the dead, God had begun to fulfill this promise.

v33: The way this verse is usually translated leaves Paul saying God gave the fulfillment of the promise He made to the father's to our children, which is a thought that is hard to explain. It leaves us wondering in what way God skipped over Paul's generation (those who were alive when Jesus rose from the dead) and gave this promise of resurrection to their children instead. But this verse can be translated with equal validity to read, "…God has fulfilled this promise to the children, raising up to us Jesus, as also it has been written…" (literal). In that case the "children" to whom Paul is referring would be the children of the "fathers," meaning all the physical and spiritual descendants of Abraham, Isaac and Jacob who have hoped in this promise. This also explains why he said God raised up Jesus "to us."

In this same verse Paul states that in Psalm 2 David was prophesying the resurrection. He quotes from verse 7 of that psalm in which we hear the Messiah reporting what the Father said to Him on the day when He established Him as Lord over the entire earth. He said, "You are My Son, today I have begotten you." Paul says that statement refers to the resurrection of Jesus Christ. By saying that He "begot" the Son on that day, the Father was not describing the origin of the second person of the Trinity, He was announcing that at the moment when the Messiah was resurrected, He would become the first member of a new race of resurrected human beings. He would be the "firstborn" son of a future family of resurrected sons and daughters. Elsewhere Paul refers to Jesus as the "firstborn from the dead" (Col 1:18), and in his revelation the apostle John also calls Him "the firstborn of the dead" (Rev 1:5).

The term "firstborn," as it is used in the Bible, generally refers to the eldest son in a Hebrew family. By virtue of seniority this person holds an honored position among his siblings, but Paul is saying that God the Father meant much more than this when He called the Messiah His "Son." He is explaining to us that in the moment of the resurrection much more took place than simply the resuscitation of a dead body or even the creation of a better body that wouldn't decay. At that instant God "conceived" an entirely new level of human existence of which Jesus was the first. In time the resurrection will affect every human, not just the righteous. Because of Jesus, both the righteous and the unrighteous will come out of the grave (1Co 15:22; Jn 5:28-29; Ac 24:15). The righteous will be resurrected at the coming of the Lord (1Co 15:23), but the unrighteous will wait until a second resurrection that takes place after a thousand-year period called the Millennium or Messianic Age (Rev 20:7-15). In His essential nature Jesus has always been, and will always be, the only-begotten Son of God, meaning that in Him the Father fully reproduced His divine nature and capacity (Jn 1:1-18; Col 1:16-17; Heb 1:1-5). But on the day when He was resurrected from the dead, another great miracle took place: by virtue of their spiritual union with Jesus, a new race of humans was born. All who place their faith in Him will share in the blessings and privileges He won by His great sacrifice, even being called "sons of God" (Ro 8:19, 23; 1Co 3:22-23; Gal 3:26).

v34: Paul's next point was to tell his listeners that because God had raised Jesus from the dead, the "mercies of David" were now available to those who believed. He quoted from Isaiah 55:3 which was a familiar passage. In that chapter God invites everyone to come to Him and to repent of their sins. If they do, He assures them He will give them the same, undeserved grace He gave to David. The Law of Moses makes no provision for deliberate, intentional rebellion. Sins done out of weakness or by accident could be forgiven, but not sins of presumption, sins done in conscious defiance of God's laws. No sacrifice was provided for this. The person who sinned with a "high hand" was left to helplessly wait for God's judgment (Nu 15:30). Yet David committed terrible sins and did them deliberately. There was no atonement for adultery and murder, only justice. But God gave him a level of mercy deeper than anything the Law of Moses could offer. Instead of running away from God because of his shame, David ran to Him. He openly confessed his sins fully acknowledging the wicked motives in his heart, and then boldly asked for mercy telling God that he was trusting in the "lovingkindness" He had promised to give His people (Dt 7:6-10). And God gave him mercy, and in doing so revealed the fact that there is a level of mercy available that is deeper than anything the Law can offer. This is what Isaiah called the "mercies of David," and Paul is telling us that through Christ these mercies are available to us. Because of the cross and resurrection there is hope for those who are enslaved to the failures of the past, those who have no excuse for the terrible things they've done.

vs35-36: Paul's third point concerning the resurrection was that it proves that Jesus is the One through whom God provides forgiveness of sins. He quotes from Psalm 16 in which David declared, "For You will not abandon my soul to Sheol; neither will you allow your Holy One to undergo decay" (Ps 16:10). In this statement we hear David confidently declare that God will not allow someone who is genuinely holy to remain in the grave. A completely holy person might die, but God would never allow him or her to undergo decay, meaning remain dead. He will bring that person back to life. David appears to consider himself to be holy enough to be included in this promise of immortality, but as Paul points out, he died and decayed in a grave proving that the level of holiness God requires must be higher than David's. Earlier in this sermon Paul mentioned that God considered David to be a very good man. He had called him "a man after My heart, who will do all My will" (v22), yet David still fell short of the necessary standard: "For indeed, David, having by the will of God served his own generation, fell asleep and was placed among his fathers, and he saw decay" (literal).

vs37-39: The fact that Jesus did not decay in the grave but rose again in a physical, but immortal, body sets Him apart from every other human being. Yes, there are accounts in the Bible of people who skipped death and stepped across into heaven such as Enoch (Ge 5:24) and Elijah

(2Ki 2:11), but those are mysterious exceptions which lack sufficient information to make any determination of whether or not the person died in the process. Regardless, it can be said of no one but Jesus that a person actually died and was buried and came back to life never to die again. This fact sets Him apart from all other human beings. He is the one God singled out for resurrection, which proves that God considered Him truly holy. Therefore, Paul announces that He is the One through whom God has made forgiveness of sins available to everyone who believes. Here's how he said it: "...but He whom God raised did not see decay. Therefore, men, brothers, let it be known to you that through this One forgiveness of sins is proclaimed, and by this One everyone who believes is justified from all the things from which you could not be justified in the Law of Moses" (literal).

v39: The phrase, "...all the things from which you could not be justified in the Law of Moses," refers to those sins done in conscious defiance of God's laws. As we noted earlier (v34) the Law of Moses provided no atonement for sins which were done deliberately, which is a very serious problem because virtually all humans at times sin deliberately. Yet the Law had no provision for such sins, nor could it remove rebellion from the human heart (Ro 8:3). So Paul's announcement would have been good news, indeed, to those in that synagogue who were aware that they had sinned deliberately and understood the rebellious nature of their own flesh.

vs40-41: Having finished proclaiming the gospel, Paul now warned his listeners of the danger of rejecting the message they had heard. He quoted from the prophet Habakkuk who had warned the kingdom of Judah that if they rejected his message, God would send Babylonian conquerors. Paul had said, "Therefore, beware [look!] so that the thing having been spoken by the prophets might not come upon you: 'Behold, you who arrogantly look down on My words of warning, be amazed and completely removed [from the land]. I Myself am working a work in your days, a work which you would not believe even if someone carefully described it to you in detail'" (Acts 14: 40-41; Habakkuk 1:5, literal). To issue such a warning indicates that Paul anticipated severe resistance, yet as we will soon see, the initial reaction by many in the congregation that day was very positive (v42). What Paul discovered as he finished his sermon was that the positive response of so many would bring a negative reaction from the synagogue leaders. And as we continue reading Luke's account of the ministry in Pisidian Antioch (vs44-50), that reaction by the leaders grew worse. When the synagogue leaders saw the crowds who came to hear Paul and Barnabas, Luke says, "...they were filled with jealousy" (v45). There was a widespread level of spiritual interest in the city including many from among their own synagogue, and they must have become afraid that their influence over the people was being stripped away by these two strangers.

v42-45: Here's how Luke described the reaction to Paul and Barnabas: "And as they [Paul and Barnabas] were going out [of the synagogue], people were asking that during the intervening week before the next Sabbath, these words would be spoken to them. And after the assembly broke up, many of the Jews and worshipping proselytes [non-Jews who worshiped Israel's God] followed Paul and Barnabas who in speaking to them persuaded them to continue [trusting] in the grace of God. And on the coming Sabbath almost all the city was assembled to hear the word of God. But seeing the crowds the Jews [synagogue leaders] were filled with jealousy and contradicted the things being spoken by Paul, [and] they were blaspheming" (literal). Their concern was not because they believed the gospel was biblically inaccurate; it was because so many people were so deeply moved by it.

v46-50: And speaking boldly with Spirit-empowered eloquence and passion Paul and Barnabas said to the religious leaders, "It was necessary that the word of God be spoken to you first, [however] since you push it away from yourselves, and [thereby] judge yourselves not worthy of eternal life, we turn to the nations [Gentiles]" (literal). Obviously, the gospel would no longer be welcomed in that synagogue, and opposition would form against anyone who openly confessed Jesus. So paraphrasing a statement made by the prophet Isaiah, the two missionaries announced that in the future they would focus their efforts on the Gentiles in the city: "For this reason the Lord has commanded us, 'I have placed you as a light for the nations, you are to be [messengers] for salvation to the end of the earth'" (Is 49:6, literal). And upon hearing this, Luke says, "...the Gentiles rejoiced and glorified the word of the Lord, and they, those who had been drawn toward eternal life, believed" (literal). That decision resulted in many people believing, and the "…word of the Lord was carried throughout all the countryside, but the Jews [synagogue leaders] stirred up alarm among the pious, well-respected women and chief men of the city, and they raised up a persecution [hunt] against Paul and Barnabas and expelled them from their borders" (literal). They took them out to the borders of their jurisdiction and demanded they leave.

v51: And Paul and Barnabas did leave, but not before "…shaking the dust of their feet upon them" (literal). This symbolic gesture meant "I don't want even the dust from this place clinging to my sandals because God's judgment against this place will be so severe." In doing this Paul and Barnabas were not merely expressing frustration at being rejected by the city, they were obeying a specific command of the Lord. Jesus had told His disciples to use this visible act to warn cities which refused to listen to their message. He said, "Whatever city you enter and they receive you, eat what is set before you, and heal those in it who are sick, and say to them, 'The kingdom of God has come near to you.' But whatever city you enter and they do not receive you, go out into its streets and say, 'Even the dust of your city which clings to our feet we wipe off… against you; yet be sure of this, that the kingdom has come near.'" (Lk 10:8-11). After explaining when and how to present this prophetic warning, Jesus also explained why God's judgment would be so severe toward those who rejected their message: "I say to you, it will be more tolerable in that day for Sodom than for that city… For if the miracles had been performed in Tyre and Sidon which occurred in you, they would have repented long ago sitting in sackcloth and ashes. But it will be more tolerable for Tyre and Sidon in the judgment than for you." (Lk 10:12-14). We should note that Jesus expected that healing the sick would accompany the preaching of the gospel. People would not only hear the truth, but they would also see God's power at work confirming the message.

Jesus made it clear that this warning needed to be delivered in a fashion people wouldn't forget. The gospel presents a person with an opportunity to receive God's grace, but if rejected, it leaves that person guilty of having deliberately refused His offer. So the gospel brings with it not only the opportunity for salvation but the potential for greater condemnation. This is because when it is proclaimed faithfully, it is always accompanied by the presence of the Holy Spirit. In various ways He confirms to that person's heart that what he or she is hearing is true. He may also confirm the gospel by performing miracles such as healing and deliverance (Lk 10:16-20). Even more important is His ministry of removing the "veil" of deception which blinds the human mind to God's truth so that an individual is able to understand and receive the message they are hearing (2Co 4:4-6; 2Ti 2:25-26). So when Paul and Barnabas arrived in a city, we can be absolutely certain that the Holy Spirit "arrived" with them, and when they proclaimed the truth, He bore witness to that truth. Under those circumstances for someone to refuse to believe, and in this case, to drive these evangelists out of their city so that no one else could be saved either required that person to willfully refuse the witness of the Holy Spirit. After shaking the dust off their feet Paul and Barnabas went on to Iconium, the next large city on the road leading east.

v52: Yet even after the apostles left, Luke says those they had led to Christ continued to be "filled with joy and the Holy Spirit." And given the circumstances they faced, their response was amazing. It shows that something truly profound had happened inside them. Even though their leaders had been ejected from the city, leaving them without any appointed eldership (Ac 14:21-23), and even though they continued to be persecuted, they thrived (Ac 14:22). Luke doesn't tell us what the apostles taught them during the few weeks or months they were there, but if we look at Paul's letters to the Thessalonians, we discover what he taught another church which faced a similar situation. He taught them to expect persecution, and as a result the Thessalonian church, like the church in Pisidian Antioch, "received the word in much tribulation with the joy of the Holy Spirit…" (1Th 1:6). In that letter Paul reminded the new believers in Thessalonica that he had warned them that they would suffer. He said, "For indeed when we were with you, we kept telling you in advance that we were going to suffer affliction, and so it came to pass as you know" (1Th 3:4). And he carefully put their persecution into perspective. He explained that it was a necessary part of every believer's life during this season of human history. Yet he also assured them that all suffering would end at the return of Jesus Christ. He said their suffering had meaning because they were enduring affliction for the sake of the kingdom of God. He told them that God saw how their faith endured in the face of persecution, and because they persevered, He considered them to be worthy citizens of

His kingdom (2Th 1:4-5). And finally, Paul promised the Thessalonian church that God would justly judge those who had afflicted them (2Th 1:6-10). If we realize that Paul and Barnabas almost certainly taught those same truths to the church in Pisidian Antioch, we can better understand why those new believers joyfully endured affliction.

Acts Chapter 14

vs1-2: Just as they had done in Pisidian Antioch, Paul and Barnabas began their ministry in Iconium by attending the synagogue on the Sabbath, and when given the opportunity, spoke about Jesus Christ. And again, just as had happened in Pisidian Antioch, a large number of Jews and God-fearing Greeks believed their message. And again those synagogue leaders who had not been persuaded by what they heard worked aggressively to stir up anger among the Gentiles toward the "brothers."

v3: Yet, rather than flee this danger, Paul and Barnabas chose to remain in that city long enough to lay a good foundation of understanding in their new disciples. In spite of the growing hostility they continued to speak out boldly, and Luke says they were able to do that because they relied on the Lord who was witnessing to the word of His grace by working signs and wonders through their hands. In other words God's power was so evident that their opponents were afraid to attack them.

vs4-5: The people of that city were divided (Lk 12:51-53). Some sided with the Jewish leaders and others with the apostles, and that tension grew until the day came when a mob was formed made up of both Gentiles and Jews including leaders from the synagogue. At some point the angry crowd began to sweep across the city with the intention of publicly humiliating Paul and Barnabas and then stoning them.

vs6-7: When they realized what was happening, rather than die needlessly, the apostles fled eastward into another part of that same region called Lycaonia. They arrived first in Lystra, which was about 20 miles south of Iconium, and then later fled from Lystra to Derbe, which was about 80 miles east of Lystra. Luke mentions that they also evangelized some of the rural areas surrounding those cities.

vs8-10: While they were in Lystra, an extraordinary miracle took place. A crowd had gathered as Paul was preaching, and in that crowd there was a crippled man who had been born lame. He must have been listening very attentively because he caught Paul's eye. Paul stared at him for a moment, discerned that he had the faith to be healed and then with a loud voice said, "Stand up on your feet!" Instantly he leaped to his feet and walked.

vs11-12: Lystra was not a large city. It was one of 13 Roman military outposts in the Galatian region and probably had no more than 2,000 inhabitants (Ray Vander Laan, "Faith Lessons," Vol. 7, "Lystra," Zondervan, 2006). So everyone in that crowd must have at least been familiar with this crippled man. They knew his disability was genuine, so when he stood up and walked, there was no possibility of fraud. This was an indisputable miracle. It could not have been faked which is why those in the crowd reacted the way they did. They were stunned and began to explain the miracle using their own religious concepts. In their Lycaonian language they shouted, "The gods, looking like men, have come down to us" (literal). They thought Barnabas was "Zeus" and Paul was "Hermes" because Paul did most of the speaking, and Hermes was the Greek god of speech. Most likely the apostles did not understand the dialect being spoken which explains why they were slow to react as this situation developed (v14). The crowd's fanatical response seems to have been influenced by a legend told in that region that Zeus and Hermes had visited that area before, but the people at that time had not welcomed them into their homes. As a result the two gods destroyed the entire population except for one elderly couple who had been hospitable to them.

The Roman poet Ovid "tells the story of an aged and pious couple of that region, Philemon and Baucis by name, who entertained Jupiter and Mercury (the Roman equivalents of Zeus and Hermes) unawares and were rewarded for their hospitality (Metamorphoses viii, 626ff)"

(F.F. Bruce, Acts, Eerdmans, reprint 1974, p291. Also: Vander Laan, see above). So when Barnabas, the Levite, who may well have looked like Zeus, and Paul, who spoke so eloquently, ministered with miraculous power, the people of Lystra assumed that those gods had returned to test them again.

vs13-15: The priest of Zeus, whose temple was located in front of the city gates, brought bulls to the area around the gates where the crowd had gathered. The animals were decorated for sacrifice covered in garlands of leaves, flowers or wool. The crowd fully intended to worship the apostles by sacrificing the bulls to them, so when this Levite and former Pharisee realized what was taking place, they instinctively grabbed their outer robes at the area around the neck and tore them in half from top to bottom. This was a Hebrew way of expressing intense grief at having been subjected to blasphemy. They were horrified that God was being blasphemed (Lev 10:6; Nu 14:6; Mt 26:65; Mk 14:63-64), so they rushed out into the crowd crying out in a loud voice, "Men, why are you doing these things? We are men, fellow-sufferers with you, preaching to turn you from these meaningless things to a living God who made the heavens and earth and the sea and all the things in them" (literal). With these words they emphatically declared their humanity, and pointed everyone's attention to the Creator, the one true God.

vs16-17: They openly acknowledged to the people of Lystra that God had allowed their ancestors to rebel against Him without disciplining them in an obvious way. Even though they had worshiped other gods and had lived in ways that violated His standards of holiness, God still sent them rain and gave them fruit-bearing seasons. But, the apostles warned, He would not withhold His judgment forever. Someday each one of them would stand before Him, and when they did, they would not be able to claim that they were ignorant that He existed. In their hearts they knew the truth because He had not left Himself "unwitnessed." It was evident from nature that there was a kind Creator who abundantly provided for them. Though they ignored Him, He still lovingly cared for them year after year. In other words, they would be without excuse on the day of judgment (Ro 1:19-20).

vs18-19: Even after challenging the crowd in such a direct way, it was only with great difficulty that Paul and Barnabas were able to restrain the people from worshipping them. Yet at that very moment, as this scene was taking place, Jews from Pisidian Antioch and Iconium arrived in Lystra and began to address the crowd. Luke does not record what they said, but it is remarkable that they were able to turn the crowd's opinion so quickly from one extreme to the other, from worship to execution. Their attack was focused on Paul. For some reason Barnabas was left untouched. We can only guess at what they said about Paul. They probably claimed that he used demonic powers to perform these miracles. Because the miracle itself could not be denied (Ac 4:16), it seems their only option would be to convince the crowd that the apostles used evil magic. But whatever line of reasoning they used, it worked. That worshiping throng suddenly turned into a murderous mob intent on stoning Paul. Stoning was a Jewish form of execution, so the crowd must have allowed the visiting Jewish leaders to perform the execution. Later Rabbinical laws, which may or may not have been observed here, carefully controlled how a stoning was done. Paul's hands and feet would have been bound, and two accusers would have pushed him off a ledge 15-18 feet high. Then each accuser would throw one stone down on his body as he lay on the pavement below (Vander Laan, see above). The bitter hatred these leaders had toward Paul can be seen from the fact that they even denied him a proper burial. When they believed he was dead, they dragged his body out of the city and left it exposed for the dogs and wild beasts to consume. That was the ultimate form of disrespect.

v20: Luke only briefly describes what happened after that. He says, "the disciples surrounded him" (literal), which surely means they prayed for Paul. Thankfully Barnabas was there to guide them, and that day they watched a miracle take place that was as great, or greater, than the healing they had seen the day before. Paul, who had been pushed off a cliff and crushed with stones, "stood up and went back into the city" (literal). It's possible to assume that he had only been knocked unconscious and then recovered, but the fact that he was strong enough to walk to Derbe the next day, a distance of about 60 miles, points to a stunning miracle. It's possible that Paul was raised from the dead.

v21: Luke does not mention any opposition in Derbe. He simply says they evangelized the city, and after making many disciples, one of whom may have been Gaius of Derbe (Ac 20:4), they turned around and retraced their steps returning to Lystra, Iconium and Pisidian Antioch. Had they continued eastward, they would have again crossed the Taurus mountains (Ac 13:14), only this time at a place called the "Cilician Gates," and the road would have led them to Tarsus, Paul's hometown. This would have been by far the shorter route back to Antioch in Syria, the place where their journey had started. So the decision to return home by the way they came was not based on their own convenience or safety. People had come to Christ in each of these cities, but Paul and Barnabas had been forced to leave before properly preparing them to face the inevitable hardships that their faith would bring.

v22: So putting their own lives at risk, they went back to reinforce (prop up) these new believers. They strengthened their "souls" by encouraging them to remain true to "the faith" that they had been taught and by warning them to expect persecution. They said it was necessary for every believer to pass through many afflictions before we enter the kingdom of God. In this context "entering the kingdom of God" refers to the moment when we depart from the evil of this present, fallen age and enter into the safety of God's presence. In practice this takes place either at death (1Th 4:13-18) or at the return of Jesus Christ (2Th 1:4-10). Such knowledge would help them endure the hardships that lay ahead by giving them a spiritual perspective of what was happening to them.

v23: In each city after spiritually preparing themselves to hear from God by means of prayer and fasting, the apostles "hand-picked" elders to lead the church. Exactly how those leaders were selected is not described here, but we need only observe the process involved in sending out Barnabas and Saul from Antioch in Syria (Ac 13:2-3) to recognize that prophetic listening must have been a major part of the way this was done. In whatever manner elders were selected, it's clear that the apostles were asking God to reveal His will. In his letters to Timothy and Titus Paul lists character qualities and spiritual gifts that are needed by anyone who becomes an elder (1Ti 3:1-7; Titus 1:5-9). Then in what must have been a gathering where all members were present, Paul and Barnabas solemnly committed them into the care of "the Lord in whom they had believed" (Php 1:6; 2Ti 1:12). Though the apostles were about to leave them, Jesus their Lord would never leave, and ultimately it was His faithful care that would carry them through the trials and temptations that lay ahead.

vs24-25: After ministering in Pisidian Antioch the apostles went south, retracing their steps back through the treacherous Taurus mountain range (Ac 13:14) to the coastal plain called Pamphylia. This time they did not bypass its major city, Perga, but spoke "the word" there before going down to Attalia, the harbor, twelve miles away. There they found a ship headed back to Antioch in Syria which brought their first missionary journey to an end.

v26: When Luke mentions that Paul and Barnabas had been originally sent out from the church in the city of Antioch in Syria, he uses an unusual a word, one that he had just used in verse 23 to describe the way the apostles trusted new believers to God. The word is "commended" (Greek: paradidomi). When used in this context, it means to place someone beside someone else, and I believe Luke chose this word to show us a profound truth. In verse 23 he told us that Paul and Barnabas "commended [placed beside] to the Lord" the disciples in the Galatian cities of Derbe, Lystra, Iconium and Pisidian Antioch. Now using this same word, he reminds us that Paul and Barnabas had themselves been "commended to the grace of God" by the Antioch church "for the work which they had accomplished [fulfilled]." In this way he is showing us that the Lord's care for His Church was being multiplied. What had been done for these apostles by their sending church, they then did for the disciples they made on their journey, and I think Luke wants us to see that those new disciples would be expected to do the same thing for those they brought to the Lord. Those who had been "commended" to Jesus' care would "commend" to Jesus' care those they led to Him. And these would in turn "commend" to Jesus' care those that they then led to Him, etc. In other words beneath all the human activity, it is ultimately Jesus who is building and upholding His Church.

v27: When Paul and Barnabas returned to Antioch, the whole church assembled to hear the report of their missionary journey. Undoubtedly they told stories of miracles and about certain individuals who came to Christ. They also must have described the persecutions they faced and the ways the Lord rescued them out of them all (2Ti 3:11). But there would have been one silent testimony in those meetings that no one could ignore: the scars all over Paul's body (Ga 6:11). They had sent out a man who had been whole in his body but received back one who had been savagely stoned. While they must have rejoiced in the glorious reports of how God "opened a door of faith to the nations" (literal), the sobering cost of opening that door stood in front of them.

v28: Luke concludes by saying "...they wore away not a little time with the disciples" (literal). Though he doesn't tell us how long this was, these missionaries would have needed time to heal physically and emotionally from the hardships they had endured.

Acts Chapter 15

v1: The success of Paul and Barnabas' missionary journey was cause for celebration in Antioch in Syria, but cause for alarm among some members of the church in Jerusalem. Over the years the gospel had made significant inroads there among priests (Ac 6:7) and Pharisees (As 15:5), and some of these still separated themselves from Gentiles as an expression of their devotion to God. They believed that the Law of Moses required them to do so. But the truth is there is no place in the Bible that requires a Jew to avoid contact with a Gentile. Yet the Bible does command a Jew to avoid contact with things unbelieving Gentiles commonly touch or do. So the simple solution for an observant Jew was to distance themselves from Gentiles. In time that practice grew into a wall of separation that demanded complete avoidance. This explains why Peter was able to say to Cornelius: "You yourselves know how unlawful it is for a man who is a Jew to associate with a foreigner or to visit him…" (Ac 10:28). His statement was correct. By that time everyone assumed it to be true even though it was not an attitude that pleased God. And it required a powerful vision to release Peter from that thinking (Ac 10:9-16). Only then could God use him to lead an entire household of Gentiles to salvation, even baptizing them with water to indicate that they were accepted as full members of the church of Jesus Christ. But that baptism caused a storm of resistance among some of the observant members of the church in Judea and Jerusalem. And at the time that crisis was only resolved by Peter explaining that God had baptized those Gentiles with the Holy Spirit before he immersed them in water (Ac11:1-18).

But cultural barriers aren't removed easily, which is why we are still encountering this one nearly 20 years later. When Paul and Barnabas went out on their missionary journey, there were still people in the church in Jerusalem who objected to mixing Jews and Gentiles in a church service. And it was to stop the multiplication of this kind of mixed congregations that certain members from the church in Jerusalem followed behind the two apostles telling their converts that, "...unless you are circumcised by the custom of Moses, you cannot be saved" (literal). Their goal was to convince the new Gentile converts to become Jewish proselytes who believed in Jesus. In their minds that would solve the problem of Jewish believers coming into contact with "unclean" Gentiles. And as we read this chapter, it is important for us to note that these men were self-appointed. Neither the apostles nor the elders in the Jerusalem church had sent them (Ac 15:23-24).

vs2-3: When they brought this false message to Antioch in Syria, Paul and Barnabas were there to confront them. The church in that city had become a center of outreach to Gentiles. Those believers had successfully put behind them the issue of fellowship between Jewish and Gentile believers, and they had even begun evangelizing Gentiles in other regions. So when those men demanded that Gentile believers in Antioch be circumcised, an angry argument took place. It appears from the way Luke words this passage that they took on a very authoritarian tone and tried to put Paul and Barnabas on the defensive by aggressively questioning them. When the church refused to submit to them, they "ordered" Paul and Barnabas, along with some others, to appear before the apostles and elders in Jerusalem so that a final judgment could be rendered concerning this question. The Antioch church agreed to submit to the decision from Jerusalem and sent along a delegation. The whole group walked over 300 miles south to reach Jerusalem, and as they passed through Phoenicia and Samaria, they stopped to meet with "brothers." Luke says they would give them detailed descriptions of the conversions that were taking place among the Gentiles, and their report produced great joy.

vs4-6: When Paul, Barnabas and the delegation from Antioch arrived in Jerusalem, they were warmly received by the entire church and began to report the "things God had done with them." But at some point during that presentation certain members of the church who had formerly been Pharisees stood up and challenged their acceptance of Gentile converts by saying, "It is necessary to circumcise them and command them to observe the Law of Moses." And since that was the matter the delegation from Antioch had come to discuss, the apostles and elders formally gathered to look into it.

vs7-11: They initially questioned Paul and Barnabas at length, and then Peter stood up and said, "Men, brothers, you know well that from olden days God chose from among you that it would be through my mouth that the nations would hear the word of the gospel and believe. And the heart-knower, God (literal), bore witness to them, giving them the Holy Spirit just as He also gave to us making no distinction between us and them cleaning their hearts by faith. Now therefore, why do you test God to put a yoke on the neck of the disciples which neither our fathers nor we were able to lift? But through the grace of the Lord Jesus we believe in order to be saved, according to that same way" (literal).

v12: When he finished, the whole congregation became silent. Peter had come down solidly on the side of Paul and Barnabas, so once again everyone gave their attention back to the two missionaries who returned to describing the amazing signs and wonders that God had done through them among the Gentiles.

vs13-18: When Peter spoke, he deliberately reminded everyone of events that had taken place many years earlier in the household of Cornelius. And he emphasized the fact that God baptized those Gentiles with the Holy Spirit (Ac 10:1-11:18). In as forthright a way as Paul himself might have done, Peter declared that Jews as well as Gentiles must be saved by the grace of the Lord Jesus, and that no one can be saved by keeping the works of the Law. Then James, the Lord's half-brother, who had become a leader among the culturally-conservative portion of the Jerusalem church, gave his opinion. He waited until Barnabas and Paul were finished speaking and then said, "Men, brothers, hear me. Simeon [Peter] described how God first visited the nations to take out a people for His name. And the words of the prophets agree with this, even as it has been written: 'After these things

I will return and I will rebuild the tent of David which had fallen, and the things belonging to it which have been overturned [ruined] I will rebuild, and I will set it up right again so that the rest of men may seek the Lord even all the nations upon whom My name has been called [who have called upon My name],' says the Lord who makes these things known from ages past." (literal).

vs19-20: In this way James was offering scriptural support for Peter's declaration. He quoted from Amos 9:11-12 using the wording from the Greek Septuagint (a Greek translation of the Old Testament). In those verses we hear God say that when the Messiah, the Son of David, comes to set up His kingdom, many Gentiles will call on the name of the Lord. Yet even though James was wholeheartedly acknowledging that righteousness is by faith, and therefore believing Gentiles should be welcomed into the Lord's church, he knew a difficult, cultural barrier still remained between the two groups. For real fellowship to take place there would need to be some restraint on the part of Gentiles as well as Jews. To ask a Jew to go into a Gentile home and ignore gross violations of God's order for marriage or to be asked to eat dishes made with animal blood was simply asking too much. Believing Jews would gladly affirm that Gentiles were clean before God through faith. They would turn their back on age-old barriers and undoubtedly would be persecuted for doing so. But if both groups were to fellowship together in church, Gentile brothers and sisters needed to bring their lives into submission to some basic biblical values. They needed to be thoughtful of their Jewish brothers and sisters just as their Jewish brothers and sisters needed to be thoughtful of them.

So James gave this pastoral advice. He said he had decided that the Jerusalem church would not trouble those who were turning to God from the nations but would write a letter that could be presented to Gentile believers which asked them to keep away from four things that were particularly offensive to Jewish believers: from food that had become ritually unclean because it had been used in the worship of idols (Da 1:8; Mal 1:7, 12); from fornication, meaning the breaking of Old Testament laws which prohibit certain types of sexual relations (Lev 18:6-23); from things strangled, meaning meat that had been slaughtered without draining the blood; and from blood, meaning dishes made with blood as one of the ingredients (Ge 9:4;

Lev 17:10-14; 19:26). God had taught His people that "life is in the blood," and for that reason He would allow them to eat the flesh of animals but not their blood. To eat an animal's blood was to consume its life, yet all life is sacred and belongs to God alone. So even those Jews who understood they were righteous by faith in Jesus Christ still considered this truth to be an overruling principle, not a meaningless ritual that could be ignored.

v21: James went on to explain: "For Moses from earliest generations has those who proclaim him in every city, being read in the synagogues on every Sabbath" (literal). He was warning the Gentile churches that tensions over these issues wouldn't go away with the passing of time. If they wanted to evangelize Jews and draw them into a common church gathering, they would need to observe these standards. For thousands of years Jews had been taught to avoid these things by the Law of Moses, and on every Sabbath in every synagogue these standards were reinforced. In other words Jews would never be comfortable fellowshipping with people who practiced such violations of the Bible. In order to reach Gentiles, Jews would need to acknowledge that salvation is by faith in Christ alone and not require Gentiles to become Jews. But to reach Jews, Gentiles would need to conform to some basic commandments of God. Otherwise a stumbling block to conversion would be placed in front of Jews, just as Jews had place a stumbling block in front of Gentiles.

v22: After Peter and James finished speaking, the apostles and elders (Ac 15:2, 6) indicated that they all agreed with James' proposal. It's possible they did this by taking a vote, but it seems more likely that individuals were asked to voice their opinions, and as they did, consensus became apparent. Throughout the process all would have earnestly sought the leading of the Holy Spirit and tested everything to see if it were confirmed by Scripture. And then once consensus was reached, the entire church was given the opportunity to signal their support for these decisions and for a proposal that two representatives from the Jerusalem church accompany Paul and Barnabas back to Antioch.

v23: These two men would carry with them a formal letter which summarized the decisions the apostles and elders had made. They wanted there to be no question in anyone's mind what had been decided. The entire assembly was troubled by the fact that self-appointed men had gone up to Antioch pretending to represent the Jerusalem church and had created a controversy and tried to undermine the authority of Paul and Barnabas. And they felt responsible to help repair the damage, so they chose two of their leading men, Judas, called Barsabbas, and Silas to carry the letter. It read: "The apostles and the elder brothers to the brothers who are from the Gentiles [nations] in Antioch, Syria and Cilicia, greetings!" (literal).

vs24-29: "When we heard that some from among us, whom we did not send, troubled you with words that tore down [sound doctrine] in your minds, it seemed good to us, having become of one mind [in complete agreement], to send chosen men to you along with our beloved Barnabas and Paul, men who have given over their lives on behalf of the name of our Lord Jesus Christ. Therefore, we have sent Judas and Silas, and when they speak to you, they will report the same things. For it seemed good to the Holy Spirit and to us to place upon you no other weight beside these necessary things: to keep yourselves away from idol sacrifices [food which has been sacrificed to idols], and blood and things strangled, and fornication [v20]. By keeping yourselves away from such things you will do well. Be strong!" (literal).

vs30-33: Luke described what happened next. He said, "Some, therefore, being released, went down to Antioch and after bringing together the multitude [of the church], they formally presented the letter. And after reading it, they rejoiced at the exhortation [call to obedience]. And being prophets themselves both Judas and Silas exhorted and strengthened the brothers with many words. And after they spent some time there, the 'brothers released them [Judas and Silas] with a blessing of peace, so they could return to the ones who sent them." (literal).

v34: "But it seemed good to Silas to remain." By the way, this man named Silas is almost certainly the same person Paul and Peter refer to elsewhere as Silvanus (2Co 1:19; 1Th 1:1; 2Th 1:1; 1Pe 5:12). "Silas" is a shortened form of the Roman name Silvanus, and like Paul, he was a Jew who was also a Roman citizen (Ac 16:37; 15:22). He will soon become Paul's partner along with Timothy (Ac 16:3) on his second missionary journey (Ac 15:40) and will help found the churches at Philippi (Ac 16:25), Thessalonica (Ac 17:4, 10, 14; 1Th 1:1; 2Th 1:1) and Corinth (Ac 18:5; 2Co 1:19).

v35: Paul and Barnabas then stayed on in Antioch. They both regularly taught in the church and with a large number of believers evangelized. Very likely there were preaching points throughout the city, and teams would also travel to other towns and villages in the region.

vs36-40: "After some days Paul said to Barnabas, 'Let us now return to look over [provide oversight to] the brothers in every city in which we proclaimed the word of the Lord to see how [well] they have kept it (literal).'" But a disagreement quickly arose between the two men. Barnabas wanted to take John Mark with them again, but Paul was still concerned that he had withdrawn from them (abandoned, deserted) on their last mission. He had left them at Pamphylia and not gone with them into the work, so Paul did not feel he was reliable and did not want to include him. Luke says, "And a sharp anger arose between them so intense it separated them from each other. And Barnabas took Mark and sailed away to Cyprus [Ac 4:36; 12:2; Col 4:10], and Paul also went out [on mission] having chosen Silas [to accompany him]" (literal).

v40: Luke specifically states that the Antioch church prayerfully committed Paul and Silas to the "grace of the Lord" before they went on their mission. It sounds like they did this in a formal way at a gathered service. But interestingly he does not say that this was done for Barnabas and John Mark. Of course it's possible the church did hold a service for them as well, and Luke simply didn't feel the need to mention it, but it's also possible that their emotions were running so high that Barnabas and John Mark left before the church had the opportunity to do so. Or it could mean that the church leaders agreed with Paul that John Mark was not yet mature enough for such demanding missionary work, and that they too thought Barnabas' decision to take him was based more on emotion than wisdom. Luke has just told us that preaching teams were regularly going out from the church (vs3, 5), so the congregation would have had the opportunity to observe Mark's courage under pressure. If by now he had overcome his earlier timidity (Ac 13:13), that change would have become evident to all.

v41: Barnabas sailed southwest to the island of Cyprus, his family home (Ac 4:36), while Paul and Silas walked up the road that led through the northern part of the province of Syria and on into the province of Cilicia. That road led them directly through Paul's home town of Tarsus. And along the way they met with churches to strengthen them.

Acts Chapter 16

vs1-2: At the city of Tarsus the road turned north again entering the Taurus Mountains at a place called the "Cilician Gates." Once through this rugged mountain range, it led west to the Galatian cities where Paul and Barnabas had founded churches (Ac 14:20-21). Derbe would have been the first city they came to and then on to Lystra, the Roman military outpost where Paul had been stoned (Ac 14:19). Luke says, "...a certain disciple was there named Timothy, the son of a faithful, Jewish woman [named Eunice, see 2Ti 1:5] and of a Greek father" (literal).

v2: This young man must have come to Christ on Paul's first visit, or shortly afterward, because believers in his hometown of Lystra, as well as those in Iconium 20 miles north, continually mentioned to Paul the good things they had seen Timothy doing.

v3: Their words must have convinced Paul that this young man had the gifting and courage to do the type of missionary work he and Silas were doing, so he invited Timothy to travel with them. Judging from the way Luke and Paul refer to Timothy's father (Ac 16:1, 3; 2Ti 1:5), it appears he was no longer involved in Timothy's life, so there was no need to obtain his permission to allow Timothy to leave Lystra and travel with the missionaries or for Paul to circumcise him. As a well-trained rabbi, Paul certainly knew how to perform a circumcision. And since their travels would take them into Jewish homes and synagogues in city after city, Paul decided it was best to circumcise Timothy so he would not be viewed as ceremonially unclean and could participate in Jewish gatherings. In Paul's mind this was merely a practical step that would open a door for ministry. It needed to be done so this young missionary would not encounter unnecessary cultural boundaries. In no way did he circumcise Timothy because he thought the young man needed to be circumcised to please God (Gal 5:3-6).

v4: When they met with the churches in Galatia, Paul, or one of his team, read aloud the letter from the Jerusalem Council (Ac 15:23-29), and they may have left a written copy so they could refer to it in the future. That official letter was extremely important because it confirmed that the gospel of "righteousness by faith" which Paul and Barnabas preached was the true gospel. It had been wholeheartedly endorsed by the apostles and elders in Jerusalem. Luke says, "...they handed over to them the opinions which had been decided by the apostles and elders in Jerusalem so they could keep [obey] them" (literal).

v5: By removing the doctrinal confusion that the false teachers from Jerusalem had sown in the Galatian churches, believers were able to again preach the gospel boldly. Doctrinal confusion always produces divisions and undermines unity. So the clear signal sent by the Jerusalem Council released a fresh season of growth. Luke tells us the churches were strengthened in the faith and increased in number daily.

v6: About 20 miles west of Pisidian Antioch, the road on which Paul, Silas and Timothy were traveling intersected a smaller road which headed north. Initially it seemed right to these missionaries to keep going west toward the highly populated costal region called "Asia." And they may have traveled some distance in that direction because Luke says they were "...cut short from speaking the word in Asia by the Holy Spirit" (literal). He does not tell us how this was done, but there are a number of ways the Holy Spirit could'd have corrected them. He may have "spoken" to one of them or imparted a "word of knowledge" (1Co 12:8) about what lay ahead, or He may have simply caused them to feel "grieved" in spirit as they walked (Eph 4:30). One way or another, they turned back and took the smaller road leading north.

The eastern part of the Roman province of Galatia and the western part of the province of Asia were populated by the descendants of an ancient kingdom called Phrygia (J.D. Douglas ed., The New Bible Dictionary, Eerdmans, 1971, "Phrygia" pp994-995). So when Luke says "they went through the Phrygian and Galatian countryside..." (literal), he may be describing the same geographical area in two ways. The area can be called "Phrygia" because the Phrygian people lived there or "Galatia" because it lay within the political boundaries of a region the Romans called Galatia.

v7: As they traveled north, the road skirted along the eastern border of a rugged hill country called "Mysia" (J.D. Douglas ed., The New Bible Dictionary, "Mysia," p856). Mysia was the name given to the northern portion of the Roman province of Asia. And that road continued north until it arrived at the city of Nicea, which was at the southern border of a heavily populated area around the Black Sea called "Bithynia." When the missionaries attempted to go further into Bithynia, Luke says "the Spirit of Jesus" did not permit them to do so. In the previous verse (v6) he identified the Holy Spirit as the One who prevented them from going into Asia, yet here it is Jesus who guides them. While it is certainly true that the Holy Spirit and the Spirit of Jesus, and for that matter, the Spirit of the Father all dwell within us (Ro 8:9, 11), Luke is probably not trying to make a theological statement about the Trinity here. Rather it is much more likely he is describing the manner in which God's guidance was communicated in that particular situation. Apparently in that moment of guidance, it was Jesus who spoke to one or more of them through a dream or vision telling them to stop traveling into Bithynia and to turn around and go back to the road that led west toward the Aegean coast. In one way or another they believed Jesus personally came to direct them (Ac 9:10; 18:9-10).

v8: From Nicea the road west ran along the southern shore of the Sea of Marmara and then followed the Aegean coast south passing through the port-city of Troas (near ancient Troy). Nearly the entire journey from Nicea to Troas, which was over 250 miles, ran along the northern border of Mysia. Luke uses a word here which means they "went beside" Mysia, meaning they didn't travel into the interior of the province or stop to minister along the way. During this portion of their journey it appears they were not aware of a particular destination. They simply kept moving forward, and when they took a wrong turn, God corrected them. At Troas this method of guidance changed. Paul received a vision directing them to go to northern Greece.

v9: When Luke describes Paul's reception of that vision, his wording indicates that it may have reappeared over the course of the night. In it he saw a Macedonian man beckoning him to come near and saying to him, "Come over into Macedonia [northern Greece]. Run to our rescue!" (literal).

v10: Up until now in this chapter of Acts, Luke has been reporting events that happened to Paul, Silas and Timothy, but he was not personally involved in these events. However, at verse 10 Luke begins to include himself in the story. Instead of telling us what "they" did, he describes what "we" did. His change in wording tells us that it was in the city of Troas that he joined this missionary team. We don't know that Troas was Luke's hometown, but we do know that when they set sail from there, he was with them. From verse 10 through verse 17 Luke includes himself, and he will do so again in Acts 20:5-15; 21:1-18 and 27:1-28:16. Since it was quite clear that Paul and his team had not known earlier that they would travel through Troas (Ac 16:6-7), Luke could not have been someone they already knew and had arranged to meet there. They must have either converted this Greek physician (Col 4:14) during their stay in the city or met him and discovered he had been converted by someone else prior to their arrival. In either case, they considered him already mature enough to join them in the next phase of their mission. And their confidence in him turned out to be well-placed. He would continue with Paul for years, and later on when others abandoned Paul during his final trial in Rome, it was Luke who stayed with him through the whole ordeal (2Ti 4:11).

vs10-11: Luke says when Paul saw the vision of a Macedonian man, "...we immediately sought to go forth into Macedonia, concluding that God had called us to evangelize them. And setting sail from Troas we had a good run [favorable winds that allowed the ship to sail straight to where they were headed] to Samothrace [about 70 miles north], and then on the following day into Neapolis [about the same distance]." Neapolis was located on the northeast coast of Macedonia and served as a harbor for Philippi, which was about 10 miles inland. A very important highway ran through Neapolis called the Via Egnatia

(Egnatian Way). It was a paved and carefully maintained military road which ran from Dyrrachium on the Adriatic Sea eastward all the way to what is today called Istanbul (Turkey). It served as Rome's main land route across northern Greece, and Paul and his team traveled west on it from Neapolis to Philippi and then to Thessalonica.

vs12-13: In spite of the fact that it was located in eastern Macedonia, Philippi had been the site of an important battle in Roman history. There in 42 B.C., Antony Octavian (Augustus) and Lepidus had defeated Brutus and Cassius, the assassins of Julius Caesar (A.T. Robertson, Word Pictures in the N.T., Broadman Press, 1930, Vol. 3, p249). To honor this victory Rome declared the city to be an official "colony," which meant it became a military outpost, and its citizens had all the same privileges as the citizens of Rome. Luke also says it was a "leading city," so it was also an administrative center for its district. Macedonia had been divided into four districts after Rome conquered it in 167 B.C. (F.F. Bruce, In the Steps of the Apostle Paul, Kregel 1995, p32). Then he adds, "...we were staying some days in this city, and on Sabbath days we went outside the [city] gate by a river where we thought there would be prayer, and sitting down we spoke to the women who had come together" (literal).

vs14-16: "And a certain woman named Lydia, a dealer in purple cloth [the color of Roman togas] from the city of Thyatira [a city in Asia Minor that specialized in dyeing purple cloth], a Gentile who worshiped God (Ac 13:43-50; 17:4, 17), was listening, and the Lord opened her heart to understand and receive the things spoken by Paul. And as she and her household were baptized, she invited us to be guests in her home saying, 'If you have judged me to be faithful to the Lord, come into my house and stay,' and she urged us so strongly she prevailed. And it happened as we were going out to the place of prayer, a certain young slave girl having the spirit of Python [divination] came out to meet us, who brought much [financial] gain to her masters by falling under a spell and giving prophetic messages" (literal).

"Python" was the name given to a mystical serpent associated with the oracle of Delphi in Greece. Greek mythology believed that when a priestess inhaled the vapors that arose from an opening in the ground at Delphi, she was actually breathing vapors from the rotting body of this serpent which had been slain by the god Apollo. They believed these vapors somehow induced a drugged trance which allowed the god Apollo to possess the spirit of the priestess and then speak through her. People went to Delphi and paid money to receive guidance from this oracle. By telling us the slave girl had the "spirit of Python," Luke is explaining that in a manner similar to the oracle at Delphi, she would fall into a trance and channel a voice from the spirit realm (a demon). By coming to her the people of Philippi believed they were receiving guidance from the "gods" without traveling 150 miles south to Delphi.

vs17-26: Luke says, "This woman, following behind Paul and us [as we walked], cried out saying, 'These men are slaves of the Most High God, who announce to you a way of salvation.' And she was doing this over the course of many days. But Paul became very troubled and turning to the spirit he said, 'In the name of Jesus Christ I command you to come out from her!' And it came out in the same hour. When her masters saw this, the hope of gain went out of them, and seizing Paul and Silas, they dragged them into the market [to make an accusation against them] before the local authorities. And bringing them before the two men who governed the colony they said, 'These men are disturbing [stirring up] our city, being Jews, and they announce customs which are not lawful for us as Romans to receive, nor do.' And the crowd rose up in support against them, and the two officials [who governed the colony] tore their garments off them and ordered them to be beaten with rods. After striking them many times [beaten times without number, 2Co 11:23], they threw them into prison ordering the jailer to guard them securely. The jailer, having received such an order, threw them into the innermost jail cell and secured their feet into the stocks. Toward the middle of the night Paul and Silas were praying a hymn to God, and the prisoners were listening to them, and suddenly there was an earthquake so great that the foundations of the jail were shaken, and all the doors were opened at once, and all the bonds were loosened."

vs27-28: "Having been awakened from sleep and seeing that the prison doors had been opened, the jailer drew his sword and was about to kill himself assuming the prisoners had escaped. But with a loud voice Paul shouted, 'Do not harm yourself for we are all here'" (literal).

According to Roman law, this jailer would have forfeited his own life for having allowed his prisoners to escape (W. Robertson Nicolle, The Expositor's Greek Testament, Eerdmans, 1983, Vol. 2, p351). In this man's case, his judgment might have been even more severe. He may have been facing some form of torture before being executed because he had been specifically instructed to guard them securely (v23). Luke notes that the man was asleep at the time of the earthquake (v27). Had he been awake and moved quickly to the gate, he might have been able to keep the unarmed prisoners inside or at least to shout for help. Regardless of how much blame the man deserved, it's obvious that he was terrified at the prospect of what would be done to him when it was discovered that his prisoners had escaped. He felt suicide was his better option. So by calling out to him, Paul mercifully prevented him from taking his own life. And apparently Paul had enough influence over the rest of the prisoners to keep them from trying to escape. In this remarkable scene we're watching God's love at work. Paul and Silas showed an amazing amount of compassion to a man who had chosen to put their feet in stocks (v24), and Roman stocks were an instrument of torture.

vs29-32: Notice; it was not until Paul spoke to him that the jailer finally called for lamps to be brought in, which may mean the entire scene Luke just described (vs26-28) took place in the dark. This may explain why the jailer did not realize his prisoners had remained in their cells, and it may mean that Paul was not able to see what the jailer was doing. He may have only perceived that the man was about to commit suicide by hearing a sword being drawn or the anguished tone in the man's voice. When lamps arrived, "the jailer rushed into Paul's cell and began to tremble, and then fell down in front of Paul and Silas. And escorting them outside he said, 'My masters [lords], what must I do to be saved?' They said, 'Believe upon the Lord Jesus and you shall be saved, and your household,' and they spoke the Word of God to him along with all those who were in his house" (literal).

What a remarkable turnaround. In one brief moment what had appeared to be defeat turned into triumph. Darkness, chains and stocks gave way to open cell doors, broken bonds and a jailer trembling, kneeling or lying face down on the ground asking how to be saved. What caused this sudden change? Undoubtedly the earthquake played a part. But earthquakes can't change the spiritual atmosphere of a place. That had already changed before the earthquake arrived (v25). Something had turned a place of despair into a place filled with the peace of God. To understand this change we need to review what happened before the earthquake occurred.

Luke tells us that Paul and Silas had their feet "secured into the wood" (literal), meaning their feet were locked in stocks. The cruelty of the jailer was remarkable. He placed men who had just been beaten until their backs and legs were bruised and bloodied into devices that forced them to sit with their legs immobile. He had been ordered to guard them carefully, but nothing had been said about restricting them, so they would have to sit on their wounds. Roman stocks were instruments of torture with leg holes placed at increasingly wider widths to make the victim miserable, and we have no idea whether or not he added to their suffering by using that feature. So who could blame these missionaries if they had spent that night in confusion? After all, they had come to Philippi in response to a vision and had committed no crime. Their only offense was setting a young girl free from a horrible, demonic possession. And their trial in front of the local authorities had been a complete violation of Roman law (vs37-38). The officers apparently felt free to humiliate and abuse them without a proper trial because they were Jews. So the fact that Paul and Silas sat in the darkness of that prison praying and singing hymns instead of giving in to discouragement shows us that they fully understood the spiritual danger they faced in that terrible moment. And they responded to that spiritual attack by engaging in spiritual warfare. They refused to give in to despair or allow unbelief a place in their hearts. They chose to not doubt their guidance or question God's protection. Instead they drove back the darkness and transformed the spiritual atmosphere by deliberately inviting the Holy Spirit to fill that jail.

Luke uses a surprising combination of words to describe their actions that night. He literally says they were praying by singing or reciting hymns to God. By specifically using the word "hymn" he is probably telling us they were singing from the Psalms, in particular from the Hallel of the Passover Seder. That would mean they were reciting or singing from Psalms 113 through 118 (Geoffrey W. Bromiley ed., Theological Dictionary of the New Testament Abridged in One

Volume, Eerdmans, 1985, p1226). And he says the prisoners were listening intently to every word. Probably because he was a physician, he chose a Greek word which was often used to describe a doctor listening to sounds in the chest or abdomen to detect disorders or pregnancy (W.R. Nicolle, The Expositor's Greek Testament, Eerdmans, 1983, Vol. 2, p350. Also: Webster's New Collegiate Dictionary, 1959, "Auscultation"). By using that word he is explaining that something profound was taking place in that inner jail. Those prisoners were listening like a doctor listens to a patient because they were being drawn to God. They were listening to every word as Paul and Silas worshiped, and the effect on them was so strong that after the earthquake opened the prison doors and loosed their bonds, not one of them rushed to escape. It appears Paul took charge of the situation and ordered all of them to remain in their places. That the prisoner's would exercise such self-restraint was totally unexpected by the jailer. When he discovered the doors had been opened, he didn't even check to see if anyone had stayed in their cells. He assumed they had escaped immediately and was so certain of it that he prepared to kill himself rather than face the punishment he was sure would be waiting for him.

This miraculous event teaches us an important lesson: It wasn't the earthquake that changed the spiritual atmosphere of that place. The earthquake didn't occur until after the power of God arrived, and the power of God arrived as a result of spiritual warfare. Paul and Silas drove back the darkness by inviting God's active presence through worship. They used the faith-filled language of the Psalms to present their need to God, and He heard them and answered with an earthquake that shook the city.

Up until that earthquake the jailer had been asleep, sound asleep. He arrived on the scene so late that all the prisoners would have had time to escape. Had he already been awake, or had he awakened quickly, he could have called for help and rushed to the outer gate to prevent any who tried to escape. But by the time he arrived, all hope of preventing an escape was gone. So the way God reached this man's heart was by the grace shown him when he arrived. Paul and Silas did not return evil for evil (Mt 5:44; Ro 12:17-21) but called out to him to prevent him from committing suicide. They even kept the prisoners from escaping. The mercy they showed him was so profound that he became overwhelmed by it. Nothing in his religion or life experience had prepared him for this. Had he been in their place, it would never have crossed his mind to do the same thing. He would have been delighted to watch his tormenter fall on his sword. For that matter, he would have fled within the first few seconds, yet these two Jews did not do what he would have done. Instead they treated him with kindness as if his life mattered. And undoubtedly the Spirit's presence still lingered there. After he called for lamps to be brought in, the astonished man surveyed the cells with their doors flung open and the prisoners still in them or gathered near Paul as they waited. And then he too was changed. He began to tremble and came and fell (face down) in front of Paul and Silas. His physical posture spoke louder than words. They had given him back his life, and he was now their "slave." Then he led them out of the inner prison, and as soon as they were outside asked, "Sirs [lords], what must I do to be saved?" In other words, "I'm already convinced that whatever you're preaching around our city must be true. God is obviously with you, and you are different from any humans I've ever met. Please tell me what you've been preaching so I can believe it and become like you." They answered, "Believe upon the Lord Jesus, and you shall be saved, you and your household" (literal). At that point he took them home so his whole family could hear the same message.

vs33-34: After Paul and Silas ministered to the jailer and his family, he led them to a place where there was water to bathe the dried blood from their wounds. When he was finished, they baptized him and the members of his family. Then the jailer "brought them up into the house" which may indicate that these things took place down at the river. Or the jailer may have lived in an upstairs apartment in or near the prison. In that case he may have led them to a nearby fountain or well and then brought them upstairs into his living quarters. Once inside, he fed them a meal. Luke literally says "...he set a table beside them." Depending on their injuries, Paul and Silas may have stood "beside" a table rather than reclining in the customary manner. While they ate, the whole family rejoiced before the Lord for their salvation. Knowing Paul, there can be no doubt their initiation into Christ included the baptism with the Holy Spirit (Ac 19:2-6), so the expressions of joy that took place in that home may well have included speaking in tongues and prophesying. Finally at some point, Paul and Silas returned to their cells or at least remained somewhere in the prison complex to await the next step in their relationship with the city. Luke mentions nothing about the other prisoners, but since they did not flee when the earthquake occurred (v28), it appears that they too waited at the jail. Undoubtedly they were hoping for leniency because they had not fled, but they also knew that this newly-saved jailer would treat them kindly in the future.

vs35-37: When morning arrived, the two men who had ordered Paul and Silas beaten and jailed (vs20-23) sent the very officers who had performed the beatings with this command: "Release those men!" They went to the jailer, and then he went to Paul. He said, "The men who govern the colony have sent an order that you may be released. Therefore, come out now and go in peace" (literal). But surprisingly, Paul replied that he would not leave. He said, "Having beaten us [bloody] in front of the people without a trial, men who are Romans, they threw us into prison and now want to throw us out [of the city] secretly. No, indeed..." (literal). And then he presented his demands, "...but let them come [here] themselves and lead us out." In effect, Paul was demanding that these leaders publicly acknowledge the injustice that had taken place, and it is very likely that he was doing this as a way of protecting the Philippian believers. If those civic leaders were not held accountable for this miscarriage of justice, the believers in that city would be subject to the same injustices after Paul and Silas left. To prevent that from happening Paul wanted to frighten them, and it appears he succeeded. He accused them of violating a very important Roman law which protected all Roman citizens from being punished without a trial. And Paul was a Roman citizen by birth (Ac 22:25-29) which made the violation of his rights even more serious. If those leaders were found guilty of abusing a Roman citizen without a formal trial, they would be removed from office and disqualified from holding such an office in the future. In fact for such a serious violation the entire city could lose its special privileges as a Roman colony (W. Robertson Nicolle, The Expositor's Greek Testament, Eerdmans, 1983, Vol. 2, p354). As it turned out, Paul's bold demand did not prevent all future persecution of believers in that city (Php 1:29-30), but it may have delayed it.

vs38-39: The officers reported Paul's demands to the leaders, and when they heard that the men they ordered to be beaten and jailed were both Romans, they became afraid and came to the jail themselves. They appealed to Paul and Silas to change their minds probably by trying to convince them it had all been a misunderstanding. Then they personally escorted them out of the jail complex and asked them to leave the city.

v40: Yet Paul and Silas refused to leave immediately. Instead they went straight to Lydia's house and gathered all the believers in the city for a final meeting. During their time in Philippi they had seen a very diverse group of people believe in Jesus Christ, yet by saying "they exhorted the brothers" (literal) at that meeting Luke is telling us how Paul and Silas viewed all of these new converts. They now thought of them (men and women) as "brothers," meaning they considered them to be members of the same spiritual family to which they themselves belonged. Regardless of someone's personal history not one was a second-class citizen. They respected everyone in the room; they loved them all, and they would feel a lifelong responsibility for their welfare (Php 1:3-5; 2:19, 25-39; 4:1-3). And as the years passed, the Philippian church proved that they felt the same way toward them (Php 1:7; 4:15-18). The final "exhortation" Paul and Silas gave in Lydia's home that day must have included a rehearsal of the central tenets of the gospel, but it also must have included the same warning they gave to other churches: "Through many tribulations we must enter the kingdom of God" (Ac 14:22).

Acts Chapter 17

v1: Paul, Silas and Timothy left Philippi traveling west on the Egnatian Way (See: 16:10-11). Luke, being a humble man, doesn't mention that he didn't go with them. He simply stops including himself in the story. He no longer uses verbs in the first person plural (we) but returns to the third person plural (they). That this change in language indicates that he remained behind is confirmed in Acts 20:5. At that verse and on through much of the rest of Acts, he will again include himself by returning to the first person plural (we). At Acts 20:4 he says Paul returned to Macedonia, and then at Acts 20:5-6 he specifically notes that Paul left from Philippi to sail back to Troas, the city where Paul originally met Luke (Ac 16:10). And when he describes that voyage, he says, "We sailed from Philippi… and came to… Troas within five days, and there we stayed seven days" (Ac 20:6). Because he does not tell us what he did or where he ministered during the next, approximately five years (Ac 18:11; 20:31) while Paul, Silas and Timothy went on to other parts of Greece and Asia Minor, we can only guess. But it seems likely that Paul left him in Philippi to pastor this new church in the same way that he would later leave Timothy in Ephesus (1Ti 1:3).

Luke says the missionaries "passed through" Amphipolis and Apollonia which probably means they only spent the night in those communities and didn't stop to preach. Amphipolis is the capital of one of the four districts of Macedonia and a commercial center (gold, silver and timber). It was located about 30 miles west/southwest of Philippi. Apollonia was a small town about 27 miles past Amphipolis. And Thessalonica was another 34 miles past Apollonia (J.D. Douglas ed., The New Bible Dictionary, pp33, 47). When they reached Thessalonica they stopped to minister. It was a very strategic place. It was the largest city in Macedonia, the seat of the Roman governor of the province of Macedonia, one of the major seaports on the Aegean Sea, and the great highway, the Egnatian Way, ran straight through it. Yet of greater significance to Paul was the fact that there was a Jewish community in that city large enough to have a synagogue.

v2: Luke reminds us that it was Paul's "custom" to attend synagogue on the Sabbath. Apparently wherever he went, if it were possible, he would participate in the local Sabbath service. Obviously in his own thinking, following Jesus Christ had not separated him from Judaism. He had not "converted" to a new religion; he had become the servant of Israel's promised Messiah. So when he attended a local synagogue, he naturally preached Christ when given the opportunity. In his own mind he was not proclaiming a new religion, nor was he trying to get them to leave Judaism; he was announcing that their promised Savior had arrived. As we saw earlier (Ac 13:16-41), the way he normally presented the gospel to Jews was to draw their attention to promises in the Scriptures about the Messiah which had been traditionally overlooked and then explain how those promises had been fulfilled by Jesus of Nazareth. Then at some point in his presentation, he would challenge his listeners to acknowledge that they had failed to live up to God's high standard of righteousness in the Law of Moses and invite them to accept God's gift of righteousness which He gives to those who believe in Jesus (Ac 13:38-39). So when Paul arrived in Thessalonica, he naturally attended synagogue, and for three weeks presented his message and "dialogued" with those who were interested. That "dialogue" must have started with a good deal of questions and answers but as time went on turned into debate and argument.

v3: In this verse Luke very concisely summarizes the main point of contention: Paul was showing the members of the synagogue that the Messiah would not only be a powerful king and deliverer, but that it was also prophesied that He would suffer and die and be miraculously raised from the dead. For many of those listening to Paul the revelation that the Messiah must suffer, die and be raised from the dead would have been a shocking reinterpretation of a familiar theme. Though there were groups within Judaism at that time which recognized that the Scriptures describe a suffering Messiah (e.g. the Qumran Community), most did not. So the discussions which followed Paul's presentations must have been lively. Having said that the Messiah must die and rise again, Luke records that Paul went on to identify Jesus of Nazareth as that Person. He would say, "This Jesus whom I am proclaiming to you is the Christ." And then he would invite people to believe and become Jesus' disciples.

v4: Luke says when Paul and Silas preached in the synagogue, some of the Jews were "persuaded and threw in their lot [joined] with Paul and Silas" (literal). But he also notes that there was a far greater response from the Greeks who had been attending the services. These were men and women who had already stopped believing in the gods of Greek mythology and had chosen instead to worship the God of the Bible. And he adds that this "a great multitude" included a large number of women from the most prominent families in the city. Very likely those who were interested attended daily gatherings that the apostles conducted so they could teach more deeply about Jesus (Ac19:9).

v5: That enthusiastic response caused the leaders of the synagogue to become very angry. They were watching a large portion of their congregation, and undoubtedly a large portion of their income and influence, begin to gather elsewhere to listen to a pair of traveling rabbis. So it's no surprise that they felt threatened. But what is surprising and sad is that they do not appear to have been motivated by concerns over religious doctrine. In other words they weren't primarily alarmed by the apostle's interpretation of Scripture. Instead their fury arose out of an intolerance for a rival. They were not going to allow anyone to challenge their leadership without a fight. And when they fought, they showed no signs of ethical restraint. They were willing to do whatever they had to do to get their people back. They were so determined to force Paul and Silas out of the city, or have them killed, that they went into the public market, hired a group of men from the do-nothings that tend to lounge around such places and organized them into a mob. And if enough people begin to march and yell, others tend to join in. So once they were able to collect enough people to make enough noise, they attracted the attention of the whole city. Then they led this mob to the home of a man named Jason who was probably providing housing for the missionaries. When they arrived at the house, someone forced their way in to search for Paul and Silas intending to drag them out so the mob could attack them.

v6: Unable to find the apostles, they seized Jason along with some other believers and dragged them to a place where public trials were held so they could accuse them of crimes before the leaders of the city. In Thessalonica the leaders of the city were called "politarchs." That was a very unusual title in that place and time, yet Luke specifically uses that term, and in 1835 archeologists discovered that word written on the ancient gates of Thessalonica (Paul Lawrence, The IVP Atlas of Bible History, Intervarsity Press, 2006, p155). This is one more example of archeology confirming the accuracy of the Bible.

v7: The synagogue leaders shouted out to the "politarchs" their accusations against Paul and Silas even though the missionaries themselves were not present. They also accused a fellow-citizen named Jason whom they said was guilty because he had taken them into his home. We have no definite information about this man named Jason, but there are some references made elsewhere in the Bible that would allow us to guess his religious background. In the conclusion of his letter to the Romans Paul mentions a man named Jason whom he associates with two other men: Lucius and Sosipater (Ro 16:21). He says those men were his "kinsmen" which means they were Jews. This Sosipater may be the "Sopater of Berea" who is mentioned in Ac 20:4. In that passage Luke places him next to "Aristarchus and Secundus of the Thessalonians" apparently because all three were from Macedonia. If so, then the Jason mentioned at the end of Romans is likely the same Jason we're reading about now. In that case he was a Jew who believed Paul's message when he preached in the synagogue (v4).

Paul and Silas, and those associated with them, were charged with the crime of "...acting in opposition to the decrees of Caesar by declaring Jesus to be another king" (literal). Those charges were unquestionably false. Paul had not come to that city to preach political subversion. He was not trying to start a rebellion. In fact he taught believers to submit to human authorities insofar as their conscience would permit them (Ro 13:1-7), and even to pray for those in authority (1Ti 2:1-4). But Paul did faithfully proclaim Jesus as the Messiah (Christ, v3) and we know from his letters to the Thessalonians that he taught them that Jesus would return from heaven to set up God's Kingdom on earth (1Th 1:9-10; 4:13-17; 2Th 1:6-10). That teaching could have been interpreted as disloyalty to Rome because the empire considered its Caesar to be divine. But there was also growing anti-Semitism. This public trial was taking place about a year or two after the Roman emperor Claudius (41-54 A.D.) expelled all Jews from the city of Rome (Ac 18:2). He may have done so out of frustration because of repeated rioting which had erupted within the city's Jewish community in response to those who were preaching the gospel. The Roman historian Suetonius made a very interesting observation about those riots. He said, "As the Jews were indulging in constant riots at the instigation of Chrestus, he [Claudius] banished them from Rome" (Suetonius, Life of Claudius, XXV.4, as quoted by F.F. Bruce, Acts, Eerdmans, reprint 1974, p368). If Suetonius mistook the name Chrestus for Christus (same pronunciation in Greek), then the charges made against Paul and Silas by the synagogue rulers in Thessalonica may have been accurate. There may have been a decree from Caesar forbidding such preaching because it caused riots. Yet the synagogue rulers in Thessalonica worded their accusation in such a way as to make the apostles appear to be political rebels against Rome. It seems they were hoping to arouse the crowd and provoke the "politarchs" to issue the harshest verdict possible.

vs8-9: And indeed their accusations produced the desired effect. The crowd and city authorities became angry and alarmed. But rather than let the situation turn violent as the leaders in Philippi had done (Ac 16:20-24), those in Thessalonica took control of the situation in a clever way. They refused to release Jason or those who were with him until they put a large amount of money in the city's custody. The purpose of that money was to threaten them financially. It was a bond which would be forfeited to the city if trouble broke out again. They were forcing them to guarantee that Paul and Silas would leave town. So even though the apostles themselves weren't present at the trial, their mission was effectively ended immediately. If they kept preaching, all those who had been forced to post bond would lose large amounts of money.

v10: Paul and Silas were hidden somewhere in the city, and after the trial was over, Jason and the others reported to them what had taken place. It was decided that they must leave immediately, so that night the church gathered and sent them to a small, remote town called Berea. It was about 50 miles southwest of Thessalonica in a different district of Macedonia which meant the authorities there would not yet have heard about the uproar in Thessalonica. And when they arrived, the missionaries went straight to the local synagogue and preached the gospel.

v11: Luke says the attitude of the members of the synagogue in Berea was far more noble (well-born) than the attitude of the synagogue leaders in Thessalonica. The root of the problem in Thessalonica was that those leaders became hostile when they felt their income and influence was threatened. It really didn't matter to them whether the gospel was true or not. But in Berea the members of the synagogue were motivated by a desire to know the truth, and they listened carefully to what was being presented. Then they carefully examined each passage of Scripture Paul and Silas presented. Luke says they "...received the Word with all eagerness [keen, active minds], and daily examined the Scriptures [to see] if it might have these things in this way" (literal). He's telling us that they approached the gospel with a combination of open-mindedness and caution. They were <u>open minded</u> in that they were hungry to know as much as they could about God and humble enough to acknowledge that there might be truths they didn't know or understand correctly. But they also were <u>cautious</u> meaning they knew they could be deceived if they relied on their own feelings to decide what was true or false. In their minds the Bible itself must be the final authority in such matters, so they engaged in diligent study undoubtedly reading each passage in its context to see if these visiting preachers were accurately presenting what each passage intended to say. And that willingness to honestly examine Scripture was all Paul and Silas needed because the truth that "the Christ [Messiah] had to suffer and rise again from the dead" (Ac 17:3, literal) is indeed taught by the prophets. Once someone sees and accepts that truth, the historical facts about the life of Jesus of Nazareth make it obvious that He is the Christ (Ac 17:3).

v12: After carefully studying the Bible many in that synagogue believed in Jesus including a significant number of Greek women and men who were highly respected in their community.

v13: When the synagogue leaders in Thessalonica heard that Paul and Silas were continuing to proclaim the Word of God in Berea, they followed them. And just as they had done in their own city, they were again able to stir up an angry mob. Either they went to the market-place and drew a crowd together (Ac 17:5), or they waded into a crowd that had already gathered to listen to Paul and began shouting accusations against him to whomever would listen. Very likely they told everyone that they had come to warn them because Paul was a political subversive who would lead them into trouble with the Roman government. And their strategy worked. They successfully instilled fear in many, and that fear quickly turned to anger. People who had been happily listening to the gospel and watching people get healed and delivered (1Th 1:5) became hostile.

vs14-15: Unlike Thessalonica (v6) Berea was a small town with no place to hide. So when the men of the church saw the situation become dangerous, they immediately rushed Paul out of town to protect him. They sent him "as far as the sea," which apparently means a group of men escorted him out to the coast, about 16 miles away. They probably chose local footpaths rather than the main roads where they might be overtaken. When they arrived, they must have put him on the first boat departing for any port, and once he was safely at sea, he could make his way to Athens. When we look at a map of ancient Greece, we discover that there was a road that ran along the coast, and it's possible that instead of escaping by boat, Paul walked 250 miles south to Athens. But since Luke makes no mention of him ministering anywhere along the way, it seems more likely he escaped by boat. With favorable winds he would have arrived in Athens within three or four days.

v15: Timothy and Silas must not have been as outspoken as Paul, and therefore, not as easily recognized because they were able to remain in Macedonia for a while longer to care for the churches (1Th 3:1-3). However, Paul did not travel alone. Some of the men from Berea graciously took it upon themselves to accompany him all the way to Athens. Obviously, they felt a need to protect him. They may not have been comfortable allowing a Jewish rabbi to travel alone in Greece. Once they arrived, they undoubtedly helped him find a safe place to stay and then felt free to return home. Before they left, Paul gave them either verbal instructions or a letter telling Silas and Timothy to join him as soon as possible.

v16: During the days he spent alone in Athens, Paul's spirit became grieved. In spite of its reputation as a center of learning and philosophy the city was full of spiritual deception. The entire place was immersed in a strong, demonic presence (1Co 10:20). The Roman writer Pliny estimated there were over 30,000 public statues of gods in Athens, and of course, that number didn't include the countless number of private shrines in people's homes (A.T. Robertson, Word Pictures in the New Testament, Broadman, 1930, Vol. 3, p278).

v17: It appears that Paul had not originally planned to conduct a mission in Athens, at least not until his partners were able to join him. But his concern for the spiritual condition of both Jews and Gentiles in that place grew so strong he couldn't help himself. It wasn't long before he felt compelled to preach. So he began dialoguing with Jews and God-fearing (worshiping) Greeks in the synagogue as well as going everyday into the large market at the center of the city to converse with whomever he happened to sit or stand beside.

v18: In the course of these discussions he met philosophers from both the Epicurean and Stoic schools of thought. The Epicureans taught that humans have no eternal existence and live in a soulless, mechanical universe. They said if the gods exist at all, they have no interest or involvement with us, and when a person finally recognizes that fact, they are set free from all the superstitions and religious activities that weigh people down. They said the main goal of life is happiness, but happiness is not found by pursuing sensual pleasure. To become happy a person must learn to avoid pain, and to avoid pain a person must escape into the inner world of the intellect. Yet even though Epicurus (306 B.C.) taught his followers not to pursue sensual pleasure, the effect of his functionally atheistic philosophy was to break down religious restraint in people and release them to engage in severe moral corruption (W. E. Caldwell, The Ancient World, Holt, Rinehart and Winston, New York, 1962, pp319, 389-390).

The founder of the Stoic school of philosophy was a Phoenician named Zeno (302 B.C.). He taught people to passively submit to the laws of nature. He said a truly wise person realizes that whatever life brings, whether it is pleasure, pain, joy or grief, those circumstances come to us because they are part of a divine plan. When Zeno spoke about a "divine plan," he was not speaking about the will of a personal god, like the God of the Bible, but rather impersonal forces that basically function arbitrarily. He pictured these forces as a divine "fire" that inhabits all of life. And since that impersonal force controls every person's life, a wise person will patiently endure whatever happens to them whether good or bad. Happiness is found by peacefully embracing one's destiny. Zeno also taught that since all humans partake of the same, divine "fire," we should consider ourselves to be "brothers and sisters" and gladly live out the obligations that the divine plan has placed on us toward our fellow human beings. True happiness is found in knowing that we are under the control of a higher, impersonal force, and therefore, we are able to exercise self-restraint over our emotions. Finally, when it comes time to die, each person should face death willingly and cheerfully because death is also a part of the divine plan (W. E. Caldwell, The Ancient World, Holt, Rinehart and Winston, New York, 1962, pp320, 389).

As these philosophers listened to Paul, some of them grew frustrated. They wanted to investigate further the amazing statements he was making. So they stepped aside from the main discussion and asked each other, "What does this peddler of someone else's ideas wish to say?" (literal). Others replied, "He appears to be a spokesman for foreign gods" (literal) because they heard him talking about someone named "Jesus" whom he claimed had risen from the dead.

v19: Taking Paul by the hand, these philosophers led him to a market-place so he could present his teaching before the "Council of Areopagus." This was a council of six, annually-elected judges who were chosen by the nobles of the city to serve as the "guardians of the established customs." Normally they met in the market-place, but because they convened on a rocky hill called the Areopagus (named after Ares, the Greek god of war) when they had to serve as judges in a murder trial, the council had come to be called the "Council of Areopagus" (W. E. Caldwell, The Ancient World, Holt, Rinehart and Winston, New York, 1962, p159).

vs19-20: In earlier times this council of elders governed the entire city of Athens, but when Paul stood before them, their authority had declined significantly until their only responsibility was investigating questions concerning religion and morals (Paul Lawrence, The IVP Atlas of Bible History, Intervarsity Press, 2006, p.156). They asked Paul, "Can we know what this new teaching is which is being spoken by you? For you are bringing into our ears some foreign things; therefore, we strongly desire to know what these things mean [wish to be]" (literal).

v21: At this point in his account Luke inserts a brief observation so we'll understand the prevailing attitude of the people Paul was addressing. He says all Athenians, including foreigners who were living in the city, spent their free time either reporting or listening to "something newer" (literal). That term probably means they researched and reported on ideas they had never heard before. Apparently this was done as a form of entertainment. They simply enjoyed hearing novel ideas. They were not engaged in a sincere search for truth. By telling us this Luke is cautioning us so that we don't mistake the council's questions to be a sincere search for truth.

vs22-23: This council of elders generally met in the Royal Portico, one of the colonnaded buildings lining the market place. When they had gathered there and asked Paul to explain his teaching, he stood up in the midst of the council and said, "Men of Athens, I have observed how much more fervently you worship the gods than do those who live in other cities because as I was walking through your streets looking up at the objects you worship, I even found an altar on which the words had been inscribed: 'To an unknown god.' This One you serve without knowing who He is, this is the God I proclaim to you" (paraphrase).

vs24-25: "The God who made the world and all the things that are in it, being Lord of heaven and earth, does not live in hand-made temples and shrines, nor does He need to be served in any way by our human hands for He lacks nothing because He is the One who gives to all of us life and breath and all things" (paraphrase).

vs26-27: "And furthermore, from [out of] one [man] He made every nation of men [people groups] to dwell upon all the face of the earth placing boundaries on their predetermined seasons [of existence] and on the frontiers of their dwelling places [the outer boundaries of the land they occupy]. And God's purpose in doing this was so that those who were seeking after Him might reach out and touch Him and find Him because the truth is He is not, and has never been, far from each one of us" (paraphrase).

v28: "For in Him we live and are moved [set in motion, originate] and continue to exist [are] as indeed some of the poets among you have said, 'For we are also His offspring…'" (literal). In order to show the Athenians that some of their own ancestors had said similar things about a supreme god, Paul quoted from two, different, Greek poets. His first quote is found in a poem by Epimenides of Crete. Epimenides wrote concerning Zeus, "They fashioned a tomb for thee, o holy and high one. The Cretans, always liars, evil beasts, idle bellies! (see Titus 1:12) But thou art not dead; thou livest and abidest forever; For in thee we live and move and have our being" (F.F. Bruce, Acts, Eerdmans, reprint 1974, p359). Paul's second quote repeats exactly the words written by a poet named Aratus of Soli (270 B.C.), a native of Cilicia, Paul's own province. In the first half of the fifth line in a poem about astronomy entitled "Phaenomena," Aratus wrote this statement, "For we are also his offspring," again referring to Zeus rather than the God of the Bible (A.G. Robertson, Word Pictures in the New Testament, Broadman, 1930, Vol. 3, p289). Obviously by quoting such passages, Paul was not trying to equate Zeus with the true God. He was demonstrating to the Athenians that he was familiar with their literature, and he was trying to find there a common truth upon which they could all agree. If he could help this council of elders recognize that there was a supreme Creator above the multitude of gods that filled their city, he would have a starting point from which he could begin to teach them about the true God.

vs29-31: Having shown these judges that some of their own philosophers had described a divine Person far too big to live in the places or objects humans might fashion for them, Paul continued, "Therefore, being God's offspring we should not think that gold, silver or stone, an engraved object produced by human skill and design, is like that which is divine. But having overlooked the times of ignorance, God now announces to all men everywhere to repent because after this [season during which men may repent] He has set up a day in which He must righteously judge all the inhabited earth by a man whom He has designated [set a boundary around], furnishing proof [that this man is the one He has chosen to be the Judge] by raising Him up from the dead" (paraphrase). Paul chose the term "times of ignorance" (Greek: agnoia) to characterize the spiritual history of Athens. For centuries the people of that city had been confused and deceived. They didn't know the true God but instead worshiped their own, invented gods. Yet Paul quickly assured them that God had not abandoned them because of those past sins. He had mercifully "overlooked" them. By saying that God "overlooked" the sins of that season, Paul didn't mean their ignorance made them morally innocent. He was explaining why, in spite of such gross sin, God withheld His wrath and was now offering them mercy. They should not interpret the fact that God had continued to provide and care for them as evidence that He was indifferent to their worship of idols, but rather as evidence of His patient love for them. He had held back the judgment they deserved in order to give them time to find Him. For hundreds of years they had "...exchanged the glory of the incorruptible God for an image in the form of corruptible man and of birds and four-footed animals and crawling creatures" (Ro 1:23). And during those centuries God indeed turned them over to the misery which naturally results from sin (Ro 1:24-25). Yet He chose to restrain the judgment they deserved in order to give them the opportunity to repent before the day comes when He will judge the world in righteousness (1Co 4:5; 2Th 1:6-10).

vs32: Paul not only warned his listeners that God's judgment was coming if they did not repent; he even identified the person through whom God would perform that judgment. He said their judge would be a man who had already lived, died and been miraculously raised back to life. God had used a resurrection from death to distinguish one man from all other human beings. And the Council listened until Paul said that. But the moment he claimed that a person rose from the dead, he lost his audience. Luke says, "...and hearing of a resurrection of dead persons, some were laughing [at him] and others said, 'We will hear you concerning this [subject] again'" (literal). In other words Paul was being dismissed. The judges had heard enough. To believe in a resurrection demands that a person believe in an all-powerful God, and to believe in an all-powerful God demands that a believer submit to

His leadership. And most of the Council of Areopagus were not ready to allow Paul to lead them any further in that direction.

vs33-34: Apparently they continued on with their council meeting after Paul left. They may have stayed to discuss how to respond to what they had just heard. But amazingly when Paul walked out of that gathering, he did not go alone. A number of people who had been listening to him were deeply touched by his words. And they stood up and walked out with him and continued meeting with him in the days that followed. Some of them came to faith in Christ, and Luke mentions two by name: one was a man named Dionysius, who was actually a member of the Council of Areopagus, and the other was a highly respected woman named Damaris. He notes that others believed as well. So Paul's sermon that day, though delivered under very difficult circumstances, still bore eternal fruit.

Acts Chapter 18

v1: While waiting for Silas and Timothy to finish their ministry in Macedonia and join him, Paul decided to travel on to the city of Corinth. It was located about 50 miles southwest of Athens, less than a day's journey by ship, near the narrow strip of land that connects northern and southern Greece. Though Athens was the cultural center of Greece, Corinth was its commercial and political center. At that point in time, it was possibly the fourth largest city in the Roman Empire (W.R. Nicoll, The Expositor's Greek Testament, Eerdmans, 1983, Vol. 2, p730). Luke doesn't tell us why Paul made the move, but Paul later mentioned that this was a very difficult season for him personally. In his first letter to the Corinthians he reminded them that he had arrived there "…in weakness and fear and in much trembling" (1Co 2:3). So he may have made the move because of hardship. It's possible his financial resources ran out in Athens, and he moved to Corinth to find work (1Co 4:9-13; 2Co 11:9, 27; 2Th 3:7-9). Luke tells us he looked for work as soon as he arrived (Ac 18:2, 3). Also at that point in time, he had not yet received any communication from Silas and Timothy, and he was deeply worried that the churches in Macedonia might not survive the fierce persecution to which they had been immediately subjected (1Th 3:1-8; 2Co 11:28-29). He did not yet know that his mission in that region had been amazingly successful (1Th 1:6-10). And the overall response to his preaching in Athens had been disappointing. Though some remarkable people came to faith, it appears that only a small group of believers were meeting in a home when he left. Luke does not mention a church there. And even after moving to Corinth Paul could easily keep in touch with believers in Athens by means of the traffic that continually flowed between the two neighboring cities.

It must have been lonely for Paul without Silas and Timothy (Ac 17:5). And in light of his description of himself as being physically weak and fearful at the time (1Co 2:3), he may have been ill or suffering from a previous injury when he arrived in Corinth (2Co 12:7-10). Being stoned in Lystra (Ac 14:19) or beaten mercilessly in Philippi (Ac 16:23) may have left him with some type of residual damage in his body. Judging from remarks he made to the Galatians, his eyesight may have been impaired (Gal 4:13-15; 6:11, 17). If indeed his eyes had been damaged in the vicious attacks, his move to Corinth would have been all the more difficult. Whatever the cause, when he arrived, he felt and appeared to the Corinthians to be weak and frightened. As a result their initial impression of him was so poor that even years later some of them still showed a lack respect for him (2Co 10:10; 12:11-12) (W.R. Nicoll, The Expositor's Greek Testament, Eerdmans, 1983, Vol. 2, p729).

v2: It was customary for young, Jewish men, including rabbis, to be taught a trade. And since Paul grew up in Cilicia, a province famous for making goat-hair tents (F.F. Bruce, Acts, Eerdmans, reprint 1974, p367), it's no surprise that he was trained in tent-making (v3). Jewish guilds formed around each particular trade, and those who worked in that trade tended to bond together with a strong sense of brotherhood even to the point of sitting together in synagogue (Alfred Edersheim, Sketches of Jewish Social Life, Hendrickson, 1994, pp170-174). So it would not have been difficult for Paul to locate the Jewish tent-makers when he arrived in Corinth. And in a busy commercial center like Corinth there must have been plenty of opportunities to find work. He soon met a man named Aquila, a tent-maker from Pontus, a region located along the southern shore of the Black Sea. In recent years Aquila had been living in Rome where he met and married Priscilla, a woman whose name implies that she was a member of a very distinguished Roman family. About a year prior to Paul's arrival the couple had fled to Corinth after the emperor Claudius (41-54 A.D.) ordered all Jews to leave the city. Claudius probably issued that order because he had grown frustrated by the rioting which was continually erupting in the Jewish community. It appears that those riots were a reaction to the growing influence of Christianity (see comments on Ac 17:7). Following the great outpouring of the Holy Spirit at Pentecost (Ac 2:10), water-baptized and Spirit-filled Jewish pilgrims must have carried the gospel there when they returned home. Then as the number of believers in Rome grew, that city began to experience the same type of violent riots that Paul was facing nearly everywhere he went.

Luke doesn't tell us if Aquila and Priscilla were already Christians before meeting Paul, but it seems likely that they were. Aquila may have heard the gospel in Pontus from pilgrims who returned after a Pentecost celebration in Jerusalem during which they were filled with the Holy Spirit. Luke specifically mentions in Acts 2:9 that people from Pontus were present on that special day (Ac 2:9). And where better for a Jewish tent-maker and an aristocratic Roman lady to meet and marry than in a church in Rome because in those communities there was "no longer any Jew or Gentile" (Gal 3:28, literal). Paul never refers to them as his converts, and both exhibit a level of maturity and partnership with Paul which seems to go far beyond what would be expected from new converts (Ac 18:18-19, 26; Ro 16:3-5; 1Co 16:19; 2Ti 4:19). However, if they were Christians before coming to Corinth, it does not appear that they began proclaiming Christ as soon as they arrived because Paul later reminded the Corinthian church that he was the one who "planted" the church in their city (1Co 3:6), and he was their spiritual "father" (1Co 4:15).

vs3-5: As soon as he arrived in Corinth, Paul needed a job and a place to stay, and this couple provided him with both. They rented a spare room to him and put him to work in their business. Initially Paul worked all week and then "dialogued in the synagogue every Sabbath… trying to persuade both Jews and [God-fearing] Greeks" (literal). But when Silas and Timothy came down from Macedonia, they brought with them a financial gift from the church in Philippi (2Co 11:7-9; Php 4:15) which released him from having to work to support himself and allowed him to devote himself to preaching.

v6: As usual Paul began his ministry in that city by preaching in the synagogue (v5). And as had typically happened in one city after another, opposition among a portion of the synagogue soon arose. To describe the confrontation Luke uses a word that pictures an army lining up in order to engage another army in battle. He may have chosen that particular word to create a picture in our minds of a particular event. Apparently the tension rose to a point where Paul was confronted by a line of angry men standing in front of the synagogue. They formed a barrier to prevent him from entering and threatened to hurt him if he tried to pass. Luke also mentions that they blasphemed, meaning they said horrible things about Jesus. Sadly such violent confrontations had already become common in Paul's ministry (Ac 13:50-51, 14:4-6, 19; 16:22-24; 17:5, 13). Since the men were Jews rather than Gentiles, Paul warned them by using a prophetic symbol drawn from the Bible: He shook the dust out of his robes. That gesture meant, "Thus will God shake you out of His robes (His heavenly kingdom) on the day of judgment (literal, see: Ne 5:13; Mt 10:14-15; Lk 9:5). And by adding the statement, "Your blood be upon your own head" he made it absolutely clear that they, not he, were morally responsible for their decision to reject Christ.

By referring to "blood" upon someone's head Paul was pointing to the biblical concept of "blood-guiltiness." It goes back to the story of Cain and Abel. After Cain killed Abel, Abel's blood "cried out to God" from the ground demanding justice (Ge 4:10-11). With this image of Abel's blood in mind, the Law of Moses viewed a person who murdered someone as guilty of defiling the land by spilling on it the victim's innocent blood, and only the murderer's own blood, by means of a just execution, could lift that curse from the land (Nu 35:33). Later on in Israel's history God used this concept of blood-guiltiness to warn the prophet Ezekiel that if he did not speak to the people about the spiritual danger they were in, God would require their "blood... from the watchman's hand" (Eze 33:6). In other words Ezekiel would be guilty of murder as though he had physically killed them. By not warning them he would become morally responsible for their spiritual death, but if he properly warned them, and they refused to listen, then he would not be morally responsible for what would happen to them. Each sinner's blood would be "on his own head" (Eze 33:4).

So by symbolically shaking out his robes at the men who confronted him and by stating that their blood-guiltiness was on their own head,

Paul announced that he had fulfilled his moral responsibility to them. In spite of all the Scriptures he had shown them, and the demonstrations of God's power that they had undoubtedly observed, they stubbornly refused to believe the gospel, and in doing so had placed themselves under potential condemnation. To die without repenting of such hardness would surely lead to God's judgment. Then he added these words: "From now on I will go to the nations [Gentiles]." He would stop trying to persuade them and focus his efforts on those who were hungry to hear the gospel.

v7: Turning away from the men who had formed a barrier Paul went into the house that was, literally, next door to the synagogue. It was owned by a man named Titius Justus. He was not a Jew. He was a Greek man who had been searching for God and whose search had drawn him to this synagogue. When he heard Paul preach the gospel, he responded in faith. By holding meetings in a home adjacent to the synagogue Paul undoubtedly hoped more Jews and God-fearing Greeks would grow curious and step inside to listen. And they did.

v8: One person who began attending those meetings and soon believed was a man named Crispus. Luke tells us he was the "synagogue ruler," which means he was the elder who supervised the services in that synagogue to ensure that everything was done in accord with tradition (J.D. Douglas ed., The New Bible Dictionary, Eerdmans, 1971, p1228). That such a man along with his whole household became persuaded that the gospel was true was a remarkable testimony to the soundness of Paul's teaching of the Bible. And the fact that their "synagogue ruler" believed must have encouraged others to follow his example. And as time passed many Corinthians, both Jews and Greeks, entered Titius Justus' house, listened to Paul preach, believed his message, and were baptized.

vs9-10: On the one hand Paul must have been delighted that so many people were coming to Christ, but on the other hand a rapidly-growing church right next door to the synagogue meant tension between the two groups would rise. Past experience had taught him that it would only be a matter of time before this growing tension would explode into violence. And as brave as he had been when facing one violent situation after another, by now all the violence may have injured him emotionally. Judging by the promise God made to him in that moment (v10), Paul had grown weary of being physically beaten. That explains why fear rose in his heart when he saw what was happening in Corinth. He dreaded the violence that he assumed would soon come. But before that fear grew strong enough to control him, Jesus Himself appeared to him at night in a vision saying, "Do not fear, but speak. Do not become silent because I am with you, and no one will hit [lay a blow on, see Ac 16:23] you to injure you, for I have many people [Greek: laos] who belong to Me in this city" (literal).

v11: Those words spoke right to the source of his fear, and Paul chose not to flee. Instead Luke says he "sat down for a year and six months teaching among them the Word of God" (literal). We learn from this exchange between the Lord Jesus and His faithful apostle that even a man as courageous as Paul could be emotionally wounded by violent persecution and as a result experience fear. Yet in that moment of weakness we observe Jesus personally come and speak to him with no condemnation but only the assurance of divine protection and great fruitfulness ahead.

v12: Paul probably had been in Corinth for about a year before a man named Gallio arrived and was installed as the proconsul of Achaia, the province which included all of Greece south of Macedonia. "Proconsuls" were senators sent by Rome to govern the peaceful provinces of the empire. "Peaceful" provinces were those which did not need a standing army, otherwise the general of the standing army governed by martial law. Based on an inscription found at Delphi (see comments on Ac 16:16), the emperor Claudius appointed Gallio in July, A.D. 51 (or possibly July A.D. 52) (F.F. Bruce, Acts, Eerdmans, reprint 1974, p374). His father was a famous teacher named Marcus Annaeus Seneca, and his younger brother, Lucius Annaeus Seneca, was a famous Stoic philosopher who at that point in time was tutoring the future emperor Nero. Gallio did not share his father's or his brother's family name because he had changed his name to honor a family friend who had adopted him and made him his heir (F.F. Bruce, Paul, Apostle of the Heart Set Free, Eerdmans, 1977, p253). He only served in Corinth for a short time before coming down with a disease (probably tuberculosis) which required him to leave the city to recuperate (F.F. Bruce, Acts).

vs12-13: The synagogue leaders, hoping to silence Paul, felt that the newly-arrived proconsul might be persuaded that Paul was preaching an illegal religion. Certain religions were formally recognized by Rome which meant they could be practiced freely. Judaism was a legally recognized religion, and since the Roman government considered Christianity to be simply another form of Judaism, it too was protected. But if the new proconsul could be convinced that the Christianity Paul taught was not a form of Judaism but rather a separate, unrecognized religion, his decision would instantly turn all the Christians in Greece (Achaia) into outlaws. So when they felt the time was right, a group of men from the synagogue rushed upon Paul, seized him and brought him to the raised, stone platform in the center of the central marketplace where Gallio was seated judging cases. Archaeologists have uncovered this platform, and it can still be seen in the ruins of ancient Corinth (F.F. Bruce, In the Steps of the Apostle Paul, Kregel Pub., 1995, p44).

v13: The crime they claimed Paul had committed was that he had persuaded people to worship God differently from way the "law" said they should worship. The way those men worded their charge left it unclear as to whether they were speaking about Roman law or the Torah (God's Law). It's possible they meant to do that hoping that Gallio would assume they meant Roman law while they would privately know they really meant the Torah. But if that was their goal, their plan backfired because Gallio thought they meant the Torah.

vs14-15: Paul was about to open his mouth to defend himself, but before he could say a word, Gallio made an instantaneous decision. He turned to the synagogue leaders and said, "If indeed he [Paul] had committed some criminal act or was using religion to financially defraud people, I would listen to what you have to say and make a reasoned judgment, but if the real reason you're here is because you're arguing about the meaning of a word and names and your own law [Torah], you handle those matters for yourselves. I do not wish to be a judge concerning these things" (paraphrase). And with those few words the plan to have the proconsul of the province pronounce Christianity to be an illegal religion failed miserably. By refusing to take up the case and by declaring that the issue that had been presented to him was merely a fight between Jews about their own internal religious matters Gallio (a very prominent Roman senator whose decision many other judges would undoubtedly follow) was affirming that Christianity was just another type of Judaism, and therefore, it was legal for Paul to do what he was doing. At that moment Christianity became formally recognized throughout the entire province of Achaia (Greece). It was now a legal form of religion, and believers were free to practice their faith with no fear of the Roman government.

Gallio had made his decision in this trial very quickly without listening to all the charges the synagogue leaders wanted to present, and he may have done so because he was already aware of the tensions in the Jewish community about Jesus Christ. He had been living in Rome when Claudius forced all the Jews out of the city (Ac 18:2), and as we noted earlier, Claudius probably did that to stop the constant rioting within the Jewish community over the preaching of the gospel. If so, then Gallio may already have formed an opinion about this matter before anyone started talking, and his decision reveals he felt that it was the synagogue leaders who were being unreasonable.

v16: After the decision was announced, either Gallio himself, or soldiers standing nearby at his order, began to forcefully shove the Jewish leaders away from the platform. That action exposed to everyone present the frustration the proconsul was feeling. He was obviously angry that this kind of religious conflict kept occurring and wanted these Jewish leaders to realize that they would not be welcomed if they brought this issue to him again. In other words, he would not tolerate in Corinth the kind of trouble that had taken place in Rome.

v17: Then something very unexpected happened. After Gallio openly displayed his frustration toward the synagogue leaders, the watching crowd felt released to express theirs. A spontaneous, mob-like action erupted right in front of the platform where the proconsul was standing. A group rushed forward and seized Sosthenes, the new "synagogue ruler" who had replaced Crispus (v8), and began to beat him. Luke describes Gallio's response this way, "And Gallio did not care about any of these things" (literal), meaning he made no effort to stop it. Clearly anti-Semitism was strong in Corinth.

Before we move on from this event, we should at least observe that the name of the synagogue ruler who was beaten that day is exactly the same as that of a man who later on became a prominent, Corinthian Christian. When Paul wrote his first letter to Corinth from Ephesus (1Co 16:8), in the very first verse he mentioned "Sosthenes, the brother" (1Co 1:1). Now there is no way to prove that this is the same man. There could have been others named Sosthenes in that city, but for a notable leader in that church to have the same name as this synagogue leader, and for Luke to name him here in Acts and tell us that he replaced Crispus after he became a Christian (v8) seems to indicate that Luke and Paul are referring to the same person. If so, then Luke gave these details about this man because he would later turn to Christ and become a prominent member of the church.

v18: Gallio's formal decision that day freed Paul from the threat of legal action. Luke says he remained in Corinth for a "sufficient" number of days, meaning he was able to stay there long enough to bring the church to a level of maturity where he felt they could carry on successfully without him. He'd been forced to leave the Macedonian cities prematurely either because the government ordered him out or a mob drove him out. As a result those churches were not ready to stand on their own which is why he left Luke, Silas and Timothy to pastor them. When Paul finally decided to leave Corinth, the circumstances were much different. He was able to say farewell properly.

Luke does not mention whether Timothy or Silas departed from Corinth with Paul, remained there or were sent somewhere else on assignment. Timothy reappears later on in Ephesus (Ac 19:22), but Silas is not mentioned in the book of Acts again. However about ten years later, Peter named him at the end of his first letter because it was Silas (Silvanus) who actually wrote down the letter as Peter dictated it (1Pe 5:12). We can only guess at where Timothy and Silas went during the years Luke did not record their activity, but it seems likely that both men accompanied Paul to Jerusalem and then travelled on with him to Antioch in Syria (Ac 15:35, 40). However, since Silas was originally from Jerusalem (Ac 15:22), he may have stayed in Jerusalem and let Paul go on to Antioch without him.

Paul would have begun his journey by walking about seven miles to Cenchrea, the eastern port for the city of Corinth. There he boarded a ship bound for Caesarea, but as Luke notes, his final destination was Antioch in Syria. Surprisingly, Priscilla and Aquila left with him. It appears they had decided to move their tent-making business to Ephesus to help plant a church (v19). When the ship stopped in Ephesus, they would stay, and Paul would travel on. Their assignment would have been to locate a home and begin working to support themselves. Paul expected to return in the future, but until then they would begin the work (Ac 18:21; 19:1).

Luke mentions that when Paul arrived at Cenchrea, before boarding the ship he performed a Jewish ritual. It was common at that time for pious Jews to enter into what was in effect a temporary form of the Nazirite vow. A person could be a Nazirite for life (Jdg 13:3-5), but someone could also be a "Nazirite" for a limited period of time. A man or a woman who was afflicted with a disease or facing some other kind of danger could enter into this special vow in order to publicly confess their hope that God would deliver them. Jewish men normally kept their hair cut (1Co 11:14), but during this vow they would let their hair grow long (Ac 21:23-24, 26). Then 30 days before offering their sacrifices at the temple in Jerusalem, they would shave their head (Flavius Josephus, The Wars of the Jews, 2.15.1, in Josephus, The Complete Works, translated by William Whiston, Thomas Nelson, 1998, p741). In fact, there was a special court in the temple complex where they could present the hair that had been cut off.

Nothing is said as to why Paul took this vow. One possibility is that he was openly confessing the Lord's promise to physically protect him while he was in Corinth (Ac 18:9-10). If so, after the Lord appeared to him in a vision, he made the vow and began letting his hair grow. The Jewish community, at least, would have understood the confession of faith he was making: God would protect him from violent attack. But when he arrived at the harbor, his time in Corinth had come to an end, and God had indeed protected him. So by cutting his hair, Paul honored the Lord for His faithfulness. He declared by that action that God had done all that He promised. Then the next step was to take that hair to the temple in Jerusalem and present it as part of a thanksgiving offering. That meant he needed to be in Jerusalem in about 30 days because that was the prescribed time-span between cutting hair and offering it. This helps explain why Paul refused to remain in

Ephesus even though the synagogue there was very interested in the gospel (Ac 18:19-21).

vs19-21: With fair winds it took about eight to ten days to sail from the west side of the Aegean Sea to the east side (Jamieson, Fausset, Brown, Acts, p.134). The ship stopped at Ephesus which was the capital of the province of Asia. "Asia" included all of what is today the western third of Turkey. It had an important harbor and major highways running into it. It was the commercial center for all of Asia Minor (Turkey), and Paul had wanted to evangelize the city much earlier, but the Holy Spirit had prevented him (Ac 16:6). Even on this occasion he was able to stay in the city only a short time because his vow required him to reach Jerusalem within 30 days. However, he did manage to visit the synagogue and proclaim Jesus as the crucified and resurrected Messiah (Ac 13:16-41), and their initial response was quite positive. They asked him to stay in Ephesus so they could continue discussing his message, but he shook his head and said, "I will return to you, God willing." Then he returned to the ship and headed for Caesarea on the coast of Israel.

v22: Paul's final destination was Antioch in Syria, not Jerusalem. After leaving Ephesus he was no longer on a mission, he was returning home, so Luke uses very few words to summarize the rest of the journey. He says, "...and after coming down to Caesarea [sailing from Ephesus to Caesarea] and going up [to Jerusalem] and greeting the church, he went down [he probably sailed north] to Antioch" (literal).

v23: The weeks or months he spent in Antioch must have been uneventful because Luke simply says, "And having spent some time there, he went forth [on his third missionary journey], first passing through Galatia and then through Phrygia, strengthening the faith of all the disciples" (paraphrase). Again Paul must have taken the road that led north out of Antioch (Ac 15:41). It went through his home town of Tarsus, crossed the Taurus mountain range at a pass called the Cilician Gates and then ran on into the great central plain west of the mountains. One by one, by following that road, he would have visited the churches that he and Barnabas founded on their first journey including Derbe, Lystra (Timothy's home town), Iconium and Pisidian Antioch. But his ultimate destination was Ephesus. Aquila and Priscilla were there waiting for him as were the elders of the synagogue. So after leaving Pisidian Antioch, he would have headed west along the Roman highway, only this time he didn't turn north toward Bithynia (Ac 16:6). He continued on until he reached Ephesus on the coast (Ac 19:1).

v24: Paul was absent from Ephesus for about a year. He had passed through on his way from Corinth to Caesarea, left Priscilla and Aquila there to start the work, spoke briefly in the synagogue and then sailed to Jerusalem. But after he left, a Jewish evangelist came to the city and began to preach about Jesus in the synagogue. That's where Priscilla and Aquila met him. The man's name was Apollonius, but people called him "Apollos." He was born and raised in Alexandria, Egypt, a city which at that time had as many as a million people about one-third of whom were Jews (David Brown, Acts, Jamieson, Fausset, Brown, Eerdmans, reprint 1982, p135). Alexandria had a fine university and one of the greatest libraries in the world, and it was also the place where the Hebrew Bible had been translated into Greek (Septuagint) about 200 years earlier (Robertson, Word Pictures in the New Testament, Broadman, 1930, Vol. 7, p306). Luke describes Apollos as a "man of words" (literal), probably meaning that he was both a diligent student and an excellent public speaker. Luke also said he was "powerful in the Scriptures" (literal), meaning God gave him spiritual insight when he read the Bible so that he truly understood what he was reading.

v25: Not only was Apollos a profound student of the Scriptures, someone had also carefully trained him in the teachings of John the Baptist, including the statements John had made about Jesus of Nazareth. And Apollos wasn't the sort of man who could hear urgent warnings about a coming judgment and just sit at home. He was impelled to go out and preach. Luke literally describes him as someone who was "boiling over in [the] spirit" which certainly meant that he was passionate about his faith, but may mean that when he preached, the power of the Holy Spirit came upon him. And Luke adds that he "spoke and taught the things about Jesus accurately [precisely, exactly]". So Apollos did not teach false doctrine, but he did have a shortcoming: his knowledge about Jesus was incomplete. And that was because John the Baptist was his only source of information about Jesus, and John's knowledge was incomplete. John had died before Jesus was crucified and resurrected, before He ascended into heaven and before He began baptizing His followers with the Holy Spirit on the day of Pentecost.

John's assignment from God had been to warn the people of Israel to get ready to face God's judgment. When people asked why he was preaching and baptizing, he answered by saying, "I am a voice of one crying in the wilderness, 'Make straight the way of the Lord,' as Isaiah the prophet said" (Mt 3:2-3; Jn 1:22-23). John expected the Messiah to immediately bring that day of judgment when everyone will be held accountable for their sins including the Jews (Mt 3:1-10). He told the Jews not to trust in the fact that they were Abraham's physical descendants. He said they needed to repent of their sins and produce "good fruit," or God would determine that they didn't belong to Him. He especially challenged very religious people to be honest about themselves and repent quickly because the Messiah would soon separate the "wheat" from the "chaff," and He would burn the chaff with "unquenchable fire" (Mt 3:10-12).

John the Baptist knew Jesus personally, in fact they were relatives and may have known each other to some degree during their childhood years (Lk 1:36, 45, 56). When Jesus came to the Jordan River to be baptized, God testified to John that Jesus was the Messiah by letting him see the Holy Spirit come down from heaven and rest upon Him. He also heard the voice of God the Father say, "This is My beloved Son in whom I am [was] well-pleased" (Mt 3:16-17). And after that John openly proclaimed Jesus to his own disciples and celebrated when many of them left to follow Jesus (Jn 3:25-30) saying, "He must increase, but I must decrease" (Jn 3:30). He even declared to them that Jesus was "the Lamb of God who takes away the sin of the world" (Jn 1:29, 36). But he never lived to see the most important events in Jesus' life, so neither he nor his disciples fully understood the gospel (Mt 11:11). Yet those disciples went out and preached what he had taught them, not just in Israel, but throughout the region going from synagogue to synagogue warning people to prepare for the coming judgment. In fact they were so effective at spreading John's message that later on, when Paul would go into a synagogue during his missionary travels, he would mention John the Baptist as part of his sermon because Jews everywhere knew about John and revered him as a true prophet (Ac 13:24-25). And when one of John's disciples brought that message to

Alexandria, Egypt, a man named Apollos became so deeply convinced that he felt he must preach it to others, and in time his travels brought him to the great city of Ephesus.

v26: When Priscilla and Aquila heard him speak in the synagogue, they quickly realized he only knew part of the truth about Jesus. He called people to repentance, but not to faith in the cross and resurrection (Ac 20:20-21). Nor did he say anything about the baptism with the Holy Spirit (Ac 19:2). It seems impossible to believe that a man from Alexandria who was as knowledgeable as he was hadn't heard how Jesus died or heard rumors about Him coming back to life (Lk 24:18-24). But if so, he clearly didn't understand what these events meant. Luke said Apollos was teaching "the way of the Lord" accurately, but when Priscilla and Aquila met with him, they explained "the way of the Lord" more accurately. In other words they filled in the information he'd been missing. They told him about the cross, the resurrection, the ascension and Pentecost. They explained why each of these things had to happen and undoubtedly showed him the same Old Testament passages that Paul had taught them (Ac 13:16-41). They must have recited for him the gospel as the apostles preached it calling people to "repent and be baptized in the name of Jesus Christ for the forgiveness of sins," and told him that the apostles assured everyone who chose to follow Jesus that "you will receive the gift of the Holy Spirit" (Ac 2:38). And they must have explained to him that God was now calling both Jews and Gentiles into His family (Eph 2:11-22), and Apollos couldn't have missed the fact that Priscilla (a Roman) and Aquila (a Jew) by their marriage were an example of this new reality.

v27-28: Armed with this this new message Apollos wanted to go directly to Greece (Achaia) to proclaim it. So the members of the Ephesian church wrote a letter of recommendation to send with him to encourage believers in the Greek churches to welcome him. When he arrived, Luke says he greatly strengthened "those who believed through [that they were saved by] grace." He strongly and publicly, one by one, exposed the errors in arguments Jewish opponents were using to discredit Christ. Luke's choice of words indicate that Apollos spoke in a loud, clear voice and used well-reasoned points to prove from the Scriptures that Jesus was the Messiah. And apparently such a strong teacher was desperately needed in Corinth at that time because some in the church had become confused. When Paul left (Ac 19:1), they became vulnerable to opponents' claims that Paul had misled them. It's likely that those who continued going to the synagogue on the Sabbath or had strong family ties were being subjected to attempts to prove that Paul had distorted the true meaning of the Scriptures. In particular those who attacked their new faith would have asserted that the Bible does not speak of a dying and rising Messiah. So when Apollos arrived, the church in Corinth suddenly had a capable, Bible teacher to represent them in public arguments as well as someone who could sit down and help those individuals who were beginning to doubt the gospel. Undoubtedly he used passage after passage from Moses and the Prophets to prove that Paul had not deceived them or taught them a foreign religion. Jesus was indeed Israel's promised Savior. Luke describes Apollos' role in Corinth not primarily as an evangelist, though he must have led many to Christ (1Co 1:12), but as a teacher who was able to explain and defend the faith that Paul had taught them. This helps us understand what Paul meant when he later wrote to Corinth saying, "I planted, Apollos watered, but God was causing the growth" (1Co 3:6). He might have added that Apollos also "weeded" by pulling out doubts which had been sown into some minds after Paul left.

Acts Chapter 19

v1: When Paul finally returned to Ephesus, Apollos was already in Corinth. On his way there Paul had walked from Antioch in Syria through the Taurus mountains at the "Cilician Gates" and into the regions of Galatia and Phrygia. Undoubtedly, he visited the churches he founded as he passed through each city, but his final destination was Ephesus. West of Pisidian Antioch the Roman highway passed through or near significant cities in the highlands of Asia Minor (Laodicea, Colossae and Hierapolis), but Paul was in a hurry and didn't stop. Aquila and Priscilla were waiting for him (Ac 18:19), and he had promised the members of that synagogue to return if God permitted him to do so (Ac 18:19-21).

Soon after he arrived in Ephesus, Paul discovered a group of men who were followers of John the Baptist. Luke takes the time to carefully describe this encounter for a reason. We are not told if these men knew Apollos before he met Priscilla and Aquila, and they taught him "the things concerning Jesus" (Ac 18:25-26), but their faith must have been very similar to what Apollos had believed earlier (vs2-4). So by listening to what Paul said to these disciples of John the Baptist and by observing how he ministered to them, we are able to discover some of the essential elements that were lacking in their faith. Luke allows us to watch Paul change disciples of John into disciples of Jesus.

v2: Paul asked them two questions. First, "Did you receive the Holy Spirit, having believed?" (literal). And they answered, "But we heard not if the Holy Spirit is…" (literal). Their reply to his question is often thought to mean that no one ever told them about the Holy Spirit, in other words they didn't know that the Holy Spirit existed. But if these men knew anything about John's teaching, it would be impossible that they knew nothing about the Holy Spirit. John's main message centered on the fact that the coming Messiah would "baptize" people with the Holy Spirit and fire (Mt 3:11-12; Jn 1:33; 3:34). The arrival of a new era of the Holy Spirit is one of the major themes of the Old Testament prophets. It is repeatedly taught that when Messiah comes, He will bring with Him the era of the Spirit, and when that happens, the Spirit of the Lord will cover the whole earth as the waters cover the sea (Is 11:9; Hab 2:14). So what those disciples must have meant by their answer is, "We had not heard that this promised blessing had arrived" (paraphrase). Obviously, a report of what happened on the Day of Pentecost (Ac 2) had not yet reached them, but neither had a report about the cross and resurrection.

v3: When he heard their response, Paul immediately asked a second question, "Into what then were you baptized?" (literal), to which they replied, "Into the baptism of John" (literal). Their answer revealed that they were sincere followers of God, and because they were disciples of John the Baptist, they may even have heard some of the things he had said about Jesus of Nazareth. But since their knowledge was limited to John's understanding of Jesus, Paul would also have known that it was likely that they did not understand why Jesus died on the cross or that each of them must make a personal choice to put their faith in Him as their Savior.

v4: Paul would have been very familiar with the ministry of John the Baptist. He had been a rabbinical student in Jerusalem when John was baptizing multitudes at the Jordan River (Ac 22:3; 26:4). He may even have been among a group of Pharisees who went down to the river to listen to John (Jn 1:19-28). If not, he surely heard the report of those who did and knew what John was preaching and why he was baptizing people. So when he heard the way these men answered his questions, he knew they had not been taught vital elements of the gospel. Above all else, he knew their knowledge about Jesus, if they had any knowledge of Him at all, was incomplete which is why we hear him say, "John baptized with a baptism of repentance, saying to the people that they should believe in the One coming after him, that is, in Jesus" (literal). While he was still alive, John had publicly declared Jesus of Nazareth to be the Messiah (Jn 1:24-34; 3:28-30), but he had been executed before Jesus died, rose from the dead, ascended into heaven and poured out the Holy Spirit on His followers. So he could not have taught his followers any of these essential truths. Knowing this, Paul must have gone on to explain them and then invite these men to place their faith in the complete ministry of Christ.

v5: Luke doesn't tell us all that Paul said before he baptized them, but in view of the fact that they were either Jews, or Gentiles who had become disciples of a Jewish prophet (John the Baptist), he must have taught them by explaining passages from the Bible just as he normally taught in a synagogue (Ac 13:16-41). And they must have believed that message because Luke says, "And having heard, they were baptized into the name of the Lord Jesus" (literal). In order to become disciples of John they had to repent of their sins and then publicly confess their repentance through water baptism. So they had already acknowledged that they were sinful and deserved God's judgment. They had already pledged to God that their new lives would produce the "fruit of repentance;" they would be marked by generosity, honesty and contentment (Lk 3:8-14). So when Paul baptized them with water for a second time, he was not asking them to reject the repentance that they had confessed when they participated in John's baptism. He was giving them the opportunity to confess their faith in the death and resurrection of Jesus for the forgiveness of their sins (Ro 6:3-5).

v6: Then immediately after baptizing them with water, Paul laid his hands on them in order to invite the Holy Spirit to come upon them in power. And just as had happened on the day of Pentecost to the first disciples, these men also spoke in tongues and prophesied. The fact that he took this deliberate action to specifically invite the Spirit to come upon someone he had just baptized shows us that he did not consider a person's initiation into the Christian life to be complete until that person actually received the Holy Spirit in a manner similar to the way believers received Him on the day of Pentecost (Ac 2:4, 38-39; 8:14-18; 10:44-48; 11:15-18).

v7: Luke doesn't give us the precise number of men involved that day but says, "And there were in all, about twelve men."

v8: During his first visit to Ephesus (Ac 18:19-21) Paul had promised the members of the synagogue that if God allowed him to return to their city, he would teach them more about the Messiah Jesus. And now Luke shows us how he kept that promise. He says Paul entered the synagogue and continued to speak freely about Christ over the course of the next three months. The words Luke chooses to describe that season tell us that Paul discussed various passages of Scripture (Ac 17:2) and tried to persuade them to believe his interpretation of a concept Luke calls the "Kingdom of God." The term "Kingdom of God" has different meanings depending on how it is used. Sometimes it refers to the place we call "heaven" (2Ti 4:18). Sometimes it refers to God's saving activity on earth (Mt 13:31-33). And sometimes it refers to the coming, Messianic Age, a glorious one-thousand-year period during which God will rule the earth through His Messiah (Ro 8:21; 1Co 15:24; Rev 21:1). In this context the term must mean the coming Messianic Age because in a synagogue Paul would have had to explain why, if Jesus was the Messiah, He hadn't brought with Him all the glories promised by the prophets. That would have been a major point of confusion for Jewish scholars. They would have asked, "If Jesus is the Messiah, where is the Kingdom of God?" And Paul would have answered this question by telling them that God's plan was to send the Messiah on two, separate occasions. At Jesus' first coming His assignment was to fulfill the prophecies that describe a suffering Messiah who dies and rises to atone (forgive) the sins of the human race. But Paul would have assured them that Jesus will come again, and at His second coming He will fulfill those prophecies which describe the Messiah ruling over all the earth.

The Old Testament often pictures the Kingdom of God as a future kingdom in which there will be peace and prosperity for Israel and the entire world. During that season, we are told, even nature will be set free from the curse that was placed on it when Adam sinned (Ge 3:17-19; Ro 8:20-21). But when Jesus came the first time, He did not bring those realities in a universal way. In the gospels we see Him minister only foretastes of those promised blessings to individuals who came to Him in faith or to meet specific needs. And that would have been a real obstacle to the faith of many in a synagogue. This was not what they had been taught to expect. So Paul would have spent much time talking about the <u>second</u> coming of Jesus (2Th 1:5-12). He would have explained that when Jesus comes again, there will be a resurrection of all believers (1Th 4:13-18), and that Jesus will sit in judgment of those who refuse to repent and believe (1Co 4:5). He would have explained that God's Kingdom will come to earth in its fullness at the proper time, according to God's predetermined plan. And he would have explained why the cross had to come <u>before</u> the arrival of the Messianic Age. He would have taught them that if Jesus had not died and risen from the dead, the entire human race would have remained under God's judgment, and therefore neither Jew nor Gentile would have been able to "inherit the Kingdom" (1Co 15:50). And he would have warned them that during the season between Jesus' first and second coming, God is calling people everywhere to repent and believe in His Son (Ac 13:40-41).

There is one additional use of the term "Kingdom of God" that we should mention here. Both Jesus and Paul taught (and demonstrated) that the blessings of this future Kingdom are available now to those who place their faith in Jesus. Since He is the promised Messianic King, when He is present, the powers of His Kingdom are present as well. So, for those of us living in this season between His first and second coming, even though we find ourselves struggling with dying bodies in a fallen world, because this King has come to live within us, we are able to experience a foretaste of those blessings. Wisdom, healing, joy, protection, provision, etc. are qualities that will fill that future Kingdom, and because Christ now dwells within each believer, we can reach out by faith and bring those future blessings into the present.

v9: It took three months for resistance to Paul's message to grow strong enough for him to feel that he had to leave the Ephesian synagogue. In other cities that threshold had been reached much earlier (Ac 13:42-46; 17:1-5, 10-13), so the Ephesians must have shown some genuine initial interest. But now Luke says, some of the members were becoming hardened and were refusing to listen. They began to loudly denounce Paul to the crowds who gathered to hear him preach. He tells us that they spoke against "the Way" which was a term the early church used to describe their faith (Ac 9:2; 19:23; 24:14, 22). Those believers probably chose that phrase because they thought of Jesus as the path to salvation. By believing in Him and following His teachings they were walking on the "way" that leads to eternal life (Jn 14:6).

Once Paul recognized that it was no longer possible to hold constructive conversations, he knew only too well the violence which might erupt if that tension continued to grow. So he stopped attending the synagogue, taking those who believed his message with him, and found a lecture hall which was available during certain hours of the day. One ancient text of Acts says Paul used that room from eleven in the morning until four in the afternoon, in other words, during the heat of the day (F.F. Bruce, Acts, Eerdmans, reprint 1974, pp388-389). The lecture hall apparently belonged to a man named Tyrannus. He must have been well-known for Luke to mention his name. The name means "our tyrant" or "our master," but Tyrannus was a common name at that time, so no judgment can be made about the man based on his name. During the years Paul spent in Ephesus he worked at his trade (tentmaking) to support himself (Ac 20:34-35), so he may have personally paid for the rent of the room.

v10: This gathering at the lecture hall continued to meet daily for two years. During that time so many people were saved, trained and sent out to preach that Luke says the entire province of Asia (the western coastal region of Turkey) heard the word of the Lord, both Jews and Greeks.

vs11-12: Not only did Paul preach and teach, but God consistently (not "hit or miss") performed powerful miracles through his hands so much so that cloths which had touched his skin, such as the handkerchiefs he used to wipe sweat from his face and the linen aprons he wore while he worked, were carried to those who were ill or tormented by demons and placed on them "to release them from their diseases and for evil spirits to go out of them" (literal).

vs13-14: Though he must have been physically exhausted from teaching as much as five hours a day on top of working mornings and late afternoons, this remarkable level of divine power continued to rest on Paul and drew the attention of religious professionals in the area. In particular a group of seven "sons," or more likely seven disciples, of a Jewish priest named Sceva, tried to imitate him. There is no record of a high priest named Sceva, and Luke is careful not to call him one. He uses words which mean Sceva's disciples were calling him that. Luke describes him as "some Jewish high priest named Sceva." The man may have been a leader of one of the divisions of priests.

This group of men traveled from place to place, and happened to be in Ephesus at the time. For a fee they would perform a religious ceremony intended to drive demons out or away from people. This practice called exorcism was fairly common in Judaism at the time. According to the ancient Jewish historian (Josephus, Antiquities, 8.2.5), part of King Solomon's great wisdom was that he had learned the skill which expels demons. Josephus said, "God taught him the art of driving out evil spirits to the profit and salvation of men" (J. Schneider, Theological Dictionary of the New Testament, Eerdmans, 1973, Vol. 5, p465) and added that he "left behind him the manner of using exorcisms, by which they never return, and this method of cure is of great force unto this day." Josephus wrote this during the first century (A.D.) and said such exorcists were still "making mention of Solomon and reciting the incantations which he composed" (Antiquities 8.2.5). This particular group of exorcists, called the "sons of Sceva," decided Paul was having better success than they, so in Luke's words, "they took hold of the name of the Lord Jesus in order to name Him over those having evil spirits" (literal). In effect they tried to command demons to leave by threatening that if they refused, they would call on "the Jesus whom Paul proclaims" to curse them. But it soon became evident that they weren't using Jesus' name because they had become His disciples, they used His name only because it appeared demons were afraid of Him. By speaking of the "Jesus whom Paul proclaims," they made it clear that they were not proclaiming Jesus, just using Him.

v15: As we read about this event, it is helpful to recall that a similar situation occurred while Jesus was ministering in Capernaum. The disciples reported to Him that they had seen a man, who was not a disciple, using Jesus' name to cast out demons, and that they had tried to stop him. Jesus told them to let him continue since the process of seeing the spiritual authority associated with His name might draw the man to faith (Mk 9:38-40). And we're never told whether that man come to faith or not, but the response by a demon in Ephesus tells us much about the faith of these seven exorcists. When they spoke the name of Jesus, the demon recognized that it was being spoken by someone who had no faith in Him. So it spoke out defiantly through the possessed man and said, "Indeed, I know Jesus, and I have heard about Paul, but who are you?" (literal).

vs16-17: Then Luke says, "And the man in whom was the evil spirit, leaping on them [like a wild animal], overpowered both of them, subdued them [and apparently tore off their clothes and beat them] so that they fled out of the house naked and wounded" (literal). This encounter, he says, became known to everyone in Ephesus, both Jews and Greeks, and the fear of God fell upon the entire city, and "the name of the Lord Jesus was being magnified" (literal).

v18: Ephesus was probably the fourth largest city in the world at that time with a population estimated at 250,000 people (Holman Bible Dictionary, Trent C. Butler ed, Holman Pub., 1991, p425). And it is significant that it was known as a center for the magical arts. Spells made from scrambled words or phrases (sometimes arranged in special patterns) or prayers (addressed to gods or angels) were written on scrolls of parchment or papyrus. Those words would then be regularly recited or placed in small cylinders and worn around the neck to bring healing, protection or prosperity. Such items sold at a high price (F.F. Bruce, Acts, Eerdmans, reprint 1974, pp391-392). In fact the use of magic was so deeply rooted in the culture and economy of Ephesus that even those who joined the church did not necessarily stop practicing it. Yet when the fear of God swept over the city because of the power being manifested through Paul, that fear swept over the church as well. Many fell under conviction and confessed in front of the whole church that they had secretly continued using magic. Luke says they even described the specific practices they used.

v19: Those who had been practicing these elaborate rituals brought their scrolls together and burned them in front of everyone, until they were reduced to ashes. And when the total value of all the scrolls that had been destroyed was calculated, it came to the staggering sum of 5,000 pieces of silver. That would be the equivalent of 5,000 times the average daily wage for a laborer.

v20: Luke summarized this season of Paul's ministry in Ephesus by saying, "Thus, by might, the word of the Lord was expanding [to more and more people] and growing more powerful" (literal).

v21: We'll soon see a riot break out in Ephesus, but before Luke describes that event, he is careful to inform us that Paul's mission in

Ephesus had been completed. He says, "When all these things [God's work through Paul] were fulfilled, Paul determined in the Spirit that he would go to Jerusalem, but first he would pass through Macedonia [northern Greece] and Achaia [central Greece] saying, 'After I have been there it is also necessary for me to see Rome'" (literal). In other words Paul wasn't driven out of Ephesus prematurely as he had been in so many other places. Yes a riot broke out, but that wasn't why he moved on. He had already been notified by the Holy Spirit that it was time to leave before all that happened.

v22: Even though Paul sensed his mission in Ephesus was complete, he didn't feel released by God to leave right away. So he sent Timothy and a man named Erastus on ahead of him to Macedonia. Timothy was already well-known in the region (Ac 17:14-15; 18:5), and it may be that Erastus was too. There's not enough information here to be certain, but there was a man named Erastus who was the city treasurer in Corinth (Ro 16:23), and a man named Erastus who at times traveled with Paul (2Ti 4:20). These two references may describe the same person which would mean that Timothy's traveling companion was the former city treasurer of Corinth. By sending two men on this mission rather than one, we observe the principle that the early church usually traveled and ministered in at least pairs. Jesus of course had modeled this principle (Mk 6:7; Lk 10:1), and His followers recognized that there is safety and strength when believers function as a team. This is why even when a traveling partner is not mentioned, we can assume that someone always accompanied Paul as he traveled.

During the years he spent in the city of Ephesus, Paul's relationship with the church in Corinth became severely strained. False religious teachers came to Corinth after he left and openly slandered him in order to gain influence in the church. They mocked his appearance and the way he spoke (2Co 10:10; 11:6). They boasted that their spiritual authority was far superior to his (2Co 10:18). They said if he were a real apostle, he would have taken offerings, and by working to provide for himself he was admitting that he did not have the spiritual right to be financially supported by the church the way the rest of the apostles were (2Co 11:7). They may even have questioned Paul's faith by asking why he hadn't been healed of a particular physical weakness (2Co 12:7-10). By reading through Paul's letters to Corinth, we can put together a picture of these opponents: they traveled from place to place and called themselves apostles (2Co 11:4, 13); they dominated and abused those they led (2Co 11:20); they aggressively collected money (2Co 11:20); they were Jews, probably from Jerusalem (2Co 11:22); they claimed that they had suffered persecution for their faith (2Co 11:23-32), and they pretended that they had received profound visions from God (2Co 12:1).

Initially Paul had tried to correct this dangerous situation by writing letters to the church. He wrote a first letter which has been lost (1Co 5:9), and the church wrote a letter to him in reply (1Co 7:1). Their letter was probably carried to Ephesus by three members of the church: Stephanas, Fortunatus and Achaicus (1Co 16:17). The letter we call "First Corinthians" is Paul's response. In it he addresses issues they raised and mentions that he was planning to come to Corinth so he could talk to them in person (1Co 16:5). Sadly, that letter did not correct the problem. In fact the influence of the false teachers continued to grow until he found it necessary to make a hurried, unplanned visit (2Co 2:1; 12:14; 13:1-2). When he got there, the confrontation did not go well, and after returning to Ephesus he wrote what he later called a "sorrowful" letter (2Co 2:4; 7:8). His original plan to visit Corinth had been to wait until a financial gift was collected for the persecuted church in Jerusalem (1 Co 16:1-4). Then when it was ready, he would sail from Ephesus to Corinth and immediately travel up to Macedonia. After ministering in Macedonia he would go back to Corinth and perhaps even spend the winter there (1Co 16:5-6). Then he would sail to Jerusalem taking their financial gift with him (2Co 1:16). But his earlier visit had changed those plans. It convinced him there was nothing to be gained by another painful confrontation (2Co 1:23). Instead he sent Titus to Corinth (2Co 2:12-13; 7:5-7) while he would go directly to Macedonia. Then after ministering in Macedonia, he would be free to spend the time he needed in Corinth (2Co 1:23; 2:1). From Corinth he would sail on to Jerusalem. But when his opponents in Corinth heard that he had changed his plans, they accused him of being indecisive, and therefore, untrustworthy (2Co 1:15-17). Yet Paul was simply adjusting his schedule to the changing situation in Corinth. Instead of allowing himself to be immediately drawn into their crisis, which would leave no time for other churches in other regions, he sent Titus to Corinth to assess the situation with the instructions that he would meet him in Troas to report his findings. But Titus was delayed in Corinth and didn't arrive in Troas on time. So even though there were many opportunities in Troas for Paul to minister, he grew so worried about what was happening in Corinth he left Troas and went on to Macedonia hoping to intercept Titus as he was traveling north to meet him (2Co 2:12-13). Paul admits that he was very worried while waiting in Macedonia for Titus, but when he finally arrived with the report that the Corinthians had repented and were actually mourning over the way they had treated Paul, he was greatly comforted (2Co 7:5-7, 13-16). After hearing this good news from Titus, he wrote the letter we call "Second Corinthians."

v23: Prior to Paul's departure from Ephesus, a riot broke out. But before we consider the details of that event, we should take note of what Luke did not tell us. Something horrible happened to Paul during the years he spent in Ephesus. The riot Luke describes in Acts (vs23-41) was noisy and exciting, but apparently no one was seriously injured. Yet there was another crisis that Luke doesn't mention that was far more sinister than that riot. Later on when Paul reflected on his time in Ephesus, he referred to it as a time of severe hardship and danger. He said he was, "serving the Lord with all humility and tears and with trials which came upon me through the plots of the Jews" (Ac 20:19). Ephesus he described as a place with a "wide open door for effective service… and there are many adversaries" (1Co 16:9). And elsewhere he added these chilling statements: "If from human motives I fought with wild beasts at Ephesus, what does it profit me?" (1Co 15:32); and "For we do not want you to be unaware, brethren, of our affliction which came to us in Asia (Ephesus), that we were burdened excessively, beyond our strength, so that we despaired even of life; indeed, we had the sentence of death within ourselves so that we would not trust in ourselves, but in God who raises the dead; who delivered us from so great a peril of death, and will deliver us…" (2Co 1:8-10). Apparently, something happened in Ephesus that was so bad Paul thought he would surely die. This may have been the occasion when Priscilla and Aquila "risked their own necks" to save him (Ro 16:3-4). Without further information we can only wonder about this trial. There is a tradition which says he spent time in jail there (F.F. Bruce, In the Steps of the Apostle Paul, Kregel, 1995, p50). Though we don't know exactly what happened, these vague references suggest that Paul paid an enormous, personal price to preach Christ to that city. And on top of it all there was a riot.

vs23-26: Just when Paul was planning to leave the city, things exploded. Luke says, "There was about that time no little trouble concerning the Way" (v23, literal) because a certain silversmith named Demetrius, who made silver shrines of Artemis, provided the craftsmen no little gain" (v24, literal). Note the play on words "no little trouble" because they feared the loss of "no little gain." Another way of saying this would be: "There was much trouble because they were in danger of losing much money." Luke has chosen his words carefully to reveal the motive behind the riot. It was money. Demetrius, who made a lot of money selling statues of the goddess Artemis, recognized that Paul's preaching was reducing the market for his products, so he decided to do something about it. He gathered the artisans who worked in the shops that fashioned these statues and warned them that they would soon be out of work if Paul wasn't stopped. He said Paul was convincing people all over Asia that Artemis wasn't a real god because "they are not gods which come into being through hands" (v26, literal).

vs27-29: Then Demetrius shrewdly moved the focus of his speech off of their income and onto civic pride, which as a theme appears to be less selfish, and therefore, makes it much easier to become outraged. Basically, he asked the craftsmen, "Are we going to let this guy disrespect our goddess?" and of course, they weren't, so they all began to chant, "Great is Artemis of the Ephesians!" until the whole city was drawn to the clamor and joined in. As the crowd swelled into the thousands, there was only one venue large enough for everyone to gather: the city amphitheater which seated 24,000 people (F.F. Bruce, In the Steps of the Apostle Paul, Kregel, 1995, p48). Somehow in the midst of all this confusion, the crowd was able to locate two of Paul's traveling companions, Gaius and Aristarchus, who were both foreigners from Macedonia. They led them into the amphitheater undoubtedly with the intention of forcing them to reveal Paul's location.

v30: During the riot Paul had been hidden in a secure place, but he was not out of communication. It's very possible Aquila and Priscilla hid him in their home or at some other site, and this was the occasion to which Paul later referred (Ro 16:3-4) when he noted that during some crisis this couple had "risked their necks" to save his life. Someone came to where he was hidden and reported what was taking place in the amphitheater, and when he learned that Gaius and Aristarchus had been seized, Paul was determined to go into the amphitheater after them. But the "disciples" who were with him would not permit him to do so. It's possible, based on Luke's choice of words here, that the way they stopped him was by refusing to leave his side. In other words, they may have said, "If you go in, we're going with you, and you can't stop us!" It was one thing for him to go alone; it was another for him to put all of them at risk.

v31: Luke's statement in this verse is remarkable. He says, "Also, some of the Asiarchs, being his friends, sent [a messenger] to him pleading with him not to give himself to the theater" (literal). Clearly Paul had some very politically-powerful friends in the city, and they knew he would try to confront the mob when he realized that his friends had been captured, and they knew he would undoubtedly be killed. The term "Asiarch" was a very distinguished title given to certain wealthy and highly respected people who had been elected by their entire city to represent them in matters concerning the whole province (Asia). Each year one of them was selected to be the honorary high priest who would lead their province in worshiping the Roman emperor (F.F. Bruce, The New Bible Dictionary, J. D. Douglas, ed., Eerdmans, 1971, p98). Amazingly, some of these individuals had become Paul's "friends." We're not told they had become "believers," but of course Paul must have preached to them, and yet they had not ended the relationship, so we can at least say they were considering Christ. Luke says more than one of them took the initiative to send a messenger to plead with Paul for his safety. So the poor and oppressed weren't the only ones in Asia interested in eternal life. There were also some powerful people who had grown to love this man and stepped in to protect him at a very dangerous moment.

vs32-33: Most of the people in the amphitheater were shouting, "Great is Artemis of the Ephesians," but some were shouting other things because they had merely been swept into the crowd by the excitement, and there was so much confusion some of the rioters didn't even know why they were there. Yet because it was about Paul, and because he was a Jew, the religious fervor being stirred at that moment might easily have turned against the entire Jewish community. To prevent that from happening, the Jews who were present picked a representative to speak on their behalf. His name was Alexander, and as he stood to speak, it's likely that he hoped to convince the crowd that though Paul was obviously Jewish, he was not truly one of them. The Jewish community had also rejected him, so they should not be blamed for the declining sales of the statues of Artemis. That was Paul's doing.

vs33-34: Alexander moved forward toward the stage and then began waving his hand up and down trying to motion to the crowd to be quiet so he could speak to them. Luke says, "He wished to defend himself to the people" (literal), but as soon as they recognized he was a Jew and knowing that Jews did not worship their goddess, they assumed that he was the one who had caused this problem. And they reacted by shouting at him with, "… one voice from all, crying out for about two hours, 'Great is Artemis of the Ephesians!'" (literal). Luke does not mention violence, but this event must have endangered the entire Jewish community by stirring up anti-Semitism.

vs35-36: The man who finally brought order to this confusion was the city clerk. The duties associated with his office included presiding over public gatherings, overseeing the city's funds and representing the city to the Roman governor (proconsul for the province of Asia) (A.T. Robertson, Word Pictures in the New Testament, Broadman, 1930, Vol. 3, p330). His speech skillfully calmed the fervor of the crowd in two ways. First, he reminded them that they were loudly making a point that no one disagreed with. He said, "Men, Ephesians, who indeed does not know that the city of Ephesus is the official guardian of the temple of the great Artemis and of that which fell down from Zeus [heaven]?" (literal). And second, he warned them to calm down and not allow their emotions to cause them to do something reckless because riots were unlawful, and what they were doing might bring on the city some form of discipline from Rome (v40).

v37: It's evident from what he said about Gaius and Aristarchus (v37) that he was already familiar with the facts of the situation. He seems to have known what Paul and his team were doing long before this. Good leaders usually know what's going on in their community, and it's quite possible the Asiarchs (v31) had also talked to him before he arrived in the amphitheater. If not, he must have taken the time to interview Gaius and Aristarchus before standing to address the crowd because it's obvious from his words he had already decided they were not guilty of a crime. He said, "For you [forcibly] led these men [here] who are neither temple-robbers nor blasphemers of your goddess" (literal).

vs38-41: Not only did the city clerk know about Paul and his team, he also knew who started the riot and named him in front of that entire assembly. He said, "If indeed Demetrius and the artisans who are with him have a formal charge to make against anyone, the courts [in the marketplace] are being led [by judges], and there are even proconsuls [available, if necessary]. Let them call one another [into court]. If you seek anything further [such as a resolution or official decision], it will be settled in a lawful assembly [not by an unruly mob like this]" (vs38-39, paraphrase). Then he added a chilling warning. He said the Romans could easily misinterpret what had just happened. They might view this chanting crowd as an act of political defiance against Rome. After all, everyone in Ephesus was supposed to be worshiping the Roman emperor, and this event might be seen by them as a rally declaring Artemis to be greater than Caesar. As the city clerk he was the one who would have to go and explain all of this to the Romans, but it would be difficult because there was no reasonable cause for such outrage. Hopefully they would believe him that this was merely a harmless disturbance. And then he announced that the meeting was over.

Acts Chapter 20

vs1-2: When the shouting finally stopped, and the riot dispersed, Paul sent word to the disciples in the city asking them to meet with him so he could say goodbye. At that gathering he encouraged, challenged and comforted them, and then hugged them and started out on his journey to Macedonia. If the only information we had was from this brief passage in Acts, we would assume Paul went directly from Ephesus to Macedonia and then down into central Greece. But as we noted earlier (Ac 19:22), much took place along the way. It appears that Luke kindly chose to omit those details because this was a very painful season for Paul, but Paul reveals them to us in his letters. We discover that he originally intended to leave Ephesus and go directly to Corinth, but because he was having such conflict with the church in Corinth, he changed his plans and sent Titus to Corinth, as his representative while he headed north, up the coast of Asia to Troas. He planned to stay in Troas long enough to evangelize and minister, yet he became so worried about Corinth he left Troas abruptly and went on to Macedonia.

vs2: By saying that Paul "passed through" the districts of Macedonia, Luke means Paul didn't remain in any one place long enough to evangelize and plant churches. On this trip he simply traveled from place to place to meet with believers, and Luke says he exhorted them (encouraged, challenged, comforted) "with many words." Then he either walked or sailed south to central "Greece" (Achaia) and spent the winter (three months) in Corinth. While there he likely visited other churches in the surrounding area such as Cenchrea (Ac 18:18) and Athens (Ac 17:34).

v3: When his time in Corinth was done, Paul's plan was to sail from Cenchrea (the harbor near Corinth on the Aegean side of the peninsula) to Caesarea (Ac 21:8). He wanted to arrive in Jerusalem in time for the festival of Pentecost (Ac 20:16). But just before his ship set sail, Paul learned that a group of Jews had boarded the ship and were planning to kill him during the voyage probably by throwing him overboard. He did have a number of traveling companions who would be on that ship with him, and they certainly would have tried to protect him in the event of an assault, but he decided the risk was too great and chose to return to Macedonia and to set sail from Neapolis, the seaport near Philippi (v6).

v4: Luke names Paul's seven traveling companions for this journey. An eighth companion would soon be added because Luke himself would join this team in Philippi (v5). The first three names he lists are from Macedonia: Sopater is from Berea (Ac 17:10-14), and Aristarchus and Secundus are from Thessalonica (Ac 17:1-9). Gauis (Derbe) and Timothy (Lystra) are both from the Galatian region (Ac 14:6), and Tychicus and Trophimus are from Asia (Ac 19:1-41).

Luke doesn't mention why Paul was traveling with representatives from all these regions, but we learn the answer from Paul's letters (1Co 16:1-9; 2Co 8:1-9:15; Ro 15:25-28, 31). We discover that he had arranged for a financial gift to be collected from the churches that he had planted and to be sent to Jerusalem to help care for the persecuted believers living in that city. Clearly, many of those who remained in Jerusalem still endured severe poverty because of their faith (Ac 2:44-45; 4:32-35; Ro 15:26). And Paul apparently preferred that the money be transported there by representatives from the contributing churches so that no one could accuse him of stealing funds. This concern for the persecuted church in Jerusalem was not new for Paul. About ten years earlier he and Barnabus transported a similar gift from the church in Antioch of Syria (Ac 11:27-30), and at that time three of the leaders of the Jerusalem church (James, the Lord's brother, Peter and John) encouraged him to continue evangelizing Gentiles, but when doing so, not to forget the suffering of their Jewish brothers and sisters. Paul gladly agreed and said it was something he was eager to do (Gal 2:9-10).

The men who accompanied Paul were either Gentiles or Jews who represented churches whose membership was mostly Gentiles, and in Paul's mind this group of men were more than simply guardians appointed to watch over the money they carried. They represented the fruit of his labors. Jesus had called him to evangelize Gentiles and Jews but especially Gentiles (Ac 9:15, 16; 22:21; 26:15-20), and he had faithfully carried out that assignment. In his letter to the Romans, written shortly before leaving on this trip to Jerusalem (Ro 15:25), he reflected on that call and described it this way: "… to be a minister of Christ Jesus to the Gentiles, ministering as a priest the gospel of God, so that my offering of the Gentiles may become acceptable, sanctified by the Holy Spirit" (Ro15:16). So while these Gentile churches were bringing an offering of money to their brothers and sisters in Jerusalem, Paul was personally presenting these Gentiles as a "firstfruits" offering to the Lord on Pentecost (the Jewish festival that celebrates the offering of the firstfruits of the wheat harvest; Lev 23:15,16) (F.F. Bruce, New Testament History, Doubleday and Co. 1971, p353). This is why "he was hurrying to be in Jerusalem, if possible, on the day of Pentecost" (Ac 20:16).

At this point in his life Paul felt that he had completed his assignment in the eastern regions of the Mediterranean, and after visiting Jerusalem he intended to stop briefly in Rome and then begin a new season of ministry in the western regions of the Mediterranean (Ro15:18-25). This trip to Jerusalem was the conclusion of one phase of ministry and the beginning of another.

v5: When he reached Philippi, Paul sent his companions on ahead to Neapolis to board a ship bound for Troas, but he remained in Philippi to observe Passover and the Week of Unleavened Bread (Lev 23:4-8). Afterward he intended to board a ship and catch up to them in Troas, but we should notice from the way this verse is worded that when he boarded that ship, he did not get on alone. It appears that after an absence of about five years Luke rejoined him (us), and apparently remained with him through the rest of his trials right up to the end of the book of Acts. Judging from Luke's use of personal pronouns, it appears that he stayed in Philippi to pastor the new church that was founded during Paul's second missionary journey (Ac 16:11-12; 17:1). This time when Paul passes through Philippi, Luke leaves with him.

v6: By noting that he and Paul left Philippi after the "days of Unleavened Bread" and that Paul wanted to be in Jerusalem by Pentecost (v16), Luke is showing us that Paul had a very limited amount of time available for the trip back. If he and Paul left Philippi on the day after Unleavened Bread, then they had exactly 42 days to reach Jerusalem. In a sense the season of Paul's third missionary journey was now over, and he had become a pilgrim on his way to Jerusalem to celebrate the festival of Pentecost. Luke tells us it took five days to sail from Neapolis to Troas and that they stayed in Troas for a week. This means that when they left that city, they had only 30 days to travel all the way to Jerusalem.

v7: Paul and Luke arrived in Troas on a Monday and undoubtedly ministered throughout the week, but Luke focuses his attention on the Sunday evening gathering held on the day before they left. He says, "On the first day of the week when we had been gathered together to break bread, Paul dialogued with them [the church], and continued his message until midnight since he was going to leave in the morning" (literal). Notice it says they assembled "to break bread," so their meal together was not just incidental. There was something important about it. The phrase "to break bread" was a common way of saying "to eat a meal," so this passage does not actually tell us that they took communion (bread & cup). But Paul's description of the gatherings in Corinth seems to picture the church sharing a common meal after which they took the "Lord's Supper" (1Co 11:20-34). And Jude mentions "agape feasts" (Jude12), and Peter mentions a common meal (2Pe 2:13), so it's safe to assume that the farewell meal held in Troas was similar.

In the Greek culture "the first day of the week" (Sunday) was not a special day. It would have been a normal work day for most of them, but for Christians it appears that by this time it had already become a special day for worship (1Co 16:2). In the future it would come to be called the "Lord's Day" (Rv 1:10) (F.F. Bruce, New Testament History, Doubleday and Co., 1971, p428). Yet even the words Luke used in this passage to identify this day give us a clue about the special meaning it already held for these early believers. He literally says they met "in the one of the weeks" which is a Hebrew way of referring to Sunday. Every one of the gospel accounts of the resurrection of Jesus uses this same phrase. Each gospel says Jesus rose on "the one of the weeks" (Lk 24:1; Mk 16:2; Jn 20:1, 19; Mt 28:1; also Ge 1:5; Ex 40:2 [The Septuagint]). So it seems that Luke was very aware that this gathering in Troas was being held on the same day of the week on which Jesus rose from the dead.

v8: Since their ship was scheduled to depart from Troas early Monday morning (v13), Paul continued teaching through the night. That meeting was held in a large, enclosed, upper room, and many brought oil lamps to provide light. Luke mentions the lamps because as a physician he obviously understood that the lamps affected the quality of the air in a closed area. And between the late hour and bad air, people could easily grow sleepy.

v9: Having pictured for us the setting of this event, Luke will now describe a remarkable miracle: a dead boy will be raised to life. Luke was in the room and observed the miracle for himself, so his description is very precise. He says a certain young man named Eutychus (Lucky) was sitting on a window sill, possibly trying to get enough fresh air to stay awake. But as time passed, and Paul kept talking, he slumped down in deep sleep and fell, probably backwards, out of the window. Luke specifically states that he fell from the third story of the building, so we won't assume Eutychus was simply unconscious or had the wind knocked out of him. Being a physician Luke undoubtedly rushed down to help but says the boy was "lifted up dead" (literal). Surely he knew how to check for a pulse, and when he did, he found there was none.

v10: As you would expect, people began to shout and wail when the news spread that Eutychus was dead. When Paul arrived on the scene, he "fell upon him, put his arms around him and held him close to his body, and [then] said, 'Stop shouting [yelling, wailing] because his life [soul] is in him'" (literal). Luke has already told us that the young man was dead, so Paul's words here should not be interpreted to mean that Eutychus didn't die but that his life had returned. What Luke is showing us here is a miracle similar to Elijah raising the widow's son (1Ki 17:18-23) or to Elisha raising the Shunammite woman's son (2Ki 4:32-36).

vs11-12: Paul then went back up to the meeting room, and a meal was served. But he only ate a small amount because he was continuing to converse with people until daylight. Before Paul left, Eutychus' family brought the boy to Paul to show him that he was alive and to express their enormous relief and gratitude. As Luke put it, "...they were not just moderately comforted" (literal).

v13: Luke, along with the seven representatives who were traveling with Paul to Jerusalem (v4), left the meeting earlier than Paul in order to board the ship before it sailed. But for some reason Paul made arrangements to walk to the next port and board the ship there. Assos was located about 30 miles south of Troas, and the two cities were connected by a paved, Roman highway. When the ship left Troas, it had to sail southwest past an extensive cape (Cape Lectum) and then turn back (eastward) to reach Assos. In fact it took longer to go to Assos by sea than if one simply walked there. Luke does not explain why Paul chose to walk instead of sail, so people have suggested all sorts of possible reasons such as needing a break from his traveling companions, wanting to be alone to pray, being tired of riding on boats or needing to take a long walk for his health. But the simplest explanation is that someone, or possibly several leaders, desperately needed to talk to him. And though he had been teaching and dialoging with people all night in a poorly ventilated room and had eaten very little, there was only one way he could give them more time, and that was by ignoring his own fatigue and inviting them to walk with him to the next port. If he wanted to be alone or pray, he could have found a quiet place on the ship which would have been much more reasonable than walking up and down hill for 30 miles. I believe what we're seeing is an example of Paul's passionate concern to disciple people. There was virtually nothing he wouldn't do to strengthen believers. So instead of leaving with the rest of his team to go to the boat where he could collapse exhausted and fall asleep, he chose to stay awake the entire next day so he could disciple or counsel someone while they walked together.

v14: Luke says, "When he rejoined us in Assos after taking him up into the ship, we came [sailed]to Mitylene [a port on an island about 40 miles south]" (literal). We can safely assume Paul slept soundly most of the way.

v15: The next day the ship left Mitylene and sailed about 60 miles south apparently putting in for the night in a sheltered cove across from the island of Chios. The day after that they sailed another 60 miles further south across a relatively open body of water to the island of Samos, and then on the last day they sailed the final 20 miles into the harbor that served the city of Miletus. The city itself lay a few miles further inland along the Maeander River, so Paul and his team must have walked from the harbor into the city.

v16: Miletus was a sizeable city located about 30 miles south of Ephesus, and because he was in a hurry to be in Jerusalem by Pentecost (v6), Paul chose to sail from Troas in a ship that docked in Miletus rather than Ephesus. Obviously, he knew that if he stopped in Ephesus, the church there would press him to stay too long.

v17: But Paul's heart wouldn't let him pass without at least saying goodbye to the elders. He knew they wouldn't see him again and felt he needed to warn them about spiritual attacks he was sure they would face after he left. Apparently, their ship was scheduled to stay in the harbor for a few days to unload cargo (Ac 21:3), or perhaps they had to wait to transfer to another ship headed southeast to the port of Patara where they would board a larger merchant vessel bound for Tyre (Ac 21:1-5). One way or another, they had enough time to send word to Ephesus and schedule a meeting. It would have taken about a day to walk from Miletus to Ephesus and then another day for the elders to walk down to Miletus to meet him.

vs18-35: When they arrived, Paul said to them (paraphrase), "'You know exactly how I conducted myself, from the day I arrived to the day I left because I stayed in Ephesus the entire time, serving the Lord with all humility and tears, and enduring the trials that came as a result of plots against me that the Jews devised because I refused to stop declaring and teaching anything that would be helpful to you, whether I was speaking in large public gatherings or in smaller meetings in homes (vs18-20).

"'While I was there, I continually witnessed to both Jews and Greeks about repentance toward God and faith toward our Lord Jesus. And now behold, having been bound by the Spirit, I am going to Jerusalem, not knowing what circumstances I will encounter once I get there, except that the Holy Spirit keeps telling me that bonds [shackles] and afflictions await me. But I don't consider my life as something that is precious and has to be protected. This is the attitude I must have if I'm going to complete the plan God has for me and fulfill the ministry I received from the Lord Jesus, which is to continue witnessing to the gospel of the grace of God (vs 21-24).

'"And now behold, I know, because God has revealed this fact to me, that all of you among whom I went about proclaiming the kingdom will see my face no longer. That's why I asked you to meet with me today. I wanted to declare to you as my witnesses that I am clean from the blood of all men, for I did not pull back from proclaiming to you all of God's will (vs25-27).

'"Pay attention to yourselves and also to the flock among whom the Holy Spirit placed you as overseers. God put you in that position of authority to shepherd the Church of God whom He protects by His own blood. I know [see] that after my departure, savage wolves will come in among you not sparing [showing no mercy toward] the flock. Even from among yourselves men will rise up speaking things that have been completely distorted in order to draw out disciples after themselves. Therefore, stay alert, remembering that for three years, night and day, I did not cease to warn each one [of you] with tears (vs28-31).

'"And now, I entrust you to the care of the Lord and to the word of His grace, which is able to build you up and give you an inheritance among all those who have been made holy [sanctified]. I did not covet anyone's gold or silver or clothing. You, yourselves, know that these hands worked hard to meet not only my needs but also the needs of those who were with me. In every way I showed you that by working hard in this manner, it is necessary to help those who are weak, remembering the words of the Lord Jesus who said, 'It is more blessed to give than to receive'" (vs32-35, end paraphrase).

vs36-38: After saying this, Paul knelt down among them and prayed, and they wept a great deal and fell on his neck kissing him over and over again. Luke notes that the deepest grief they suffered came when Paul told them they would never see him again. Then they walked with him back to the ship.

Acts Chapter 21

vs1-2: When it came time to leave Miletus, Luke says, "We had to tear ourselves away because they kept clinging to us" (literal). But once they got underway, the winds were favorable, so the ship was able to sail all the way to the island of Cos about 50 miles south. The next day they covered a full 70 miles to the island of Rhodes, and on the final day they sailed 60 miles east to the port of Patara. There they boarded a merchant vessel bound for Phoenicia and put out to sea.

v3: The entire journey from Patara to the port of Tyre was about 400 miles. Near the halfway point they passed the island of Cyprus, which Luke describes as rising up (from the horizon) on the left side of the ship, and then says they left it behind as they sailed to the coast of the province of Syria. Apparently, they reached the coast somewhere north of Tyre and sailed south before arriving at the port. The ship was scheduled to remain in port for a week to unload its cargo.

v4: The stopover gave Paul and his team time to contact the disciples who lived in the city. Years earlier Paul had passed through Tyre on his way to the Jerusalem Council (Ac 15:3), so he may have known where to start looking. Gatherings were arranged, and Luke mentions that during their time there Paul was repeatedly given prophetic warnings telling him not to enter Jerusalem.

vs5-6: When it came time to leave, all the believers including women and children walked with them to the ship and then knelt down to pray together on the beach. After everyone hugged the disciples, the team boarded the ship, and the people returned to their homes.

v7: Paul and his team still had one more day on the ship. They had to sail the final 30 miles south to the Greek city of Ptolemais (modern Acre). There they disembarked and chose to walk the rest of the way. While they were in Ptolemais, they contacted the believers who lived there and remained an extra day to fellowship with them.

vs8-9: On the following day they walked 35 miles down the coast to Caesarea and stayed in the home of Philip, the evangelist. Luke reminds us that this man named Philip was not Philip the apostle (Mt 10:3) but one of the "seven," meaning he was one of the seven deacons who were chosen by the Jerusalem church shortly after Pentecost (Ac 6:1-6; 8:4-13, 26-40). He also notes that he had four, unmarried daughters who were all prophetesses.

v10: Luke tells us Paul and the team remained in Caesarea several (more) days, but in view of the fact that there were only about five days left until Pentecost (Ac 20:16), it's not likely they stayed more than two nights because it was normally a two-day walk from Caesarea up to Jerusalem. If we count down from the day Paul left Philippi, which was immediately after the week of Unleavened Bread (Ac 20:6), Paul must have reached Jerusalem no more than a day or so before Pentecost.

vs10-11: While they were in Caesarea, Luke says, "...a certain prophet named Agabus came down from Judea, and coming to us and picking up Paul's belt, he bound his own feet and hands and said, 'These are the things the Holy Spirit says, "The man to whom this belt belongs the Jews in Jerusalem will bind in this manner and deliver him over into the hands of the nations [Gentiles]"'" (literal).

vs12-13: Then he tells us, when they heard the things Agabus said, Agabus, along with Paul's team of representatives and the believers who lived there, begged (exhorted) Paul not to go up to Jerusalem. But he answered, "What are you doing weeping and crushing my heart, for

I am prepared not only to be bound but even to die in Jerusalem for the name of the Lord Jesus" (literal).

v14: Since they could not persuade him to change his mind, they quieted down saying, "May the will of the Lord be done!" (literal).

vs15-16: When their time in Caesarea came to an end, they packed up the supplies they would carry with them and walked up to Jerusalem. Some of the disciples from Caesarea went along in order to guide them to the home of a man from Cyprus named Mnason with whom they might find lodging. Luke adds he was an "early disciple," meaning his faith may have gone as far back as the time of Pentecost.

vs17-18: When Paul and his team arrived in Jerusalem, the leaders of the church welcomed them gladly. The next day Paul went into a formal meeting with James (the Lord's half-brother) and the elders, and he took his entire team with him.

vs19-21: After warmly greeting the assembled leaders, Paul began to describe one by one the things God had done among the nations through his ministry. When he finished, James and the elders glorified God and then said, "Behold, brother, how many myriads [countless thousands] there are among the Jews who have believed, and all are uncompromisingly committed to practicing the Law. But they have had people come and tell them about you saying that you teach apostasy from Moses, that in nation after nation you tell all the Jews to not circumcise their children or continue walking in our traditional religious practices" (literal).

vs22-24: "How should we respond to this situation? Surely they will hear that you've come. So do what we tell you to do: There are four men in our church who have placed themselves under a Nazarite vow. Take them to the Temple and be purified along with them and then pay for the offerings that they are required to present to the Lord before they can shave their heads and complete their vow [Nu 6:13-21; sin, burnt, grain, drink and peace offerings]. Then everyone will know that there is no truth to the things they have been told about you, but that you yourself walk in an orderly way, keeping the Law" (literal).

v25: "But concerning Gentiles who have believed, we already sent out a letter that stated our decision about what we require of them [Ac 15:23-29], namely to keep themselves from eating food which has been sacrificed to idols or from drinking blood, and also from what is strangled [eating the meat of animals that were strangled in order to keep the blood in them rather than slaughtering them and draining the blood, Lev 17:10-14], and [finally] from fornication [participating in any of the wide assortment of un-biblical sexual arrangements which were common among the Gentiles, Lev 18:1-24]" (literal).

v26: The next day Paul, having been purified with them (a ritual bath), took the men and went into the area of the temple called the court of the Nazarites to give notice to the priests of the day when their vow would end. On that day they would present themselves to the priests bringing with them the necessary offerings which included a 50 shekel "gift" from each man (Josephus, Antiquities, 4.4.4). At this point we should remind ourselves that Paul had made that same vow five years earlier in Corinth (Ac 18:18) and then traveled to Jerusalem to present the same required offerings (Ac 18:22). So by taking this vow Paul was not doing something which violated his conscience. For him it was not a means of earning righteousness but an expression of faith, an act of worship. By taking a Nazarite vow he could show the believers in Jerusalem that he did not reject such things though he had already made it clear in his letters that his understanding of the purpose of the Law and his reason for performing such rituals changed dramatically when he put his faith in Christ (Gal 3:19-26).

vs27-28: The four men gave notice to the priests that their vows would end in a week, which meant that they would spend those final seven days in the temple. They would remain there the entire time. Small chambers were provided along the inner wall of the court of the women in which people could live while fulfilling the final seven days of their Nazarite vows. By living in the temple courts, a person would be protected from accidentally coming in contact with something that would make them ceremonially unclean (Thomas M. Lindsay, Handbook for Bible Classes and Private Students, Acts of the Apostles, T&T Clark, Edinburg, 1885, Vol. 2, pp113, 114). Tradition required that the Nazarite vow be kept for at least a month (Mishna, Naz. vi), so the four men undoubtedly had been keeping this vow for a while.

But tradition also allowed them to invite someone to join them for their final week, especially if that person was willing to pay for their expenses.

During those seven days they would have continued to refrain from eating or drinking anything produced from grapes, going near a dead person or cutting their hair (Nu 6:3-6). It seems likely that they spent the time in prayer and worship (Ac 24:12, 18). But just as that week was coming to an end, Jews from "Asia" (which almost certainly meant they were from the region around Ephesus) spotted Paul in the temple. Roman historians claimed that no less than two million Jews crowded into Jerusalem during such feasts (G. Campbell Morgan, The Acts of the Apostles, Fleming H. Revell, 1924, p483), and since this was the time of the feast of Pentecost (Ac 20:16), it's no surprise that Jews from Ephesus were present, nor that they were still furious at Paul for the humiliation they suffered in the amphitheater (Ac 19:23-41).

Those who recognized Paul began to shout, stirring up the crowd of worshippers around them, warning everyone that there was someone present in the temple who had committed an outrage against God. They grabbed Paul with their hands and began to call for help saying, "Men, Israelites, come and help us; this is the man who has been preaching to all men everywhere against our people and the Law and this place...." And then they added a blatant lie, because if believed, it would bring with it the death penalty. They cried out, "...and he also brought Greeks into the temple and defiled this holy place."

v29: Luke tells us that these men were already aware that Paul was in the city before discovering him in the temple. They had seen him earlier with Trophimus (Ac 20:4), a Greek citizen of Ephesus. So they must have been watching for him among the crowds at the temple, and when they saw him there, Luke says they "assumed" he'd brought Trophimus into the restricted area with him. He had not done so, yet they made no attempt to verify the charge. Gentiles were welcomed into the temple as far as the court of the Gentiles, but no further. In fact a barrier had been erected in front of the steps leading into the inner courts with a sign posted on it in Latin and Greek that warned Gentiles not to pass on threat of death (F.F. Bruce, Acts, Eerdmans, reprinted 1974, p434).

v30: Within an instant a wave of anger swept through the crowd of worshippers and then out into the city. A mass of people ran toward Paul, laid hold of him and dragged him out of the temple. The Levitical temple-police quickly shut the doors (beautiful gate) that separated the inner courts from the court of the Gentiles (Rienecker/Rogers, Linguistic Key to the Greek New Testament, Zondervan, 1980, p322).

v31: Then while the mob was trying to beat Paul to death, someone ran up to the Roman fortress located at the northwest corner of the court of the Gentiles and reported to the commander (Claudius Lysias, Ac 23:26) that a riot was underway, and the whole city was in turmoil. Herod the Great had placed that fortress there when he built the temple. He'd named it the Antonia Fortress in honor of his Roman patron, Mark Anthony. It was connected to the temple grounds by two flights of stairs that ran directly down to the covered walkways that lined the outer walls of the court of the Gentiles. It was there so soldiers could pour onto the courtyard at a moment's notice, and the Romans kept a legion (1,000-3,000 soldiers) stationed in that fortress at all times (Josephus, Wars, 5.5.8).

v32: As soon as the Roman commander heard the report, he personally led a group of soldiers and centurions (officers in charge of a hundred soldiers) down the stairs, across the courtyard and straight toward the mob. When the mob saw him coming, they stopped beating Paul.

vs33-34: The commander grabbed Paul, ordered his soldiers to chain both his arms and then turned to the crowd and asked who this man was and what he had done that caused such an uproar. But different people in the crowd shouted out different answers, and there was so much confusion he couldn't determine anything for certain, so he ordered his men to take Paul into the fort.

vs35-36: When they reached the bottom of the stairway that led up to the fort, the soldiers picked Paul up and carried him up the stairs because the crowd had followed them menacingly across the courtyard and grew violent when they saw Paul being taken away. Apparently, some reached out and tried to grab him while everyone was screaming, "Away with him!" (Lk 23:18), which meant "Kill him!" not "Take him out of here!"

vs37-38: When the soldiers reached the top of the stairs and were about to take him into the fort, Paul turned to the commander and spoke to him in Greek, politely asking, "Am I permitted to say something to you?" His respectful tone and eloquent Greek surprised the commander who, based on the violent reaction of the crowd, assumed Paul was a notorious criminal who had been caught trying to sneak into the temple. Several years earlier a Jewish, false prophet had come up from Egypt, organized a large band of followers and led an attack on the Roman fortress. That attempt had failed, but during the confusion the leader had conveniently disappeared leaving his followers to face the Roman soldiers alone. Four hundred men had died in that tragedy, and two hundred were taken captive. So the commander thought Paul might be that Egyptian prophet who had been discovered by the crowd trying to sneak into the temple and the people were all venting their fury at him (F.F. Bruce, Acts, Eerdmans, reprint 1974, p436; Josephus, Antiquities, 20.8.6; Wars 2.13.5).

In responding to Paul, the Roman commander mentioned that the Egyptian prophet had been associated with a group called the "Assassins" (literally "dagger men;" "Sicarii" in Hebrew). At this point in Israel's history there was a growing movement of radical Jews who carried razor-sharp daggers hidden in their robes and would attack their victims suddenly in the middle of the day. When the victim fell to the ground, they quickly mixed into the gathering crowd and pretended to be shocked at what had just happened. And their strategy often worked allowing them to escape undetected. And this type of terrorism had grown to become a major problem in the city. Many Romans and pro-Roman Jews were slain this way every day (Josephus, Antiquities, 20.8.6; Wars, 2.13.3), so suspicion and fear were rampant.

v39: Paul wasted no time denying that he was the Egyptian prophet. Instead he rapidly presented his credentials saying, "I am indeed a Jew, a citizen of Tarsus in Cilicia, a well-respected city," and then he quickly added, "I beg you, allow me to speak to the people." Amazingly, the commander gave him permission. He probably thought the crowd had made the same mistake that he had and would calm down when they learned Paul's true identity.

v40: He allowed Paul to stand at the top of the steps in order to address the crowd, presumably while Paul was still handcuffed between two soldiers. Paul motioned with his hand for silence, and the crowd grew quiet. Many were probably hoping to discover why they were rioting. Paul spoke to them in a loud voice using Aramaic, the common Hebrew dialect spoken in Israel. His accusers from Ephesus (Asia) were primarily Greek-speakers, so they may have had some difficulty understanding him, but Paul knew what he was doing. This was the chance of a lifetime to preach Christ to tens of thousands of Jews in their heart-language. So he didn't scold, and he didn't argue for his innocence. Filled with compassion and respect he shared with them his testimony; he told them the story of how he came to Christ.

Acts Chapter 22

vs1-4: Paul said, "Men, brothers and fathers, hear my defense which I now present to you." Luke notes that when they heard him address them in their Hebrew dialect (Aramaic), a hush fell over the crowd. Paul then went on to tell them that he was a Jew, born in Tarsus in the province of Cilicia, but raised in Jerusalem, and that he had been taught a very strict interpretation of the Law. Gamaliel the Elder, a highly respected rabbi (Ac 5:34-40), was his mentor. He said he had been as uncompromisingly devoted to God as "all of you are today." In fact, he had been so zealous that he had tried to destroy a movement made up of the followers of Jesus called "the Way." He hunted them down, arrested them and even put women in prison as well as men.

v5: He encouraged them to talk to Caiaphas, the former high priest, or any of the elders who had been part of the Sanhedrin during those years because they would be able to confirm that what he was saying was true. He said he had even travelled beyond Israel to pursue "the Way." The religious leaders had written letters of introduction on his behalf to the synagogue leaders in Damascus (Ac 9:1-2) and asked them to allow him to arrest any Jews who were following Jesus in that city and transport them back to Jerusalem where they would receive the "vengeance" they were due.

vs6-10: Then he told the crowd how he met Jesus. He said it happened when he was travelling toward Damascus. About noon a light came out of heaven and shone around him, and when he fell to the ground, he heard a voice say, "Saul, Saul, why are you pursuing [hunting] Me?" And he had asked, "Who are you, Lord?" and the One speaking to him replied, "I am Jesus, the Nazarene, whom you are pursuing." He said those traveling with him were able to see the heavenly light, but they weren't able to understand what the voice said. They only heard a sound. Then he revealed that he had asked Jesus, "What will I do, Lord?" and that Jesus had told him to go into Damascus and there he would be told the plans God had for him.

vs11-16: Paul told the crowd that the light was so brilliant it left him blind. Those who were traveling with him had to lead him by the hand into the city. In Damascus he met a man named Ananias. Ananias was a Jew who was very careful in his obedience to the Law of Moses and highly respected by all the other Jews in the city. He came and stood at Paul's bedside and said to him, "The God of our fathers has hand-picked you beforehand to know His will, and to see the Holy One and hear an utterance from His mouth because you will be His witness to all men of the things which you have seen and heard." Then Ananias said, "Now here's what you're going to do: you'll rise up from this bed and be baptized and wash away your sins calling upon God, in Jesus' name, to forgive you" (paraphrase).

vs17-21: Paul said he then left Damascus and returned to Jerusalem. While praying in the temple he was suddenly overwhelmed by God's presence and saw Jesus and heard Him say, "Hurry, get out of Jerusalem quickly because they will not receive your testimony about Me." Paul admitted that he argued with the Lord reminding Him that everyone in the city knew he had gone from synagogue to synagogue beating and imprisoning those who believed on Jesus, and that he had even overseen the stoning of Stephen. But Jesus didn't change His mind. He told Paul, "Go, I will send you to the distant nations [Gentiles]."

vs22-23: Luke says the crowd in the courtyard listened to Paul up to his final statement about being sent to the Gentiles, and then their fury erupted again. They called for his death saying a person like him shouldn't be allowed to live. They shouted and waived their robes and threw dust in the air since no stones were available on the smooth pavement of the courtyard.

v24: It's likely the commander could not understand what Paul was saying in Aramaic, even though someone was probably translating for him. So when the crowd again exploded in fury, he assumed Paul must have lied to him and decided to take him into the fort and torture the truth out of him. Now, even the Roman commander was angry at Paul and ordered him to be scourged. Many terrible things had been done to Paul over the years, but never this (2Co 11:23-25). If he survived, it would leave him crippled for the rest of his life. That's what Pilate had ordered to be done to Jesus in that very same fort, and then paraded Him in front of the crowd declaring, "Behold, the man!" (Jn 19:5). In fact, scourging was so brutal it was against Roman law to scourge a Roman citizen no matter what they had done.

v25: The soldiers dragged Paul into the fort, tied leather straps around his wrists and probably his ankles, and then they began to pull him over or around a post in order to expose his back to the whip. As this was taking place, in fact at the very moment that he was being "stretched forward," Paul spoke to the centurion who was standing nearby. He asked, "If a man is a Roman and not condemned, is it lawful for you to scourge him?" By asking this question he was declaring himself to be a Roman citizen and claiming the legal protection that citizenship gave him. The commander already knew that he was a citizen of Tarsus (Ac 21:39), but apparently that did not necessarily mean he was actually a Roman citizen.

vs26: But when Paul indicated he held that high honor of citizenship, the soldiers stopped instantly. To violate the rights of a Roman citizen was a very serious matter and could subject them to severe punishment (Ac 16:35-39). And it was very unlikely that anyone would make that claim falsely because once that lie was discovered, that person would be executed immediately and horribly (J. Rawson Lumby, Acts, Cambridge Greek Testament. Cambridge Univ. Press, 1904. p392). So the centurion went straight to the commander and asked him with alarm why he had ordered him to do something so illegal because "… this man is a Roman."

vs27-28: The commander approached Paul and said, "Tell me, are you a Roman?" And Paul answered, "Yes." The commander was surprised and possibly unconvinced. After being beaten by a mob, Paul must have looked ragged and bloodied, not like someone from a prestigious social background. He challenged Paul's claim by saying, "I acquired this citizenship by paying a great sum of money," to which Paul replied, "But I, indeed, was born one." That meant that his parents were Roman citizens, which probably indicates that they, or some earlier ancestor, had done something notable on behalf of Rome and had been honored with citizenship. Or at least the family was wealthy enough to purchase the right of citizenship and pass it on to their children. What the commander suddenly realized was that Paul had a powerful family behind him who could demand an investigation.

v29: Paul's statement hit like a bomb. Immediately, the soldiers backed away from him. They had already gone too far. Even the commander was afraid because he had given the order to scourge him. If Paul decided to press charges, there could be trouble.

v30: This left the commander in a very difficult position. He still didn't know what Paul had done to cause such a riot, but now that he knew he was a Roman citizen, torture was no longer an option. And Roman law forbade him to hold Paul without cause, yet the Jewish authorities would be furious if he let him go. So the next day he ordered the Sanhedrin to assemble, and after removing Paul's chains brought him down to meet with them. Luke doesn't say where the meeting was held, but it could have been either in the council house itself, located west of the temple and connected to it by a bridge, or at the east end of the portico of Solomon (also called the Royal Stoa) along the south wall of the court of the Gentiles (Leen and Kathleen Pitmeyer, Secrets of the Jerusalem Temple Mount, Biblical Archeological Society, Wash. D.C., 1998, pp43-44). Then he left Paul standing in the midst of them and withdrew to a nearby gallery where he could listen to the charges made against Paul and also Paul's defense against those charges.

Acts Chapter 23

v1: Paul spoke first. He stared at the court members seated around him, possibly recognizing a number of them, and then began to speak. He said, "Men, brothers, I have been living as a good citizen before God, with a perfectly clear conscious right up to this very day" (paraphrase).

v2: At that time the high priest was a man named Ananias (Hananias). A grandson of Herod the Great nominated him to that office, and he served in that role from A.D. 48-59. He was a man of very bad character who as high priest had been so cruel to the Samaritans that he was summoned to Rome in A.D. 52 to answer charges against him (A. T. Robertson, Word Pictures in the New Testament, Broadman, 1930, Vol. 3, p398). The historian Josephus reports that he would send his servants to the threshing floors and violently, if necessary, seize for himself the tithes meant for the common priests. Josephus said some of the older priests actually died of starvation as a result (Josephus, Antiquities, 20.9.2). This encounter with Paul probably took place around A.D. 60, and six years later when the Jewish revolt against Rome broke out (A.D. 66), Jewish insurgents would find him hiding in an aqueduct and put him to death (Josephus, Jewish Wars, 2.17.9). Paul's last contact with the Sanhedrin had been nearly 30 years earlier, so he would not have recognized Ananias.

vs2-5: His opening statement infuriated the high priest, and Ananias ordered someone standing beside Paul to hit him in the mouth (Jn

18:19-23). Paul responded angrily saying, "God is going to strike you, you whitewashed wall! Do you sit there to judge me according to the Law and then unlawfully order me to be hit?" One of the men standing beside Paul challenged him saying, "Do you [dare to] harshly scold God's high priest?" to which Paul quickly replied, "Brothers, I didn't know he was the high priest," and then to show his own submission to the Law of Moses he added, "…it is written, 'You shall not speak evil of a ruler of your people'" (Ex 22:28). Apparently, the high priest was not wearing his formal robes at this meeting, nor was he sitting in his usual place (F.F. Bruce, Acts, Eerdmans, reprint 1974, p45).

v6: It was now obvious that Paul had no hope of receiving a fair trial from this high priest. Any appeal for justice was pointless because Ananias, and the Sadducees who supported him, clearly hated not only Paul's faith in Jesus but everything he believed about God. Yet among that gathering of elders there was a minority of Pharisees, and Paul, having been raised a Pharisee (Ac 26:5; Php 3:5), still held much in common with them. In his mind their faith was an expression of true, biblical Judaism. They were a religious movement who believed the Bible and zealously tried to obey it. Yes, most of them had failed to recognize the Messiah, Jesus, and yes, many were making the fatal error of trying to establish their own righteousness rather than receiving the gift of God's righteousness by faith, but Paul's love for them and loyalty to them was still strong (Ro 9:1-5; 10:1-3; 11:1-2, 28-32). Even after all that had taken place over the past years he had not stopped hoping that they would repent and believe. So in that dark moment surrounded by godless enemies, Paul reached out to these Pharisees for help. Over the previous 24 hours he had been savagely beaten by a mob; he had barely escaped being scourged by Roman soldiers; he had spent the night in jail; he had just been hit in the mouth while trying to testify in front of Israel's high court and now found himself standing in front of a high priest so evil that the man was arguably demon-possessed. In that moment of desperation he decided to plead for help from his Bible-believing brothers by crying out, "Brothers, I am a Pharisee, a son of Pharisees, and I am being judged for the hope and resurrection of the dead."

vs7-8: When the Pharisees heard those words, they responded immediately, and actually, so did the Sadducees. Both groups stood up, physically moved apart from each other and started yelling. Paul's words had struck a nerve. Whatever polite behavior was required of them when the Pharisees and Sadducees sat together in the Sanhedrin, beneath the surface there lay bitter differences of opinion and deep distrust. Luke tells us the Sadducees completely rejected the concept of a physical resurrection of the dead and the existence of angels or demons, while the Pharisees confessed all those things (Mt 22:23; Mk 12:18; Lk 20:27). Undoubtedly, the Sadducees wanted to avoid entering into a religious debate with the Pharisees about those issues, so they were probably shouting something to the effect that Paul wasn't on trial because of doctrinal errors but because he was a troublemaker who had been dividing synagogues everywhere by preaching his Christian heresy. They probably focused on the fact that day he had been charged with violating temple restrictions (Ac 24:5-6). But apparently, the Pharisees had instantly become suspicious that the real reason the temple authorities wanted to prosecute Paul so severely was his biblical faith. In other words they suspected Paul would have been treated differently if he had been a Sadducee rather than a Pharisee.

v9: In the midst of that noisy confusion, scribes representing the Pharisees stood up and began to argue fiercely to defend Paul. They declared, "We find nothing evil in this man…," and then added these words: "…and if a spirit spoke to him or an angel" (literal). That statement seems to mean: "And who knows whether or not the spirit of someone who died or an angel spoke to him. And we Pharisees believe such things can and do happen because there are examples of such things in the Bible. So it's possible that Paul is telling the truth." Their mention of a "spirit" likely refers to Jesus speaking to Paul on the road to Damascus (Ac 22:6-10). If so, then they were announcing that they neither accepted nor rejected Paul's report but acknowledged that it might be true. And for Paul that was very good news. It meant the Pharisees were unwilling to condemn him as a fraud or label him as someone who was demonically deceived. They were remaining open to the idea that he was actually telling the truth and that what had happened to him may have been from God. Clearly, they were not going to vote to condemn him.

v10: That decision ignited an even greater uprising with both sides grabbing at Paul. Apparently, the Pharisees were trying to rescue him from the Sadducees, and the Sadducees were trying to prevent him from escaping. The Roman commander, observing all of this from the gallery, grew frightened for Paul's safety because it looked like he was going to be torn apart, so he ordered his soldiers to go down and rescue him and return him to the fort.

v11: Luke says that night the Lord Jesus appeared to Paul (literally "stood by him"). He began by speaking a command we often hear Him use in the gospels which can be translated as "Be of good cheer" or "Take courage" (Mt 9:2, 22; 14:27; Jn 16:33). And then He said, "…for as you have fully witnessed to the things concerning Me in Jerusalem, so it is also necessary for you to witness in Rome." Those few words contained a great amount of information: Jesus told Paul he did not need to fear; He told him that he had already accomplished what he had been sent to Jerusalem to do, and He told him that he wasn't going to die in Jerusalem because God still had work for him to do in Rome. Though none of Paul's physical circumstances changed in that moment, his courage instantly returned. And as we watch him face the coming trials, we will see in him an amazing confidence.

vs12-13: During that night as Paul was receiving comfort from the Lord, somewhere else in the city a band of more than 40 men were meeting to devise a plot to assassinate him. We're not told who they were, but most likely they were not Pharisees since the Pharisees had rallied to his side during the meeting of the Sanhedrin (v9). Luke calls them "the Jews," which in this case points toward the Sadducees or others associated with the high priest. Paul's nephew applied the same title to this group when he reported their plot to the commander (v20). He told the commander that Paul's intended killers were a group of men who "came out of them" (v21), so most or all may have been Sanhedrin members. Undoubtedly, many of them must have been very frustrated when Paul was forcibly taken out of their midst by soldiers. And some may have huddled afterward to arrange a private meeting where they could discuss the matter more freely. We learn here (v14) that more than 40 men swore an oath that they would neither eat nor drink until they had killed Paul. And the making of this type of oath had very dangerous consequences. It required each man to pray that God would curse him if he ate or drank anything before Paul was dead. We should keep in mind that during those years assassination had become a daily event in Jerusalem (Ac 21:37-38), so had they succeeded, they might easily have blamed religious zealots and escaped the fury of the Roman commander. However, since the plot failed (vs31-33), we're left to wonder how they backed out of this oath and returned to eating and drinking.

vs14-15: When morning arrived, they approached the chief priests and elders and told them, "We cursed ourselves with a curse, [vowing] to taste nothing until we kill Paul. Now, therefore, you appear before the commander with [the rest of] the Sanhedrin to request that he bring Paul down to you, as if you were going to investigate the matters concerning him more thoroughly, and before he comes near [where you're meeting] we'll be ready to kill him" (paraphrase).

v16: Then Luke reports an amazing intervention by God. He says Paul's nephew (the son of his sister) heard about the planned ambush. It would have been a very carefully guarded secret known only to those who planned it or were going to carry it out or to the chief priests and elders to whom they later revealed it (v14). And the reason the secret would have been guarded so closely was that Paul would have an armed escort on his way to that meeting. So Roman soldiers were likely to be killed in the attack, and that would bring a terrible retaliation from Rome on anyone who was caught, which raises the question of how Paul's nephew could have heard about it.

Luke calls Paul's nephew a "young man," but he used the same term to describe Saul of Tarsus (Paul) when he oversaw the stoning of Stephen (Ac 7:58), and Paul had to have been in his late twenties or even thirties to have risen to that level of authority. So it's possible that this nephew, who came from the same prestigious family Paul did, may have also been involved with the Sanhedrin just as Paul had been at that age. But surely people would have known that this young man was Paul's nephew, so either he accidentally overheard a whispered conversation, or someone on the Council wanted to stop the assassination and deliberately leaked the information to him. Up to this point in the book of Acts Luke has made no mention of any of Paul's family, but that omission could be because most of his family were estranged from him over his new faith, not because he had no relatives in the city. At least he had a nephew in the city who was willing to risk his life to rescue him, and that young man went into the fort, asked permission to meet with his uncle and then reported the plot to Paul.

vs17-18: Paul asked one of the centurions to come near so he could speak to him. He told him, "Lead this young man to the commander because he has something to report to him." The centurion did as Paul asked. He took Paul's nephew to the commander and said, "Paul, the prisoner, called me to him and asked me to bring this young man to you because he has something to tell you" (literal).

vs19-21: The commander took him by the hand and led him back to a place where they could talk privately. Then he asked him, "What is it you have to report to me?" and the young man said, "The Jews have agreed together to ask you to bring Paul down to the Council tomorrow morning as if they were going to investigate something about him more thoroughly. So don't be persuaded by them because more than 40 of them are waiting to ambush him, men who have cursed themselves [by vowing] that they would neither eat nor drink until they kill him. And they are ready now waiting for the order from you" (literal).

vs22-24: The commander responded by dismissing the young man after ordering him to "tell no one that you reported these things to me" (literal). Then he selected two centurions whom he trusted to perform this task and ordered them to "prepare 200 soldiers, 70 horsemen, and 200 spearmen to go as far as Caesarea [70 miles]" (literal). He told them they were to leave Jerusalem at about nine o'clock in the evening and were to have "beasts standing by," meaning there were to be horses or mules saddled and ready for Paul and the soldier to whom he was chained. The plan was to bring Paul out at the last minute, put him on one of the mounts and then leave immediately so that no one would know he had been transported out of the city until it was too late. They wanted to move him secretly at night, so he would be miles away and surrounded by a large, armed force before any attack could be arranged. The commander was rescuing Paul by sending him to the Roman governor in Caesarea.

v24: At that time the governor of Judea was a man named Marcus Antonius Felix who had been installed in that office in A.D. 52. He was a brutal and greedy man whom the Roman historian Tacitus described this way: "With savagery and lust he exercised the powers of a king with the disposition of a slave" (Tac., Hist. v.9). During his stay there he married Drusilla, a daughter of Herod Agrippa I (E.M.B. Green, The New Bible Dictionary, J.D. Douglas, ed., Eerdmans, 1971, p421). Finally in either A.D. 59 or 60 the emperor Nero recalled him to Rome. That helps us put a date on these events. Since Luke tells us Felix imprisoned Paul for two years, and in the next chapter we will observe Felix being replaced by Festus (Ac 24:27); we can be reasonably sure that Paul's night-time journey to Caesarea took place in either A.D. 57 or 58.

vs25-29: The commander, Claudius Lysias, wrote a letter which the soldiers were to present to the governor when they arrived in Caesarea. He needed to explain why so many soldiers were required to guard one man, and he also wanted to carefully reinterpret the order of events surrounding Paul's arrest so the fact that he had placed a Roman citizen in chains and nearly scourged him without a trial would be hidden. His letter leaves the impression that he rescued Paul after learning that he was a Roman citizen and then arranged a meeting between Paul and the Sanhedrin to try to determine the charges being made against him. He said he had concluded that the root of the problem was a debate over Jewish theology and that Paul had done nothing to justify being executed or imprisoned.

vs30-32: He ended his letter by saying, "And when it was revealed to me that there was a plot against the man, I immediately sent him to you, ordering his accusers to speak to him in front of you" (literal). In other words, as a Roman citizen, Paul had a right to hear for himself what his accusers were saying about him, and then to be allowed to defend himself against those charges.

v31: Following their commander's orders, the soldiers put Paul on a horse and traveled by night to Antipatris, a town about 35 miles from Jerusalem. The next day the foot soldiers were permitted to return to Jerusalem because the final 27 miles to Caesarea was through open country and out of danger (F.F. Bruce, Acts, Eerdmans, reprint 1974, p461).

vs33-35: When the military escort arrived, they handed the commander's letter to the governor and presented Paul. After reading the letter Felix asked from which province Paul came because his jurisdiction extended only to certain providences. When he learned that Paul's home was in the Roman province of Cilicia, he knew he had the authority to decide the case so he spoke to Paul and said, "I will hear what you have to say after your accusers arrive." Then since Paul was a Roman citizen and had not been convicted of any crime, he ordered him to be held in the same building where he himself was living, one that had originally been Herod's palace. The ruins of that beautiful palace can still be seen among the ruins of ancient Caesarea today. They are located on a rock ledge right next to the sea. Judging from the language Luke uses, we cannot be certain that Paul was placed in a jail cell while he was there. He may simply have been confined to the area of the soldiers' quarters.

v35: Paul was kept in custody in Caesarea for two years. During that time the governor allowed Paul's friends to visit and care for him. In fact Felix himself frequently summoned Paul and conversed with him (Ac 24:23-27). And since Philip the evangelist and his family lived in that city (Ac 20:8-9), and since years earlier a powerful outpouring of the Holy Spirit had taken place in the home of a Roman centurion named Cornelius (Ac 10-11), it's likely that there was a sizeable church in the city and that Paul stayed busy during those years ministering to a steady stream of visitors.

Acts Chapter 24

vs1-2: Five days later, Ananias (the high priest) arrived from Jerusalem accompanied by some members of the Sanhedrin and a Roman lawyer named Tertullus. The lawyer immediately began to make accusations against Paul to the governor, so Felix quickly assembled a formal trial because Paul had a right as a Roman citizen to hear the charges being made against him. When the tribunal gathered, Tertullus began his remarks by flattering the judge.

vs3-8: He told Felix, "Through you we have obtained much peace, and through your forethought reforms have come to this nation. Most excellent [strongest] Felix, with thankfulness we gladly welcome the reforms you brought to every area in the life in this nation. But so that I will not interrupt [cut in to] your busy schedule any further, I beg you to be merciful and listen to us briefly. We have found this man to be like a contagious disease. He's been starting riots among the Jews throughout the entire, inhabited earth. He is a leader of the sect called the Nazarenes, and he tried to violate the holy restrictions of the temple [by bringing a Gentile into its courts] (Ac 21:28-29). That's why we seized him. We wanted to judge him according to our own law, but Lysias, the commander, with much violence took him out of our hands and led him away. And Lysias can fully confirm these charges we're making against Paul because he also examined him" (paraphrase).

vs9-13: At that point the elders who came from Jerusalem with Ananias spoke up affirming that these charges were all true. Then the governor nodded his head toward Paul to indicate that it was his turn to speak. Paul addressed his response directly to Felix. He said, "Knowing that you have been a judge to this nation for many years, I cheerfully [feel confident that I can] defend myself concerning these matters" (paraphrase). And his defense was quite simple. He told Felix that he had arrived in Jerusalem only 12 days ago, and during that time hadn't assembled a crowd or dialogued with anybody, not in the temple or a synagogue or any place else in the city. He told Felix he knew the governor could investigate to see whether or not what he was saying was true, and he encouraged him to do so. He said his accusers, however, would not be able to prove the charges they were making against him.

vs14-15: Yet he admitted there was something he needed to confess to the governor. It was the fact that he did indeed worship the God of Israel's fathers according to "the Way" (an early term commonly used to refer to Christians; Ac 9:2, 19:9, 23, 22:4, 24:14, 22). Then he explained, "…which they [his accusers] call a 'sect,'" meaning in this case a group which had separated itself from mainstream Judaism and taught false doctrine. To make it clear to Felix that this was absolutely a false charge, he added, "I believe all the things that have been written in the Law and the Prophets, having a hope in God, which these men themselves expect to receive, that there is going to be a resurrection of both the just and the unjust" (literal). For Paul to say that about this group of elders meant there must have been Pharisees present because Sadducees didn't believe in a resurrection (Ac 23:8).

v16: Regardless of what the Roman governor would or would not decide in this case, a spiritual question was being debated in this trial that the governor did not yet understand, and all the Jews in the room knew it. The real debate was about whether or not Paul was an apostate Jew who deserved to be executed according to the Scriptures. The high priest and Sadducees believed the mob had done the right thing when they tried to beat Paul to death. Those among them who actually believed in God felt that divine justice was sadly interrupted when the Roman troops took him out of their hands. So Paul's statement here about his faith is his answer to that spiritual charge. In effect he was repeating what he said to the Sanhedrin several days before

(Ac 23:1). His remarks were directed to the religious leaders, not the Roman governor, and what they heard him say was something like this (vs14-16): "I have already judged myself. I have examined my own motives and tested my actions against the Word of God, and my conscious is clear. I have not turned away from true Judaism. I have not abandoned the God of our fathers. I have not forsaken the Scriptures. My faith is strong, and I am fully prepared to stand before God as all of us will do at the coming judgment" (paraphrase). And here in his own words is the way he concluded that defense: "...and in light of this [the resurrection and coming judgment] I myself always maintain a blameless ["unstumbled"] conscience toward God and men" (literal). He had made that same claim when he testified before the Sanhedrin, and Ananias had responded by ordering a servant to strike him on the mouth (Ac 23:1-2) because if Paul's claim was true, then Paul was the one who was truly following Israel's God, and they were the rebels.

vs17-21: After defending himself theologically, Paul returned to defending himself legally before the Roman governor by saying, "After many years I arrived [in Jerusalem] to present alms [gifts for the poor] to my nation, and having been ritually purified to present offerings, and that's what they found me doing in the temple, not trying to assemble a crowd or start a riot. But there are some Jews from Asia who ought to be standing here in front of you to present charges if they have something against me. Or let these men themselves declare what unrighteous deed they discovered when I stood before the Sanhedrin other than this one statement that I shouted out while standing among them, 'I am being judged before you today concerning the resurrection of the dead.'"

vs22-24: At this point Felix had heard enough. He finally understood the real motivation behind this trial. This was not the first time he had heard about Christianity. He already knew about Jesus and the movement called "the Way" (v14), so he didn't need to listen to any further arguments. The root of this conflict was religious intolerance, but he didn't have the political courage to say that, so he postponed his decision. He simply adjourned the trial saying, "When Lysias the commander comes down [from Jerusalem to Caesarea], I will investigate the matters concerning you more thoroughly" (literal). Then he ordered the centurion to keep Paul in custody, but to "loose" him (probably from his bonds), and not prevent his friends from meeting with him or providing for his needs.

v24: Realizing that Felix had no intention of prosecuting this case any further, the religious leaders returned to Jerusalem. And since Paul had obviously committed no crime against Rome, Felix should at that time have released him. But he didn't want to offend these influential, religious leaders, so he tried to appease Roman law and them by leaving Paul in a relaxed form of custody for the next two years (v27). Luke tells us that only a few days after the trial was over, Felix arranged for a private meeting with Paul so that he and his (third) wife Drusilla could hear him explain his faith in the Messiah Jesus. Drusilla was Jewish and may have been the one who pressed for the interview. She was one of King Agrippa's (Agrippa I, A.D. 37-44) five children. Bernice and Agrippa II, who will interview Paul at a later date (Ac 25:13), were her sister and brother. Their father (Agrippa I) had been the brutal king who ordered the death of the apostle James (Ac 12:1), tried to kill the apostle Peter (Ac 12:3-4) and then died only a short time later in a sudden and very gruesome manner (Ac 12:21-33). Though she had been only five years old when those events took place, at some point she must have discovered the circumstances surrounding her father's death (J. Rawson Lumby, Acts, Cambridge Greek Testament for Schools and Colleges, Cambridge Univ. Press, 1904, p.414) and may have come to that meeting with some troubling questions in her heart.

vs25-27: Luke says Paul "dialogued" with them concerning "righteousness, self-control [of our passions and desires] and the coming judgment" and reveals that during the conversation Felix grew extremely frightened and decided he had heard enough. And as he had done before (Ac 24:22), Felix handled the situation by refusing to make a decision. He said, "For now leave, but I'll send for you later on" (literal). Then, over the course of the next two years, he sent for Paul and talked with him more often than he really wanted to because, as Luke explains, he was hoping Paul would offer him a bribe. Then at the end of those two years (in either A.D. 59 or 60), the Roman emperor, Nero, replaced him as governor with a man named Porcius Festus. The Jewish historian Josephus wrote that Nero removed Felix because of the brutal way he put down a riot that erupted between Jews and Gentiles in the city of Caesarea (Josephus, Jewish Wars, 2.13.7, Antiquities, 20.8.7.9; also: F.F. Bruce, Acts, Eerdmans, reprint

1974, p474). Knowing that when he returned to Rome, he would give an account to Nero for the way he had governed Judea, and knowing that he would need the religious leaders in Jerusalem to speak positively about him to the emperor, Felix departed for Rome without releasing Paul even though he knew he was innocent.

Acts Chapter 25

vs1-3: Three days after arriving in Caesarea to take up his new position as governor, Festus went up to Jerusalem to meet with the chief priests and other prominent, religious leaders. By this time Ananias (Ac 24:1), the man who had been high priest when Paul was first arrested, no longer held that office. He had been replaced by a man named Ishmael (Josephus, Antiquities, 20.8.11). Yet the religious leaders in Jerusalem had not forgotten about Paul, and when they met with Festus, they restated their charges against him and begged the new governor to do them a "favor." They asked him to transport Paul from Caesarea to Jerusalem so they could interview him again. And just as they had done two years earlier (Ac 23:12-14), they planned to assassinate him along the way.

vs4-5: Festus replied that Paul was indeed still in custody, and since he intended to return to Caesarea in a few days, he invited them to send representatives to accompany him back to his palace. He said when they arrived he would assemble a formal, court hearing, place Paul before them and "...if there is anything improper ["out of place"] in the man, let them present charges against him" (literal).

vs6-7: Eight or ten days later Festus returned to Caesarea, and representatives from the Sanhedrin must have accompanied him because the day after he arrived, he went into the courtroom, sat down on the judgment seat (bema) and ordered Paul to be brought in. When he arrived, hostile witnesses came forward, stood in a circle around him and began to accuse him of many serious crimes. But they were unable to prove any of them.

v8: So when his opportunity to speak in his own defense finally came, Paul said, "I have not sinned in any way against the Law of the Jews, nor against the temple, nor against Caesar" (literal). Though Luke doesn't mention the specific charges that were made that day, Paul's response indicates that they must have accused him of blasphemy, violating the temple (by bringing in Gentiles) and some sort of violation of Roman law.

v9: If the Jewish authorities had been able to convince the governor that Paul had actually violated temple restrictions, Festus might have handed Paul over to them to be judged by the Sanhedrin. But they were unable to provide any proof. Yet among the many charges they presented that day, there was an accusation that Paul had committed some sort of crime against the Roman emperor, and from a Roman perspective that charge was far more serious than any violation of Jewish law. If proven, it would take Paul out of Jewish jurisdiction and make his case a matter of Roman law. And in their zeal the Jewish authorities made that tactical mistake. They accused Paul of everything they could think of and in doing so accidentally crossed a line. They charged him with a crime that only a Roman court could decide (F.F. Bruce, Acts, Eerdmans, reprint 1974, p477 footnote).

Rome had removed Felix, the previous governor of Judea, in part because Jewish leaders had made complaints against him. So Festus did not want to start out in his new assignment by arousing their anger. And it appears from Luke's account that he was unaware of the fact that this same group of leaders had tried to arrange Paul's murder two years earlier (Ac 23:12-15). And their proposal to move the trial to Jerusalem seemed harmless. He would still serve as Paul's judge in order to give the appearance of fairness, and by giving into their request, he might gain some political support. Hopefully by doing them a favor, they would be less inclined to file complaints against him as they had done to Felix. Had Festus actually suspected that Paul committed a crime against Caesar, he would have acted immediately. In effect by suggesting that Paul go to Jerusalem, he was saying, "He isn't guilty as far as Rome is concerned, but I'm willing to let the Sanhedrin try to prove that he committed a religious crime worthy of death."

When Paul declared his innocence (v8), Festus responded by asking, "Are you willing to go up to Jerusalem to be judged there before me concerning these things?" (literal). His question exposed his attitude. There was simply no reason why he could not have made a decision based on the information he already had. Judging Jewish religious matters wasn't part of his assignment. Yet he was proposing that he would sit as Paul's judge in such a trial. While trying to appear impartial, he was obviously more interested in gaining political advantage for himself than ensuring that Paul received justice.

vs10-11: Paul knew why these leaders wanted his trial moved to Jerusalem. He knew he wouldn't survive the trip. Though he was quite ready to die for Jesus (Ac 21:13), there was nothing to be gained by allowing himself to be meaninglessly murdered. And he was now convinced that Festus would overrule any objection he might make to the location of the trial and order him to be transferred to Jerusalem. Then once Festus announced his verdict in Jerusalem, the trial would be over, and it would be too late for Paul to make an appeal. So his answer to Festus' question about going to Jerusalem was his only chance to escape the plot against his life. As a Roman citizen he had the right to appeal that this life-or-death case be conducted in Rome and his verdict be announced by the emperor. One of the most precious rights given to a Roman citizen was stated in a law which "forbade any magistrate vested with imperium [Latin: rule] or potestas [Latin: power] to kill, scourge, chain or torture a Roman citizen, or even to sentence him ["in the face of an appeal"], or prevent him from going to Rome to lodge his appeal there within a fixed time" (F.F. Bruce, Acts, Eerdmans, reprint 1974, p363).

Every Roman citizen had the right to make this appeal at any stage in their trial by formally stating, "I appeal to Caesar" (Latin: Caesarem appello). And the judge would announce, "You have appealed to Caesar, unto Caesar you shall go" (Latin: Caesarem appellasti; ad Caesarem ibis) (G. Campbell Morgan, Acts, Revell, 1924, p511). So when he realized that his life was in danger, and Festus did not have the courage to give him justice, Paul announced, "I am standing before

Caesar's judgment seat (Greek: bema) where I ought to be judged because I have committed no crime against the Jews, as you indeed know better [than you are willing to admit]" (Ac 25:18-20). If I am someone who has committed a crime and have done anything worthy of death, I do not refuse to die. But if not one of these things of which they accuse me [is true], no one can give me to them as a favor. I appeal to Caesar!" (paraphrase).

v12: Then, after talking with his own council of advisors, Festus granted to Paul his right of appeal. On the one hand it must have been a relief to Festus to have this difficult case moved out of his jurisdiction, but on the other hand Paul's appeal had the potential to embarrass the governor. Rome would quickly recognize that Paul was not guilty of any serious offense against their laws, so they would question why Paul had felt it necessary to appeal his case to the emperor. Why didn't Festus simply pronounce him innocent and release him? For that reason the new governor needed to come up with a reasonable explanation as to why he had delayed justice for this particular Roman citizen.

v13: Some days later, Herod Agrippa II (the great-grandson of Herod the Great) and Bernice, his sister, arrived in Caesarea to welcome the new governor. His father, Herod Agrippa I, had ruled Judea from A.D. 41-44, but he had been only seventeen when his father died, and those in Rome who counseled the emperor Claudius did not consider a seventeen-year-old to be mature enough to take his father's place. Later on Claudius granted him the title of "king," but he was only given limited authority over a small kingdom east of Lebanon called Chalcis (A.D. 45). Some years after that (A.D. 53) Nero gave him a larger kingdom, north and east of Israel, which included the city of Caesarea Philippi near Mount Hermon. He made that city his capital and renamed it "Neronias" in honor of Nero (F.F. Bruce, Acts, Eerdmans, reprint 1974, pp481-482).

Since the Romans held all the real political power in the region, Jewish "kings" were only allowed to exercise a limited authority over local, internal matters. The primary benefit of being such a "king" was that they received a steady flow of income from their landholdings. However, Agrippa II had been given an additional form of authority. From A.D. 48-66 he governed the concerns of the temple in Jerusalem, appointed the Jewish high priests and was the custodian of the special robes used by the high priest on the Day of Atonement (F.F. Bruce, Acts, reprint 1974, p481). He remained loyal to Rome during the Jewish War for independence (A.D. 66-70) and as a result was rewarded with a larger kingdom but left Israel and moved to Rome where he died childless, about A.D. 100 (F.F. Bruce, The New Bible Dictionary, J.D. Douglas, ed., Eerdmans, reprint 1971, p523). He was the last Jewish king.

When Paul met him, Agrippa II was in an incestuous relationship with his sister Bernice (Berenice) who was a year younger than he (E.M.B. Green, The New Bible Dictionary, J.D. Douglas, ed., Eerdmans, reprint 1971, p142). Prior to this relationship with her brother, she had been married to her uncle, the king of Chalcis, a small kingdom east of Lebanon. That marriage lasted only a few years, and when her uncle died, she became her brother's mistress. Then partly to escape the rumors about that relationship, she married the king of Cilicia (Paul's province) but soon deserted him and moved to Rome with the intention of rejoining her brother who now lived there. However, an unexpected circumstance changed her plans. During the final stages of the Jewish War (A.D. 66-70), she had attracted the attention of Titus, the Roman general, who soon after that became emperor. So when she arrived in Rome, instead of moving in with her brother Titus took her as his wife though he never actually married her (F.F. Bruce, Acts, Eerdmans, reprint 1974, p482, footnote).

vs14-27: (paraphrase) "Agrippa and Bernice did not leave Caesarea right away but stayed on for a number of days. During that time Festus took the opportunity to discuss with the king the situation concerning Paul. He told him, 'There is a certain man here whom Felix left behind as a prisoner. While I was in Jerusalem, the chief priests and elders of the Jews brought charges against him asking me to issue a judgment against him declaring him guilty. I told them that it's not the custom of Roman law to decide in favor of anyone before the person who has been formally accused might be given the opportunity to face his accusers and defend himself against the charge. So when the religious leaders assembled here in Caesarea, I acted immediately. The next day I sat down on the judgment seat and commanded this man be brought into the courtroom (vs14-17).

"'When those presenting formal charges stood to speak, they brought no specific example of the type of evil which I had assumed he must have done, but rather certain questions about their own religious fears and about someone named Jesus who had died, but whom Paul claimed is alive. And I, being confused by the debate about these matters, asked if he was willing to go to Jerusalem to be judged there concerning them. But when Paul appealed for protection until he could receive the emperor's decision, I ordered that he be guarded until I was able to send him to Caesar.' Agrippa responded to Festus saying, 'I would also like to listen to the man for myself,' to which Festus replied, 'Tomorrow you shall hear him (vs18-22).'

"The next day Agrippa and Bernice entered Festus' auditorium in an elaborate parade meant to honor them. They were accompanied by commanders of the troops stationed in Caesarea as well as the most distinguished leaders of the city. When Festus gave the command, Paul was brought in. Then the governor raised his voice so everyone could hear him and said, 'King Agrippa, and all those who are gathered here with us, behold this man about whom multitudes of Jews have approached me, both in Jerusalem and here in Caesarea, crying out that he should not be allowed to live any longer. But [when I investigated his case] I discovered that he has done nothing worthy of death. Yet [in spite of that fact] he still chose to appeal to the emperor [which it is his right to do as a Roman citizen], so I decided to send him. However, [this leaves me with] no solid facts that I am certain are true to put into the letter that I will send with him to the 'lord' [emperor], which is why I brought him before [all of] you and most of all before you, King Agrippa, so that after this examination has taken place, I may have something to write because it seems illogical to me to send a prisoner [to Rome] without indicating the charges which have been made against him'" (vs23-27, end paraphrase).

Acts Chapter 26

vs1-3: Agrippa then turned toward Paul and said, "You are allowed to speak on your own behalf." Paul raised his hand, and in doing so he was taking the formal posture that ancient speakers traditionally assumed in order to honor their audience. In effect, it was a salute. On several occasions in the past we saw him raise and lower his hand to call for silence (e.g. Ac 21:40), but this situation is different. He was not calling for silence, he was beginning his defense by showing respect to that distinguished gathering. Then, addressing his remarks to the king, he said, "Concerning all those things of which I am being accused by Jews, King Agrippa, I consider myself blessed that I am going to defend myself before you today since you are the one most knowledgeable among all the Jews about our customs and the questions [being discussed here] which is why I beg you to patiently listen to me" (literal).

vs4-8: "So then, all Jews know my personal history from my youth onward, which from the beginning has been lived out among my own people and in Jerusalem. Having known me from the very beginning, if they were willing to testify [under oath], they would have to admit that I lived as a Pharisee following after the strictest school of thought in our form of spiritual discipline. And now I am being judged [by my accusers] because I stand on the hope of the promise which God made to our fathers to which our twelve tribes earnestly reach out in worship, night and day, hoping to arrive at that goal, and it is because of this hope that I am being accused by the Jews, O King. Why do all of you consider it to be unbelievable that God raises dead people?" (literal).

vs9-10: After challenging Agrippa (and everyone else in the room) to ask himself why he found it so difficult to believe that God would raise the dead, Paul returned to telling his own story. He said that as a Pharisee he assumed God wanted him to stop the spread of Christianity. It wasn't enough that he personally didn't believe that Jesus of Nazareth was the promised Messiah, his conscience impelled him to try to prevent anyone else from believing in Him either. And when the chief priests granted him the authority to pursue and persecute any followers of Jesus he could find, he performed his assignment with tireless zeal. He said he put many "saints" in jail, and when they were brought to trial in a religious court, he was a member of the jury who voted on whether or not to execute them, and he voted for death.

v10: The Greek words Luke uses in this verse picture how that voting was conducted. He records Paul as literally saying, "...and when they were being lifted up [tried and executed], I put down a stone." The word Luke uses for "stone" does not mean the larger type of rock one might throw at someone to execute them, but rather a small, smooth pebble, the kind that were used in ancient voting. To cast a vote, a member of a jury would get up and place either a white stone (innocent; Rev 2:17) or black stone (guilty) into a jar, and then the votes would be counted (A.T. Robertson, Word Pictures in the New Testament, Broadman, 1930, Vol. 3, p446). By confessing this Paul is accepting full, moral responsibility for his actions. Not only had he arrested people, but their innocent blood was on his head because he had personally participated in the decisions that brought about their execution (Ac 8:1).

v11: Up to this point in his defense Paul described only the persecution he conducted in the city of Jerusalem, but now he would reveal that his growing hatred for Christ had propelled him far beyond Jerusalem. He said he systematically examined every synagogue in the region and then expanded his search to foreign cities. Any suspect he captured who refused to renounce Christ would be stretched out on the ground and whipped with a leather whip up to 39 lashes (2Co 11:24). As he beat his victim, Paul said that he demanded that they blaspheme Jesus and described himself during that horrible process as "raging against them" like someone who is insane.

vs12-13: Finally, his campaign against "the name of Jesus" (v9) led him to the city of Damascus. The chief priests in Jerusalem had empowered him with the authority to act on their behalf, and as he and his companions were traveling toward the city, suddenly, at mid-day he looked down the road and saw a light from heaven shining brighter than the sun itself. In fact it shone so brightly that, even though it was the middle of the day, the ground around them was illuminated by it.

v14: All of them fell to the ground and heard a voice speak to them, but Paul's companions only heard a noise; they didn't understand the words that were being spoken (Ac 9:7; 22:9). Paul explained that the voice spoke to him in the Hebrew dialect that was commonly spoken in Israel called Aramaic (Ac 21:40). It said, "Saul, Saul, why are you pursuing [hunting] Me? It's hard for you to kick against the goads" (literal). There are two powerful images in that statement that we need to understand. The first pictures Paul as a hunter pursuing his prey, and the second as a farm-animal, such as a horse, mule or ox, pulling a wagon. In order to prevent that animal from kicking the wagon-box with its hind feet, sharp stakes were mounted on the front of the wagon. With those stakes in place when the animal kicked backwards at the wagon, it immediately injured itself, and the behavior was soon stopped. So before He even introduced Himself to Paul that day, Jesus showed him how his behavior looked from God's perspective: God saw him as both a vicious hunter and a stubborn mule.

On this particular occasion as he presented his case before king Agrippa, Paul disclosed everything the Lord said to him during that encounter, and we discover comments addressed to him personally that we have not heard before in the book of Acts (Ac 9:4-6; 22:7-10). One of these is the statement about "kicking against the goads." This is a very enlightening remark. Jesus used it to expose an attitude hidden in Paul's heart. He was revealing something that only He and Paul knew existed there which is that Paul had been plagued with painful doubts when he was violently persecuting Christians. We don't know what caused those doubts, but we can guess. Had he seen the depth of faith in those believers who refused to renounce Christ even when they were being whipped or stoned? Did Stephen's shining face still haunt him (Ac 6:15; 7:55-56)? Could he sense how evil his dark rage against Christ had become? Yet every time the Holy Spirit had tried to reveal the truth about Christ to him, he had reacted stubbornly, hardening his heart and growing ever more hostile. He had kept on "kicking against the goads" even though he wounded himself more deeply each time.

Jesus' comment that day indicates that there may have been a lingering suspicion in the back of Paul's mind that he might be wrong, and these followers of Jesus might be right. Yet every time such thoughts arose, he repressed them and became more aggressive. If this is so, it may be why Jesus did not confront Paul with the gospel during that first encounter on the road to Damascus. He didn't ask him to confess His death and resurrection. He just stood there in His glory and asked Paul why he'd been such a hypocrite.

vs15-16: Since Jesus did not introduce Himself before confronting Paul, sooner or later Paul had to ask the question, "Who are you, Lord?"—not because he had no idea who this glorious person must be, but because he felt more like a guilty man asking a judge to announce a verdict he knows is coming—to which Jesus responded, "I am Jesus, whom you are pursuing [hunting]." There's no missing the irony here. Paul had been pursuing Jesus like a hunter stalking his prey, but now that he'd found Him, he discovered how desperately small, weak and helpless he was before this divine Son of God. Then, without waiting for Paul to say anything more, Jesus told him to stand on his feet to receive his assignment. There would be no discussion about whether Paul did or did not believe. Like Jacob, he had wrestled with the Lord and lost (Ge 32:24-32). The very fact that his life was being spared and his sins forgiven should, and did, provide all the motivation he would need to obey the commands he was about to receive. But when he stood to his feet, he was totally blind (Ac 9:8), so that simple act of rising and standing at attention would have required an extra effort. And then Jesus commissioned him into His service by saying, "...for this reason I have appeared to you, to appoint [handpick] you [to be] a servant and witness of those things about Me which you have already seen [His resurrected glory] and also of those things in which I will appear to you [in the future]" (v16, literal; see Ac 18:9; 23:11; 2Co 12:2).

Paul's report to Agrippa that day contained more information than similar reports he gave elsewhere (Ac 9:3-8; 22:6-11) which causes some people to think he must have added statements that the Lord later spoke to him through Ananias (Ac 9:10-19). But there's nothing in the text to suggest that. It seems more likely that, because of his great desire to reach this troubled king's heart (vs2, 7, 13, 19), he presented to him a full, unabridged version of everything the Lord said on that occasion.

vs17-18: Paul also explained to Agrippa that the Lord told him that He was going to send him into dangerous situations, but that He would repeatedly rescue him from these. There would be times he would be rescued from Jews, and times he would be rescued from Gentiles, but Jesus would send him to both groups in order "to open their spiritual eyes so that they would be able to turn from darkness [ignorance, deception] to light [God's revealed truth] and from being dominated by the authority of Satan to [call upon] God, so that they might receive forgiveness for their sins and an inheritance [their allotted portion] among those who have been sanctified [made holy, cleansed of sin] by faith in Jesus" (paraphrase).

vs19-20: He then assured the king that he did not disobey those commands given him during that heavenly "sight" (It is important to note that what Paul saw on the road to Damascus was not a vision. He actually saw Jesus in His resurrected glory; 1Co 9:1; 15:8). He said he went first to the Jews, whether they lived in Damascus (Ac 9:19-25), Jerusalem (Ac 9:26-30; 22:17-21; Gal 1:18) or even in the rural countryside of Judea, and then to the Gentiles. And everywhere he went, he announced that people should repent and turn to God and show their repentance by "doing works worthy of repentance." The term "works worthy of repentance" points to the transformative changes in attitudes and behaviors that take place when a person truly repents and turns to God. Paul strongly rejected the idea that anyone could earn their salvation by doing good works (Ro 3:20), but in this statement we hear him make it clear that he still expected believers to produce good works because good works are the fruit of a transformed heart. When a person changes inside, the way they live will naturally change also.

vs21-23: Paul explained that when he met Jesus, he did the very same things he was now telling others to do: he repented, turned to God and began doing "works worthy of repentance." In his case that meant going out and preaching the gospel to Jews and Gentiles (vs17-18). So he explained to Agrippa, it wasn't because he was a troublemaker that some Jews seized him in the temple and tried to beat him to death; it was because he was doing what the Lord had told him to do. And just as He had promised, Jesus came to his rescue which was why Paul was able to declare, "Until this day I stand witnessing, to both small and great, to nothing beyond the things the prophets and Moses said were going to happen: that the Messiah must suffer [before coming again to set up God's Kingdom on earth], and that He would be the first person resurrected from the dead and by His resurrection proclaim light [spiritual revelation] to both the Jewish people and the Gentiles" (paraphrase).

v24: As Paul was saying these things in his own defense, Festus suddenly interrupted him. In a loud voice he said, "Paul, you're talking like someone who's gone insane. All your intense study of the Jewish Scriptures has driven you mad" (paraphrase). It was probably Paul's statement about the Messiah being resurrected that produced such an emotional reaction from the governor. Festus was a Roman, and from his perspective the fact that Paul was obviously convinced that a dead man named Jesus had come back to life and even claimed that he had seen Him alive was proof that Paul must be crazy. His own religious and philosophical background had taught him some wild, mythological tales about Jupiter and dozens of other Roman gods, but he didn't actually believe any of those strange stories. But Paul was different. What shocked Fetus was the <u>faith</u> he saw in Paul. Here was a highly-trained, religious scholar who actually believed what he was saying. He wasn't just rehearsing religious doctrine. You could see the earnestness in the expression on his face and the intensity in his eyes. You could even feel it. This prisoner was actually hoping to persuade a king and a governor to believe that a dead man had come back to life. And when that realization hit him, Festus had to make a quick decision about Paul. Either Paul was right, or Paul was crazy. And Festus chose to believe Paul was crazy because if Paul was crazy, he didn't have to repent and follow Jesus.

vs25-26: Paul didn't react to that insult in anger; he remained respectful and replied to the governor using his formal title, "Most

Excellent [strongest] Festus." But he did disagree with him. He said, "I am not speaking like someone who's insane. I am uttering carefully-worded statements which are true and arise from a sound, rational mind" (paraphrase). And then he quickly turned his attention back to Agrippa. Throughout this entire discourse he spoke primarily to the Jewish king, and now we discover why: He sensed that Agrippa might come to faith in Christ. So he assured the king that he had hidden nothing from him, and added that he was confident the king already had extensive knowledge about Christianity because it would have been impossible to hide such events from him. After all, neither Jesus nor His church were secretive about their ministry or their message. None of these things were "done in a corner."

vs27-28: At that point Paul dared to press the king to personally respond to what he'd heard. He asked him if he believed the prophets, meaning the prophetic writings in Scripture, particularly those that speak of the coming Messiah. And then without waiting for an answer, he declared, "I perceive [see] that you believe!" Judging from that statement it appears Paul discerned some amount of genuine faith present in Agrippa (Ac 14:9). At that moment the Holy Spirit must have been revealing to the king the truth of what he was hearing. And amazingly Agrippa acknowledged that he was, indeed, under conviction by saying, "If I keep listening to you a little while longer you'll persuade me to do a Christian [action]," by which he probably meant be water baptized (literal).

v29: Filled with compassion and encouraged by this admission that the king's heart had softened a bit, even though he was not yet fully convinced, Paul exclaimed, "I pray to God, whether in little or much [time], not only you but also all those who are listening to me today would become the same kind [of believer] as I am except for these bonds" (literal).

vs30-32: After Paul said that, the king, the governor, Bernice and all the guests who were sitting with them stood up and walked away. After withdrawing to a distance where they could discuss Paul's case privately, they said to one another, "This man is doing nothing worthy of death or imprisonment." And at some point in that discussion Agrippa turned to Festus and said, "This man could have been released if he had not appealed to Caesar." Clearly, he didn't know that Festus had already refused to release Paul though he knew he was innocent and would have sent him into a situation where he would have been assassinated.

Acts Chapter 27

v1: Judging from the way Luke describes the process of sending Paul to Rome, it appears Festus consulted the provincial council to make those practical arrangements. Luke says, "And when it was decided to sail us to Italy, they handed over both Paul and some other prisoners to a centurion named Julius…" (literal). As the governor of a Roman province, Festus had a council available to him made up of various officers and some young men sent from Rome to gain experience in provincial government. They were there to consult the governor on important decisions, especially those involving Roman law (Ac 25:12), and he could seek their advice whenever he chose, but the responsibility to make final decisions belonged to the governor alone (F. F. Bruce, Acts, Eerdmans, reprint 1974, p479).

Luke also introduces us in this verse to Julius, the centurion who will transport Paul to Rome. As their journey to Rome progresses, Luke will show us what a remarkable man he was. Here he tells us that Julius was a member of a special army unit called the Augustan Cohort. That title, along with his rank, indicates that he was an officer of a highly-trusted unit which at times may have guarded the emperor himself. Apparently at that time it was stationed in Caesarea to protect Festus, the governor. Josephus, the ancient historian, specifically mentions that a troop of horsemen by this name was stationed at Caesarea (Josephus, Jewish Wars, 2.12.5).

v2: Festus and his council made the decision to send Paul to Italy even though it was very late in the season for navigation. The weather during those months became treacherous. It was considered dangerous to sail on the Mediterranean from about September 14th until November 11th, and then after November 11th, all navigation came to a complete halt until the winter was over. In verse nine Luke mentions that by the time they arrived at the island of Crete, the Day of Atonement (the fast) had passed. And if this journey took place in A.D. 59, then the Day of Atonement fell on October 5th (F.F. Bruce, Acts, Eerdmans, reprint 1974, p506). Paul had already been held in Caesarea for over two years, so there is no apparent reason that his transport to Rome could not have been delayed until spring when travel became safe again. But it seems that after he preached the gospel so bluntly to Festus and Agrippa (Ac 26), Festus wanted to get rid of him as quickly as possible. So rather than waiting four months until travel would be safer, Festus ordered that Paul, along with some other prisoners, be put on a ship right away.

Based on Luke's description, by the time the prisoners left Caesarea, strong, westerly (or northwesterly) winds were blowing, and regular shipping had stopped. During the safer months for navigation their ship would have first gone to Alexandria, Egypt and from there would have sailed directly to Rome. But by that time of the year they were forced to board a smaller, Greek vessel which would try to work its way north running along the coast. Then once they reached the southern coast of Asia Minor (Turkey), they hoped to find winds and ocean currents that would carry them west. Throughout his description of this voyage Luke uses the first person plural (we/us/our) indicating that he accompanied Paul on this trip. And he must have kept a daily log because his descriptions of what happened along the way are detailed and accurate, clearly those of an eye witness.

Luke mentions that Aristarchus, a Macedonian man from the city of Thessalonica, was with them on this journey. Since Aristarchus had been with Paul in Ephesus (Ac 19:29) and had traveled with him to Jerusalem two years earlier (Ac 20:4), it's possible that he was devoting himself to caring for Paul during that season of Paul's life. He may have continued to help him during the years in Caesarea, and Paul mentions him in two of the letters he wrote as a prisoner in Rome describing him as his "fellow-prisoner" (Col 4:10; Phm 2:4). So this loyal friend may have ended up joining Paul in jail.

v3: The ship carrying Paul and his friends arrived at the ancient harbor of Sidon, nearly seventy miles north, the day after it left Caesarea. The Christian community in that city had probably been in existence since early believers fled Jerusalem after the stoning of Stephen. Luke lists the region of Phoenicia as one of the places to which those refugees carried the gospel (Ac 11:19). And Paul had already made contact with that church when he passed through on his travels between Jerusalem and Antioch in Syria (Ac 11:30; 12:25; 15:3; 18:22). The major road that ran along the Mediterranean coast passed right through Sidon so, as you might expect, Paul, who traveled that road numerous times, already had friends there. When the ship docked, Luke says Julius, the centurion in charge of Paul, treated him very kindly by allowing him to leave the ship and go into the city to receive care from his friends. Undoubtedly a soldier accompanied him (Ac 28:16), but obviously Julius already trusted and respected Paul.

v4: We're not told how long the ship stayed in Sidon. It probably remained in the harbor only long enough to unload its cargo and take on more. Then once they put out to sea, the captain headed north toward the east coast of the island of Cypress. Strong, westerly winds were already blowing hard, and he wanted to find shelter by sailing close to the eastern shore of the island. Luke says the winds were "contrary" (against them).

v5: When they reached the southern coast of Asia Minor, they were able to turn west by catching the westward current that flows along that coast and any helpful breezes that might come off the land. Staying close to shore and resting at anchor whenever necessary, they would have slowly worked their way down the coast of Cilicia, Paul's home province, and then past Pamphylia, a small province he visited during his first missionary journey (Ac 13:13). Luke's choice of words tells us that the ship next sailed across a stretch of open ocean before arriving at Myra in the province of Lycia, one of the main ports for the large ships that regularly carried grain from Egypt to Rome (F. F. Bruce, Acts, Eerdmans, reprint 1974, p502).

v6: At Myra they needed to change ships because the small vessel they were on would continue north along the west coast of Asia Minor

(Turkey) on its way back to its home port of Adramyttium (v2). So the centurion searched the harbor for a ship bound for Italy and found a merchant ship carrying wheat to Rome. In better weather that ship would have been able to sail directly to Rome, but it appears it too was having to work its way west along the southern coast of Asia Minor to escape the strong, westerly winds. Egypt was a major source of grain, and there was an entire fleet of ships whose primary business was to transport Egyptian wheat to Rome. These were huge, merchant ships able to carry many tons of grain along with hundreds of passengers. The largest of these that has been found by archeologists measures 150 feet long, with a beam width of 50 feet (Thomas V. Brisco, Holman Bible Atlas, Holman Publishers, Nashville, 1998, p256). The historian Josephus mentions that he sailed to Rome in A.D. 63 in a ship that was carrying 600 passengers (Josephus, Life, 3).

vs7-8: Luke says it took their ship "many days of sailing slowly" to reach the western-most port of a long, thin peninsula that stretches out into the Aegean Sea from Asia Minor. Cnidus (modern Knidos) is basically an island connected by a thin strip of land to the main peninsula. That thin strip of land forms two harbors, one on the north and one on the south. To sail west of Cnidus meant that a ship must enter the southern part of the Aegean Sea, and the winds were still so strong that even this large, merchant ship could do nothing but tack hard to the south hoping to reach the shelter of the southern coast of the island of Crete. Luke says they drew close to Crete at its northeastern tip, a place called Salmone (modern Cape Sidero), and then sailed along the southern shore of the island until they came to a place called "Fair Havens" (literally: Good Harbors, modern Kaloi Limenes).

v8: This small harbor was adequately sheltered from northern and westerly winds, but if a strong wind came from the south or the southeast, a ship might find it necessary to move to a more sheltered portion of the harbor. Yet full shelter was available, and that place is still used today as a marina with freighters anchored offshore. Luke mentions there was a city nearby named Lasea, and its ruins have been located a few miles east of the harbor.

v9: Luke doesn't tell us exactly how long they remained in Fair Havens only that they stayed "...a sufficient amount of time," which probably means until the ship owner's patience ran out. Summer was long past, and fall had arrived, so it was very dangerous to sail out into the open waters of the Mediterranean because the weather could change very quickly. And by that point in time the crew realized they would have to wait out the winter season before traveling on. The ship would have to remain at anchor in the safety of a harbor for the next three months, and that realization caused a discussion to take place among those in charge as to whether they should remain in Fair Havens or try to move to another harbor on the island.

v10: And while that debate was going on, God gave Paul a vision of what would happen if the ship left that harbor. So armed with this prophetic knowledge, he repeatedly warned them that they should not attempt to change locations. He said, "Men, I see [behold] that this sailing is going to be with unnecessary damage and much loss, not only of the ship's cargo and of the ship itself, but also of our lives" (literal).

v11: Now in this verse, Luke shows us that the centurion was the person who held the senior rank on that ship. As an officer of the Roman army and someone who was accompanied by an unspecified number of armed soldiers, he would be the one who made the final decision. The captain (who was probably also the owner of the ship) and the helmsman (the man who steered the ship) had their own, strong opinions about what should be done, and they wanted to move the ship, but they had to convince the centurion before they could act.

vs11-12: They told him that the harbor they were in was "not well placed" because it might be exposed to winter storms, and they wanted to move the ship another 30 to 40 miles further west to a place called Phoenix (modern Foinikas and Lutro). Phoenix actually provided a double harbor, one on either side of a small peninsula which they said would give them better protection from southwest or northwest winds. However, it should be noted that the harbor they were in at the time also had excellent protection from southwest or northwest winds, so if that actually was their major concern, moving the ship made no sense. They surely had to admit that leaving Fair Havens involved risk because soon after departing, they would have to turn sharply north exposing them to the wind for about 10 miles before turning west again. And we should keep in mind that while this conversation was taking place, a strong, westerly wind was still blowing. Yet they persisted, and Paul's voice was outnumbered. Most of those who counseled the centurion advised him to risk the move, and their voices prevailed.

v13: Then a remarkable turn of events took place. The strong, westerly wind that had been troubling them died down, and a gentle, south wind began to blow. And that was exactly the wind they needed in order to sail around the nearby cape and move north. So thinking that if they acted quickly, they could reach Phoenix before the wind changed again, they hoisted the anchor and began to sail as close as they could to the shore for safety.

vs14-15: But soon after they left the harbor, a violent typhoon swept across the island from the northeast and drove them helplessly away from shore and out into the open ocean. Luke uses an ancient, nautical term to describe that wind. He calls it the "Euraquilo," which meant "north-one-third-east wind" (F.F. Bruce, Acts, Eerdmans, reprint 1974, p509). It struck so suddenly that even though they had stayed close to shore, they had no time to find shelter and drop anchor. They must have heard a roaring sound and looked up to see a violent wind sweeping down the hillsides of the island and then felt it slam into the side of the ship. At that point there was no resisting its power. The ship was unable to turn its bow into the wind, so the helmsman swung the rudder around until the wind was at their back and they began to run with the wind. At that point they had no choice but to let it carry them wherever it would.

vs16-17: It blew them past a small island named "Clauda" (modern Gavdos) which lies about 30 miles to the southwest, but almost all of its shoreline is rocky and rises steeply from the water, so trying to land there in that gale meant crashing on the rocks. However the helmsman was able to steer the ship into some calmer water on the southwest side of the island. He couldn't draw close enough to the island to find shelter, but as they passed by, they were able to pull in the rowboat which they had been towing behind them. Undoubtedly the waves had filled it with water, but when it was bailed out, the sailors could use it to wrap great loops of rope around the hull of the ship to keep its planks from separating. Ancient ships could be shaken apart by a violent storm.

v17: The sailors, who knew where they would come ashore if the wind kept blowing from that (northeast) direction, were terrified because they were headed straight for an area of the northern coast of Africa called Syrtis Major (modern Gulf of Sirte). That stretch of shoreline has a sandy shelf that runs far out into the sea, and if the ship ran aground in that sand with such huge waves breaking over its stern, it would be beaten to pieces and swamped. Luke then explains how the captain managed the storm. He says, "…letting down the vessel, they were thus carried along." His words mean either that they towed a "sea anchor" behind them or lowered some or all of the sails to slow the rate at which they were moving. They probably did both but may have left up some small amount of sail so they could continue to keep the bow of the ship aimed as far to the northwest (away from Syrtis Major) as possible.

vs18-19: On the next day, since they were still being violently driven toward the African coast by the storm, they began to throw cargo overboard. By the third day they became desperate to lighten the ship even more because it was leaking badly and riding lower and lower in the water, so it appears the sailors (probably assisted by some of the passengers) lifted up the heavy main mast of the ship and threw it overboard.

v20: Then after doing everything they could to lighten the ship except throw the tons of wheat still in the ship's hold overboard (v38), they drifted for many days. And Luke says that terrible winter storm did not let up but continued to press heavily "upon them." He says the sky above them was so heavily covered with clouds that they didn't get a glimpse of sun or stars the entire time, and "all hope that we might be saved was now being stripped away" (literal).

vs21-26: During the storm everyone went without food, probably because they were too seasick and frightened to eat. But toward the end of their journey Paul stood up in their midst and said, "Men, indeed you should have obeyed me and not set sail from Crete and incurred this unnecessary damage and loss. And now I advise you to be of good courage, for there will be no throwing away of your life, but only of the ship. For there stood by me this night an angel of the God to whom I belong, and whom I also serve, saying, 'Fear not Paul; it is necessary for you to stand before Caesar, and behold, God has graced to you all those sailing with you.' Because of this, be of good courage, men, for I believe God that it will be exactly as it has been spoken to me, but we must run aground on a certain island" (literal).

The angel's statement that God had "given" Paul all those on board the ship indicates that he, along with Luke and Aristarchus, had been earnestly interceding in prayer. An earlier prophecy had already declared that if they left the harbor at Fair Havens, all lives would be lost (v10), yet clearly Paul understood that word as a warning, not a fatalistic pronouncement of doom. He knew that in God's eyes that prophesied loss of life was a warning of what would happen if He didn't intervene to save them rather than a "judgment" He wanted to impose. So Paul went to his knees and fought for the people on that ship in prayer until an angel arrived with the announcement that the spiritual battle had been won. The ship would not sink but rather would run aground on an island, and no one would drown. Paul relayed this message to everyone on board, and by now it had surely become abundantly clear that he truly heard from God. They had foolishly disregarded his first warning, but when he prophesied this second time, his words must have sparked hope in many hearts.

vs27-28: On the fourteenth night of the storm the sailors recognized they were nearing land. Luke says for two weeks they had been "carried about in the Adriatic Sea." Today the term "Adriatic Sea" is applied only to the sea east of Italy, but in those days that title was applied to the entire central region of the Mediterranean (F.F. Bruce, Acts, Eerdmans, reprint 1974, p515). Over the past two weeks they had drifted 476 miles from the little island of Clauda, near Crete, to the northeastern coast of the island of Malta, which means the wind carried them about 36 miles every 24 hours. And it must have been the sound of waves crashing on Malta's rocky shoreline that alerted them in the dark of night that they were finally approaching land. Immediately they let down a lead weight on the end of a cord to measure the depth of the water and found that it was 20 fathoms, or 120 feet, deep. Then, after drifting a short distance, they took another measurement and found the water was now only 15 fathoms, or 90 feet, deep, and that rapid change of depth told them they were moving toward land, not just passing by. And undoubtedly as time went on, the growing sound of waves breaking on the shore became unmistakable.

v29: It was good to discover that they were close to land, but we need to remember that they were still being violently driven forward by a powerful wind, and the roaring sound they heard through the darkness came from waves crashing against rocks. Anyone who has watched storm waves crash against a rocky shore understands why those experienced sailors were terrified. At that moment it appeared that their journey was about to end with the ship being smashed to pieces. Sheer rock walls rise straight up out of the ocean in some places along the island of Malta, and there are long stretches of beach strewn with huge boulders in others. And to make matters worse, rocky reefs are scattered everywhere just beneath the surface. So desperate to keep the ship from being dashed against the rocks, the sailors threw four anchors from the back of the ship hoping to catch hold of the ocean floor before they collided with whatever lay ahead. And even if they did not hold the ship back, the anchors would at least keep the prow of the ship aimed toward the shore so they would not come in sideways. Then Luke says, the sailors "prayed it would become day." It was still too dark to see the shore, so they waited anxiously and begged whatever gods they believed in to bring the morning light.

vs30-32: Obviously they had no confidence that those anchors would protect the ship because they soon devised a plan to escape in the ship's rowboat. Sadly in that moment of crisis, instead of fighting to protect their passengers, they chose to abandon hundreds of people leaving them to be helplessly dashed against the rocks. But there was no way for them to escape unnoticed, so as they lowered the boat into the sea, they told the passengers they were getting in the rowboat so they could cast out anchors from the front of the ship, which of course made no sense, but it appears that lie worked until Paul discerned the truth and went to the centurion and soldiers and warned them. He said, "Unless these men remain in the ship, you cannot be saved [from drowning]" (literal). And the soldiers responded by slashing the ropes and letting the boat fall away. Given their situation, it seems it would have been wiser to pull the rowboat back on deck since they would soon need it. But when those frightened soldiers realized what was happening, they reacted with understandable emotion. They quickly eliminated any possibility of escape.

vs33-36: Then while it was still dark, before the first light of morning arrived, Paul began to encourage everyone to eat something. The passengers and crew had all gone without nourishment for two weeks, so he said to them, "Today is the fourteenth day you've continued without bread, eating nothing, while you wait [for disaster to strike]. Now I exhort you to take nourishment, for this will be the beginning of your salvation [rescue], for not a hair of one of your heads will perish" (literal). Then with everyone watching, he took bread, gave thanks to God, broke it and began to eat. And amazingly, after he said that, everyone became joyful and also began to eat. Their response shows the level of trust Paul had earned by that time.

v37: And so that we won't miss the magnitude of what's taking place, Luke adds, "And we, all who were in the ship, were 276 souls." In other words hundreds of lives, "souls," were rescued because of the prayers and leadership provided by Paul.

v38: Luke tells us that everyone ate until they were no longer hungry and then threw the rest of the wheat into the sea. Apparently the ship owner's valuable cargo of wheat was the last thing to go overboard, but if they were to survive they must lighten the ship so it would ride as high as possible in the water. Hopefully they could make it over any reefs hidden beneath the surface and run the ship onto the shore where everyone could climb out safely.

v39: When daylight finally grew bright enough to let them see the shoreline, no one recognized where they were, but they were able to see an inlet with a stretch of shoreline smooth enough to try to drive the ship onto it. And after some intense discussion among themselves, they decided to try.

v40: The plan required as much speed as possible, but they were still dragging four anchors (v29) which by then must have been dragging along the floor of the sea, slowing the ship's approach to shore. So when the decision was made to try to beach the ship, the sailors didn't try to hoist the anchors back on board, they simply unhitched the ropes and left them in the sea. But since those were the only "brakes" they had to slow the ship down, once they were gone, the only hope they had was to gain enough speed to carry them over the rocky reefs and then to steer between the rock walls on one side and massive boulders on the other. To regain control of their ship, the sailors loosened the leather straps that they had tied to the steering oars during the storm in order to hold them in place while the ship was drifting. Ancient ships often had two steering oars (rather than a single rudder) located on either side of the stern which were usually connected by a wooden yoke (crossbar) so they could be turned in unison. But a sailing ship which has no sail to catch the wind cannot be steered; it drifts helplessly. So in order to regain the ability to steer the ship, they hoisted a small sail, located at the bow, to catch the wind which was still blowing forcefully at their backs. And then taking hold of the steering oars, they aimed for shore (W.E. Vine. Expository Dictionary of New Testament Words, Fleming H. Revell, reprint 1966, p120).

v41: The shoreline Luke describes here fits a place that can still be seen along the northeast coast of Malta, and the titles "St. Paul's Island" and "St. Paul's Bay" are still used for that area. A small island is located about 100 yards offshore with rock walls that rise straight up from the sea, and the shore of the mainland is a combination of rock walls and enormous boulders. There is a narrow passage through those rocks, and just west of that gap along the shore, there is a flat shelf of rock. And Luke says the sailors aimed the ship toward that narrow passage with the hope of reaching that rocky shelf. But before they could reach the shore, the ship's prow slammed onto a reef, stuck fast and remained immovable. Meanwhile powerful waves continued to crash against the back of the ship, tearing it apart.

v42: They were probably no more than 50 yards offshore when this happened, so with the stern breaking to pieces, everyone would have to quickly go over the side and swim for shore or drift in clinging to any object that floated. This meant the soldiers would have to remove the chains that had been placed on the prisoners, and that worried the soldiers. They envisioned someone trying to escape by swimming ahead and reaching the shore first. And if someone did escape, Roman law would severely punish the soldier responsible, probably by executing him.

v43: Yet Julius, the centurion in charge of transporting these prisoners to Rome, wanted to spare Paul's life. He had been kind to Paul since the trip began (Ac 27:3), and after all that had happened during the past two weeks, Paul must have risen even higher in his esteem. Luke does not disclose anything about the centurion's faith, but it's not out of the question that Paul had been witnessing to this man along the way. Whatever his reason, Julius forbade his soldiers from killing the prisoners and eliminated the risk of escape by ordering his soldiers who were able to swim to be the first ones to jump overboard so they would be on the beach when the prisoners arrived.

v44: After that, everyone else on board jumped over the side and made their way to land, some swimming, and some clinging to planks or loose debris they found floating in the water as the ship was breaking apart. Luke concludes his description of the shipwreck with these words, "And thus, it happened that they all escaped safely onto the land" (literal). In other words, "This is how God fulfilled His promise to preserve every life" (vs 22-26, 34).

Acts Chapter 28

vs1-2: Even after they all arrived safely on shore, they still had no idea where they were. Thankfully, some people who lived on the island saw the shipwreck and came down to help. The local people spoke a language no one on the ship understood. It was probably a dialect of Phoenician (J. Rawson Lumby, The Acts of the Apostles, Cambridge Univ. Press, 1904, p448). Yet somehow the two groups were able to communicate, and Luke says, "…we learned that the island is called Melita [Malta]." Those who came down to help the castaways welcomed them warmly and were unusually kind. They must have brought with them some dry wood and hot coals because in spite of the pouring rain and cold wind, they were able to light a bonfire. There was probably a place nearby with some sort of shelter from the storm.

v3: Paul must have been free to move about because at some point he left the warmth of the fire to go in search of more wood. He found some dead bushes and collected a large bundle of them, but in the process he didn't notice that there was a snake in one of the bushes. And probably because of the cold weather the snake did not react immediately. But when Paul went to put the pile of brush on the fire, the snake felt the heat and struck at him driving its fangs into his hand and not letting go. At this point we should remember that Luke was a doctor and would have had quite a bit of knowledge about snakes and snake bites. Snake bites were very common in ancient, agricultural societies. And what's significant here is that Luke did not use the general term that includes all types of snakes when he described the snake that attacked Paul; he used a Greek word that specifically means a viper (or adder), which is a very poisonous variety of snake. He also used a medical term to describe the way that viper struck Paul's hand. The word means the snake fastened onto his hand and introduced poison into it (Rienecker/Rogers, Linguistic Key to the Greek New Testament, Zondervan, 1980, p343).

v4: Luke says the "beast" hung there on Paul's hand until he shook it into the fire. When those who lived on the island saw what happened, they said to one another, "This man is indeed a murderer whom having been rescued out of the sea, [the goddess] Justice did not allow to live" (literal). Both the ancient Greeks and the Romans believed in a goddess who was responsible to enforce moral fairness in the human race. Today many of us might still recognize the Roman depiction of her as a blindfolded woman with a scale in one hand and a sword in the other. So when those residents of Malta saw Paul escape a shipwreck only to be bitten by a venomous snake, that was proof in their minds that this goddess had weighed him in her scales and found him guilty of death. So if the sea didn't kill him, she would swing her "sword" and send a deadly viper.

vs5-6: But Paul shook the snake loose and let it fall into the fire, and he didn't appear to suffer any negative reaction to its poison. Yet those residents were sure the venom would have an effect, so they watched him closely expecting the hand to swell up and become inflamed (Luke again uses a medical term for this), or that Paul would suddenly collapse and die (another medical term). But as time passed, nothing happened; he showed no harmful symptoms at all. And then at some point they completely changed their minds and decided he must be a god.

There has been much discussion among students of the Bible about the fact that today there are no species of snakes on the island of Malta with venom strong enough to kill a human. This fact is taken by some as proof that no species of viper existed there 2,000 years ago, even though many species of animals have gone extinct over the course of history. And in light of Luke's statement that the snake was a viper, in order to believe that it was not a viper, a person must assume two things: first, that Luke, a trained physician, did not know the difference between a viper and a non-venomous snake; and second, that a population that had lived on that island for centuries had not yet recognized the fact that when that type of snake bit them, nothing happened because they clearly thought Paul was going to die from that snake's venom. Actually, both of those assumptions are based on the idea that human beings who lived in the distant past were naïve and easily misled, which, of course, isn't true. What is far more likely to have happened to that species of snake is that as the human population expanded to cover the entire island, as forests and wooded areas were cleared and cultivated, and as non-native species were introduced through shipping and other means, it became extinct. A glance at a list of extinct or endangered species shows us how tragically possible this is. And since Luke has proven to be very reliable in the facts he reports, we would be wise to trust him here as well and assume that Paul was, indeed, struck by a viper.

There is one more observation we should make about Paul's encounter with the snake: It fulfills one of the promises the Lord Jesus made in the final verses of the gospel of Mark. After commanding His disciples to "Go into all the world and preach the gospel to all creation," He listed certain "signs" that would accompany them and prove that the message they preached was from God (Mk 16:20). One such sign was that "… they will lift up snakes…" (Mk 16:18), and they will not hurt them. The idea behind that statement is that God will protect Jesus' disciples from being harmed during accidental encounters with wild animals as they "go into all the world." This promise, and the one that follows it about drinking poison (Mk 16:18), was not meant to be used as a test of one's salvation but as an encouragement to believers to fearlessly carry the gospel into dangerous places. And it seems we're watching that promise at work for Paul. He was bitten by a viper but not hurt, and the inhabitants of the island took it as a sign that he was divinely protected.

v7: One of the main landowners in that part of the island was a man named Publius. Luke says he was the "protos" or "first man" of the island. That title is very unusual. It is not found in literature or inscriptions outside of Malta, but archaeologists have found two inscriptions that contain that title on Malta (F.F. Bruce. Acts. Eerdmans, reprint, 1974, p523). The island was so small that the Romans placed it under the jurisdiction of the neighboring larger island of Sicily (J. Rawson Lumby, Acts, Cambridge Univ. Press, 1904, p450), and it may be that instead of sending someone from Rome to such a remote place, they chose one of Malta's citizens to serve as their local representative and gave him that title. It's not certain what duties Publius performed, but he was the one who welcomed the castaways and took responsibility for their well-being. He even personally housed and fed them for three days.

Christian tradition states that Publius went on to become the bishop of Malta and later served as the bishop of Athens (Jamieson, Fausset, Brown, A Commentary, Eerdmans, reprinted March 1982, Vol. 3, p184; and W. Robertson Nicoll, The Expositor's Greek Testament, Eerdmans, reprinted August 1983, Vol. 2, pp540-541). That tradition can't be proved, but given all that took place on Malta during Paul's stay, it would not be surprising if Publius did become a believer. He watched the miraculous healing of his father followed by months of listening to Paul preach and watching him pray for the sick, and that level of exposure to the power of God would have a strong influence on anyone. And judging from the way he treated the castaways, it appears he was a kind and generous man even before he met Paul.

v8: It so happened that Publius' father was quite ill. Luke uses medical terms to describe the man's condition, and what we learn is that he was experiencing fits of high fever and dysentery (severe diarrhea). We're not told how the man's need was brought to the attention of Luke and Paul, but it's possible that when Publius learned that Luke was a physician, he told him about his father and asked if he could help. It appears that Luke was already in the room with the sick man when Paul arrived because he tells us the father was "lying down" when Paul entered. It's easy to imagine a natural progression of events which began if Luke saw the man first, diagnosed his condition and then said something to the effect, "There's not much I can do beyond encouraging you to have him continue to drink water, however I am traveling with a man who has been powerfully used by God to heal the sick. Would you like me to ask him to come and pray?" We don't know the actual sequence of events that allowed Paul to pray for Publius' father, but we do know that he was invited to come, entered the man's room, went directly to the his bedside, began to pray and then at some point during that prayer laid his hands on him, and the man was healed.

v9: The report of that healing spread rapidly across the island, and from then on during the entire time Paul remained on the island, those who were weak and sickly came to him and were healed. And it's impossible to imagine that Paul, Luke and Aristarchus were not evangelizing at the same time. So during those winter months they were able to lay the foundation for a church unhindered. They enjoyed the protection and support of the "protos" (first man) and were guarded by a security team of Roman soldiers. We don't know if Paul wore a chain during those days, probably not, but almost certainly there was a Roman soldier stationed nearby at all times. And we shouldn't overlook the spiritual impact Paul's ministry must have had on the soldiers who guarded him. As we noted earlier (Ac 27:1), the centurion was an officer of an elite group of soldiers who at times may have guarded even the emperor's own household. In one of the letters Paul wrote during his imprisonment in Rome, he mentioned that the gospel had spread into the "praetorian guard" (Php 1:13) and to "those of Caesar's household" (Php 4:22). What we're watching take place here on Malta may help to explain how the gospel got a foothold in the Roman military.

v10: As God worked His wonders among them, the people who lived on the island showed their thanks in many ways. Luke doesn't tell us exactly how they did this; he simply says, "...they honored us with many honors," which likely means they brought gifts to them. Those "honors" probably included a meal or favorite food, a handmade item that held a special meaning, or given the fact they probably lost everything in the shipwreck, someone may have sewn warm clothing for them or woven a blanket. It's easy to imagine what those thankful moments must have been like. There may have been tears in the eyes of individuals or family members who were grateful beyond words for the miracle God had done for them. And when the time finally arrived for Paul, Luke and Aristarchus to board a ship bound for Rome, the people provided everything they might need for the trip: food, clothing and possibly even some money for expenses. Such generosity goes far beyond what people normally do when they're merely being polite. That moment looks much more like a church saying goodbye to their pastor.

v11: The shipwreck occurred along a rocky section of the island's northeast coast, but the main harbor for the island lies several miles to the south (modern Valletta). That harbor is actually a remarkable complex of harbors and today is filled with marinas and docking facilities for large ships. The winter season that prevented ancient navigation usually ends during the early weeks of February, so as calmer weather approached, the centurion arranged for passage to Rome on another Egyptian ship, probably another wheat-freighter. That ship had also spent the winter in Malta and would leave with the first signs of spring. At this point Luke does something very unusual: he tells us the name of the ship. On its prow there was a "sign" (a figurehead or painting) that depicted two mythological figures: Castor and Pollux. Those two gods were believed to be twin brothers born to a human woman named Leda and fathered by the god Jupiter (Greek: Zeus). Sailors would sacrifice to Castor and Pollux seeking favorable winds, and the two mythological figures were referred to by a Latin title that means, "sons of god" (Zeus) (Charles M. Gayley, ed., Classic Myths in English Literature, Gim and Co., Second Ed., Boston, 1894, pp281-283). Why Luke mentions this isn't clear, but he may have found it humorous (or prophetic) that they were escorted to Rome in a ship named "sons of god" (Gal 3:26).

vs12-13: Syracuse, the first port on the way, was an ancient Greek colony on the island of Sicily about 80 miles north of Malta. The ship remained there three days, probably waiting for a wind that would allow them to sail up the straits between Sicily and the Italian mainland because Luke says when the ship left Syracuse, it had to "go around," which probably means they had to zigzag back and forth up the straits to reach Rhegium (modern Reggio de Calabria), a distance of about 80 miles. Rhegium was a harbor on the Italian side of the Strait of Messina, and they stayed in that harbor for a day before a south wind came up to carry them through the strait and allow them to complete the final 200 miles in two days. Their final destination was Puteoli (modern Pozzuoli, in the Bay of Naples), the main port for Alexandrian wheat ships (F.F. Bruce, Acts, Eerdmans, reprint 1974, p526).

v14: Then somehow, while still in Puteoli, they met Christians who lived in the city. You would have expected the soldiers to march their prisoners off the ship and either place them in a local jail, if they had to stay there for a while, or immediately begin walking the final 140 miles to Rome. But they didn't. They stayed in Puteoli for seven more days apparently because the local Christians asked them to stay. Luke says, "Having found brothers [there] we were begged by them to remain seven days, and in this manner we went to Rome" (literal). This statement can only mean that Julius, the centurion, agreed to stay an extra week in Puteoli so Paul, Luke and Aristarchus could minister to the church. And if that doesn't indicate that he had become a believer, it at least means he had become very supportive of Paul.

v15: The city of Rome consumed as much as 150,000 tons of grain per year, so there was a constant flow of traffic between Rome and the port city of Puteoli where the grain ships docked (Paul Laurence, The IVP Atlas of Bible History, IVP Academic, 2006, p167). So during the week they spent in Puteoli someone sent notification to the churches in Rome that Paul was in Italy and would leave the port on a certain day. And word of his arrival spread quickly among the churches, and groups of believers, probably some of Paul's friends as well as church leaders, walked a day or two south along the main highway to meet him. They knew he would be traveling along the Via Appia (Appian Way), so some came out as far as the Appian Forum (modern Tor Tre Ponti), 43 miles south, while others stopped sooner at a place called Three Inns (modern Cisterna di Latina), about a day's walk from the city.

After leaving Puteoli the centurion would have led his group north and east along a highway called the Via Campana to where it intersected with the Via Appia at the town of Capua (modern Santa Maria Capua Vetere; see Capua Porta Napoli) (Thomas V. Brisco, Holman Bible Atlas, Holman Publishing, Nashville, 1998, p257). Luke tells us that as they approached Rome, Paul looked up and saw believers waiting for him along the road; he uttered thanks to God and was greatly encouraged. Clearly, their warm greeting meant that the church in Rome would not reject him because he arrived in chains or because of the gospel he preached which was based on the righteousness of faith (Ac 15:1-2; Ro 2:16; 16:25). Luke doesn't mention by name those who came out to meet them, but when Paul wrote to the churches in Rome three years earlier, he closed his letter by greeting those he knew in Rome (Ro 16:3-16). His list began with Priscilla and Aquila, who by that time had returned to Rome (Ro 16:3), and he mentioned a church which met in their house. If physically able, those two, dear "fellow workers in Christ Jesus" would have come out to meet him, and their faces would have been a most welcomed sight.

v16: The Praetorian Guard was headquartered in a huge, brick barracks in the northeast section of Rome (Paul Laurence, The IVP Atlas of Bible History, IVP Academic, 2006, pp166-167), and normally Paul would have been taken there to await his trial. But when they arrived in the city, Paul was allowed to stay in a private home (possibly with Priscilla and Aquila) rather than being placed in a cell. Julius, the centurion, undoubtedly reported to a superior officer as soon as they arrived and probably handed Paul over to a guard, but his report to his superior officer about Paul must have been very favorable because the Roman government allowed Paul to stay in a rented house for the next two years (v30). Of course, his right hand would have been chained to a soldier (v20), but having a different guard sitting next to him each day would have provided Paul with a marvelous opportunity to evangelize and disciple members of the praetorian guard (Php 1:13).

vs17-19: Three days later, probably on the Sabbath when Jewish leaders were gathered at a synagogue service (Ac 9:20; 18:4, 19), Paul sent a representative to invite them to meet with him. He wanted to explain several things to the Jewish community: first of all, that he had not done anything criminal, nor violated any Jewish religious laws; and second, that he had not appealed to Caesar in order to tarnish the reputation of the high priests or the Sanhedrin. This second point mattered a great deal because the political climate for Jews in Rome had become very dangerous. About ten years earlier all Jews had been banned from the city because they had been involved in so many religious riots (see notes: Ac 17:7; 18:2), and they had only been allowed to return a few years before this. And there was also a growing hostility toward the Roman government in Israel, so the last thing the Jewish community living in Rome wanted to hear was that Paul had come there to make accusations to the emperor against the religious leaders in Jerusalem. This may be why it appears no representatives were sent from Jerusalem to testify against Paul at his trial. Political tensions were so high for Jews that they didn't want to argue their differences in front of Nero. However, Paul did feel free to tell the Jewish leaders who came to visit him about the injustices he had endured. He said the religious leaders in Israel delivered him over to the Romans without cause. And even after the Romans examined him in a trial, found that he had done nothing deserving the death penalty and wanted to release him, those leaders still continued to speak against him until he was forced to seek relief by appealing to Caesar.

v20: He said that was why he had asked them to visit him. He was actually summoning them as witnesses to hear his declaration of innocence, and he also wanted to put their minds at ease that he wouldn't stir up trouble for the Jewish community. Then he added this statement, "… and it is because of the hope of Israel that I have this chain around [me]" (literal). He had made that same claim on earlier occasions: First, when he stood before the Sanhedrin (Ac 23:6), and later, before King Agrippa (Ac 26:6-7). He said the real reason the leaders in Jerusalem opposed him so strongly was because they opposed his faith, in particular his belief in the resurrection of the dead.

vs21-22: The synagogue leaders replied that they had not received letters about him from Judea, nor had anyone traveling from there brought a bad report about him. But considering the seriousness of the situation, they felt it would be worthwhile to meet with him so he could tell them what he thought about the movement based on the teachings of Jesus because it was being "spoken against everywhere." Obviously, their comment reveals that the dividing line between Jews and Christians had already grown quite deep.

v23: A day was arranged when they could meet with Paul at his lodging, and a large number of the synagogue leaders came. The meeting lasted all day, from "morning to evening," as Paul carefully laid out before them what he believed. Luke says he "solemnly witnessed" to them as if he were testifying in a court of law. He explained "the kingdom of God" and tried to persuade them to believe "the things concerning Jesus from both the Law of Moses and the Prophets." In other words he turned to the promises found in Scripture that speak of Israel's Messiah and showed them that it had been prophesied that the Messiah must suffer and die and be raised from the dead <u>before</u> coming back to rule over an earthly kingdom. To most Jews this would have been a radically different teaching from that which they had learned from their elders. Most of Judaism was waiting for a powerful Messiah who would set up the Kingdom of God on earth (Mt 3:11-12). They had no concept of Him suffering as the atonement for their sins and then rising from the dead, so those issues would have been the focus of much of their discussion that day (Ac 13:26-39; 26:22-23). And God's inclusion of believing Gentiles into His kingdom would also have been very controversial.

vs24-27: During the course of the day some of the elders became convinced that what Paul was showing them in the Scriptures was true, and they believed in Jesus, but others did not. And once again, as had happened in city after city, the gospel divided that Jewish community. What began as an orderly presentation sadly dissolved into loud disagreement. And then Luke says, those who rejected Paul's teaching "loosed themselves from Paul," and as they left, he warned them that their rejection of Christ was a symptom of the fact that they were stubborn toward God, and that stubbornness would only produce further spiritual damage. To make his point, he quoted from something God said to Isaiah when He called him to be a prophet (Isa 6:9-10). God had asked Isaiah the question: "Whom shall I send, and who will go for Us?" and Isaiah had responded by saying, "Here am I. Send me!" And then the Lord told him to "go," but along with that commission He added something very troubling. He warned him that his ministry would fail to change the destructive course of the nation. He said that most of the people would not listen to him, not because they didn't understand what he was saying, but because they did not want to repent. They would deliberately close their spiritual eyes because they did not want to see what God was trying to show them; they would make their spiritual ears "heavy" by refusing to hear what He was saying to them; and their hearts would grow "fat" (literal), meaning they would become increasingly satisfied with things as they are. In fact, God said the spiritual condition of the nation was so bad that Isaiah's preaching would only serve to make most of his listeners worse. They would become more resistant to God, not less. So when Paul compared those who walked out on him to Isaiah's generation, he was warning them that they were rejecting a message that their hearts knew was true. He was telling them that by deliberately turning away from God's promised Savior, it would become harder for them to hear God's truth in the future. In fact, Jesus Himself used this same passage to describe the resistance He faced so often during His ministry (Mt 13:10-16).

And Isaiah's warning would have been extremely familiar to Paul's audience. Not one of the elders would have missed his meaning. He was saying that they were reacting just like Isaiah's generation and in doing so were proving that they were truly the spiritual children of those stubborn fathers. He said, "The Holy Spirit spoke well [accurately] through the prophet Isaiah to your fathers…" (v25).

v28: And then Paul added one more element to his prophetic warning. He informed the elders that God had already sent this "salvation" to the nations (Gentiles). He said, "Therefore let it be known to you that this salvation of God was sent to the nations, and they will hear" (literal). By that point in time he had been preaching the gospel for almost 30 years, and everywhere he went it was Gentiles rather than Jews who came to Christ in large numbers. So his words were more than a simple statement of fact. They contained a prophetic warning that by rejecting Christ these elders were forfeiting their proper place of leadership in the kingdom of God. The tide of Gentiles pouring into the church was swelling, not declining, and as time went on, they would vastly outnumber the very people to whom the Messiah, first of all, belonged. Paul is pointing to the same situation Jesus illustrated by a parable about guests invited to a dinner (Lk 14:15-24). Those who had been invited first had refused to come, so the master of the household (God) sent out his servants to invite others: the poor, the crippled, the blind and the lame, in other words the very people Israel's leaders considered unworthy. But since there was still room after these came, the master of the household sent his servants out to the "highways" and along the "hedges" so that his house would be full. In this parable the people of Israel are those who were first invited, and the Gentiles are those found on the highways and along the hedges.

v29: Verse 29 is not found in many of the ancient manuscripts of the New Testament, but since it simply states what obviously must have happened, there is no reason to overlook it. It says, "And when he had said these things, the Jews departed having much dispute among themselves" (literal). Can there be any doubt that's exactly what occurred?

vs30-31: With these two verses Luke brings his history of the early church to an end. Apparently he stops writing while Paul is still waiting for his case to be reviewed by Caesar Nero. He tells us that for two full years Paul was allowed by the Roman government to stay in a rented house or apartment, and it appears Luke stayed with him during that time. Why Paul's case took so long to come to trial isn't said. There may have been a long list of cases in front of him, but it's also possible that the Roman court was waiting for a representative from the Sanhedrin to come from Jerusalem to press charges. Undoubtedly there was a limited window of time for Paul's opponents to present their case, and if no representative arrived, Paul would have gone through some sort of formalities and then been released (F.F. Bruce, Acts, Eerdmans, reprint 1974, pp534-535).

That the Roman government itself did not consider Paul dangerous is made clear by the fact that they allowed him to remain in some form of house arrest for years. It's almost certain that during those years a soldier had to be assigned to guard him, and stationing a soldier next to Paul everyday was expensive. It would have been much cheaper to simply throw him into a crowded cell. But they didn't, and that fact tells us that in their judgment he had committed no serious crime. Nor did they consider his message to be dangerous because he was given complete freedom during that time to proclaim his Christian faith to all who came to visit him. But that level of tolerance toward Christians would change dramatically only a few years later. A fire would sweep through the city of Rome (A.D. 64), and the emperor Nero would viciously turn against all Christians (F.F. Bruce, Acts, Eerdmans, reprint 1974, p535 footnote). But when Luke ends the book of Acts, there is no sign of such hostility. Paul is still in rented quarters, "… proclaiming the kingdom of God and teaching the things concerning the Lord Jesus Christ with all boldness, unhindered [without any legal restraint]" (literal).

Acts Bibliography

Chapter 1

Bruce, F.F. The Book of the Acts. Grand Rapids, MI: Eerdmans, reprint 1974.

Edersheim, A. The Life and Times of Jesus the Messiah. Vol. 2, E.R. Herrick and Co., 1853-1890.

Vamosh, M.F. Daily Life at the Time of Jesus. Herzlia, Israel: Palphot Ltd., PO Box 2, 2001.

Vine, W.E. An Expository Dictionary of New Testament Words. Revell, 1966.

Chapter 2

Edersheim, A. The Temple: Its Ministry and Services. Eerdmans, reprint 1988.

Josephus, F. "Antiquities." The Complete Works. Translated by William Whiston, Thomas Nelson. 1998.

Vamosh, M.F. Daily Life at the Time of Jesus. Herzlia, Israel: Palphot Ltd., PO Box 2, 2001.

Chapter 3

Edersheim, A. The Temple: Its Ministry and Services. Eerdmans, reprint 1988.

Harrison, R.K. "Deuteronomy." The New Bible Commentary. Edited by J.D. Douglas, Revised, Eerdmans, 1971.

Chapter 4

Edersheim, A. The Temple: Its Ministry and Services. Eerdmans, reprint 1988.

Hall, D.R. "Annas." The New Bible Dictionary. Edited by J. D. Douglas. Eerdmans, 1962.

Chapter 5

Gelston, A. "Sadducees." The New Bible Dictionary. Edited by J.D. Douglas. Eerdmans, 1962.

Thompson, J.A. "Sanhedrin." The New Bible Dictionary. Edited by J.D. Douglas. Eerdmans, 1962.

Chapter 6

Lumby, J.R. Cambridge Greek Testament for Schools and Colleges: Acts. Edited by J.J.S. Perowne, Cambridge Univ. Press, 1904.

Chapter 7

Bruce, F.F. "Acts." The New International Commentary on the New Testament. Edited by Gordon D. Fee, Eerdmans, reprint 1974.

Chapter 8

Bruce, F.F. The Book of the Acts. Grand Rapids, MI: Eerdmans, reprint 1974.

Gelston, A. The New Bible Dictionary. Edited by J.D. Douglas, Grand Rapids, MI: Eerdmans, 1971.

Vine, W.E. Expository Dictionary of New Testament Words. Fleming H. Revell, 1966.

Wiseman, D.J. The New Bible Dictionary. Edited by J.D. Douglas, Grand Rapids, MI: Eerdmans, 1971.

Chapter 9

Aharoni, Y. and Avi-Yonah, M. The Macmillan Bible Atlas. New York: Macmillan Publishing Company, 1968.

Douglas, J.D., ed. The New Bible Dictionary. Grand Rapids, MI: Eerdmans, 1971.

Glueck, N. Rivers in the Desert. New York: Farrar, Straus and Cudahy, 1959.

Knowling, R.J. The Expositor's Greek Testament. Vol. 2, Edited by W. Robertson Nicoll, Eerdmans, reprint 1983.

Payne, D.F. The New Bible Dictionary. Edited by J. D. Douglas, Grand Rapids, MI: Eerdmans, 1971.

Rienecker, F. and Rogers, C. Linguistic Key to the Greek New Testament. Zondervan, 1980.

Chapter 10

Lumby, J.R. The Acts of the Apostles. Cambridge Greek Testament, Edited by J.J.S. Perowne, Cambridge: University Press, 1904.

Chapter 11

Brown, D., Fausset, A.R., Jamieson, R. A Commentary: Critical, Experimental, and Practical on the Old and New Testaments. Vol. 3, Eerdmans, reprint 1982.

Josephus, F. "Antiquities." The Complete Works. Translated by William Whiston, Thomas Nelson, 1998.

Morgan, G.C. The Acts of the Apostles. Fleming H. Revell, 1924.

Chapter 12

Rienecker, F. and Rogers, C. Linguistic Key to the Greek New Testament. Zondervan, 1980.

Chapter 13

Howson. "Acts." Quoted by Brown, D. A Commentary: Critical, Experimental, and Practical on the Old and New Testaments. Vol. 3, Eerdmans, reprint 1982.

Rienecker, F. and Rogers, C. Linguistic Key to the Greek New Testament. Zondervan, 1980.

Wheaton, D.H. The New Bible Dictionary. Edited by J.D. Douglas, Grand Rapids, MI: Eerdmans, 1971.

Chapter14

Bruce, F.F. The Book of the Acts. Grand Rapids, MI: Eerdmans, reprint 1974.

Vander Laan, R. "Lystra." Faith Lessons DVD Series. Vol. 7, Zondervan, 2006.

Chapter 16

Auscultation. In Webster's New Collegiate Dictionary. 1959.

Bruce, F.F. In the Steps of the Apostle Paul. Kregel, 1995.

Bromiley, G.W., ed. Theological Dictionary of the New Testament Abridged in One Volume. Eerdmans, 1985.

Douglas, J.D. ed., "Mysia," The New Bible Dictionary. Eerdmans, 1971.

Douglas, J.D. ed., "Phrygia." The New Bible Dictionary. Eerdmans, 1971.

Nicolle, W.R. The Expositor's Greek Testament. Vol. 2, Eerdmans, 1983.

Robertson, A.T. Word Pictures in the New Testament. Vol. 3, Broadman Press, 1930.

Chapter 17

Bruce, F.F. The Book of the Acts. Grand Rapids, MI: Eerdmans, reprint 1974.

Caldwell, W.E. The Ancient World. New York: Holt, Rinehart and Winston, 1962.

Douglas, J.D. ed., The New Bible Dictionary. Grand Rapids, MI: Eerdmans, 1971.

Lawrence, P. The IVP Atlas of Bible History. Intervarsity Press, 2006.

Robertson, A.T. Word Pictures in the New Testament. Vol. 3, Broadman, 1930.

Chapter 18

Brown, D., Fausset, A.R., Jamieson, R. "Acts." A Commentary: Critical, Experimental, and Practical on the Old and New Testaments. Vol. 3, Eerdmans, reprint 1982.

Bruce, F.F. The Book of the Acts. Grand Rapids, MI: Eerdmans, reprint 1974.

Bruce, F.F. In the Steps of the Apostle Paul. Kregel Pub., 1995.

Bruce, F.F. New Testament History. Doubleday and Co., 1971.

Bruce, F.F. Paul, Apostle of the Heart Set Free. Eerdmans, 1977.

Douglas, J.D. ed. The New Bible Dictionary. Grand Rapids, MI: Eerdmans, 1971.

Edersheim, A. Sketches of Jewish Social Life. Hendrickson, 1994.

Josephus, F. "Antiquities." The Complete Works. Translated by William Whiston, Thomas Nelson, 1998.

Nicoll, W.R. The Expositor's Greek Testament. Vol. 2, Eerdmans, 1983.

Pitmeyer, K. and L. Secrets of the Jerusalem Temple Mount. Washington, D.C.: Biblical Archeological Society, 1998.

Robertson, A.T. Word Pictures in the New Testament. Vol. 7, Broadman, 1930.

Chapter 23

Bruce, F.F. The Book of the Acts. Grand Rapids, MI: Eerdmans, reprint 1974.

Green, E.M.B. The New Bible Dictionary. Edited by J.D. Douglas, Eerdmans, 1971.

Josephus, F. "Jewish Wars." The Complete Works. Translated by William Whiston, Thomas Nelson, 1998.

Robertson, A.T. Word Pictures in the New Testament. Vol. 3, Broadman, 1930.

Tacitus. The Histories.

Chapter 24

Bruce, F.F. The Book of the Acts. Grand Rapids, MI: Eerdmans, reprint 1974.

Josephus, F. "Antiquities." and "Jewish Wars." The Complete Works. Translated by William Whiston, Thomas Nelson, 1998.

Lumby, J.R. Cambridge Greek Testament for Schools and Colleges: Acts. Edited by J.J.S. Perowne, Cambridge Univ. Press, 1904.

Chapter 25

Bruce, F.F. The Book of the Acts. Grand Rapids, MI: Eerdmans, reprint 1974.

Bruce, F.F. The New Bible Dictionary. Edited by J.D. Douglas, Eerdmans, reprint 1971.

Green, E.M.B. The New Bible Dictionary. Edited by J.D. Douglas, Eerdmans, reprint 1971.

Josephus, F. "Antiquities." The Complete Works. Translated by William Whiston, Thomas Nelson, 1998.

Morgan, G.C. The Acts of the Apostles. Fleming H. Revell, 1924.

Chapter 26

Robertson, T.A. Word Pictures in the New Testament. Vol. 3, Broadman, 1930.

Chapter 27

Brisco, T.V. Holman Bible Atlas. Nashville: Holman Publishing, 1998.

Bruce, F.F. The Book of the Acts. Grand Rapids, MI: Eerdmans, reprint 1974.

Josephus, F. "Jewish Wars" and "The Life of Flavius Josephus." The Complete Works. Translated by William Whiston, Thomas Nelson, 1998.

Vine, W.E. Expository Dictionary of New Testament Words. Edited by Fleming H. Revell, 1966.

Chapter 28

Brisco, T.V. Holman Bible Atlas. Nashville: Holman Publishing, 1998.

Brown, D., Fausset, A.R., Jamieson, R. A Commentary: Critical, Experimental, and Practical on the Old and New Testaments. Vol. 3, Eerdmans, reprinted 1982.

Bruce, F.F. The Book of the Acts. Grand Rapids, MI: Eerdmans, reprint 1974.

Gayley, C.M., ed. Classic Myths in English Literature. Boston: Gim and Co., 1894.

Laurence, P. The IVP Atlas of Bible History. IVP Academic, 2006.

Lumby, J.R. The Acts of the Apostles. Cambridge Univ. Press, 1904.

Nicoll, W.R. The Expositor's Greek Testament. Vol. 2, Eerdmans, reprinted 1983.

Rienecker, F. and Rogers, C. Linguistic Key to the Greek New Testament. Zondervan, 1980.

Pastor Steve's Reference Books

Here is a list of the reference books to which I turn most often when I'm doing a verse by verse study. I normally preach from the New American Standard version of the Bible, but rely heavily on my own translation of the text. So you'll find listed here many research tools designed to help a student understand the original meaning of a Hebrew or Greek word. You'll also find numerous Bible atlases because I find it very helpful to picture in my mind where a particular event is taking place. Time spent reconstructing the scene brings it to life. Though I don't mention it in the list, satellite photography, accessed through the internet, makes available a new level of precision and clarity. We can almost visit the places we're studying.

Of course, there are many other references available, but these are ones that helped me in preparing this commentary.

1. The NASB Interlinear Greek-English New Testament by Alfred Marshall (Zondervan)
2. Novum Testamentum Graece, Nestle-Aland, eds. (Deutsche Bibelstiftung, Germany)
3. A Textual Commentary on the Greek New Testament by Bruce Metzler (United Bible Societies)
4. Analytical Greek New Testament by Barbara and Timothy Friberg (Baker Book House)
5. The Interlinear Hebrew/Greek English Bible by Jay P. Green, Sr. (Associated Publishers and Authors, Wilmington Delaware 19808)
6. A Parsing Guide to the Greek New Testament by Nathan E. Han (Herald Press, Scottsdale, Pa, 15683)
7. New Testament Greek for Beginners by J. Gresham Machen (The Macmillan Co.)

8. A Manual Grammar of the Greek New Testament by H.E. Dana and Julius R. Mantey (The Macmillan Co.)
9. Theological Wordbook of the Old Testament, R. Laird Harris, ed., Gleason L. Archer, Jr. and Bruce K. Waltke, assoc. ends (Moody Press)
10. The Septuagint Version of the Old Testament and Apocrypha (Zondervan)
11. A Handy Concordance of the Septuagint (Samuel Bagster and Sons)
12. New American Standard Exhaustive Concordance of the Bible, Robert L. Thomas, ed. (Broadman and Holman)
13. The Exhaustive Concordance of the Bible by James Strong (Abingdon Press)
14. Greek English Concordance to the New Testament by J.B. Smith (Herald Press, Scottsdale, Pa, 15683)
15. A Linguistic Key to the Greek New Testament by Fritz, Rienecker, Cleon L. Rogers, Jr. ed. (Zondervan)
16. An Expository Dictionary of New Testament Words by W.E. Vine (Fleming H. Revell)
17. Word Pictures in the New Testament by Archibald Thomas Robertson, 7 volumes, (Broadman)
18. A Lexicon Abridged from Liddell and Scott's Greek-English Lexicon (University Press, Oxford)
19. Theological Dictionary of the New Testament Abridged in One Volume by Geoffrey W. Bromiley (Eerdmans)
20. Theological Dictionary of the New Testament by Geoffrey Bromiley, Gephard Kittle, ed. (Eerdmans)
21. The New Bible Dictionary, J.D. Douglas, ed. (Eerdmans)
22. The Zondervan Pictorial Encyclopedia of the Bible, Merrill C. Tenny, ed., Steven Barabas, assoc. ed., 5 volumes (Zondervan)
23. The Macmillan Bible Atlas by Yohanan Aharoni and Michael Avi-Yonah (Macmillan)
24. The Moody Atlas of the Bible Lands by Barry J. Beitzel (Moody)
25. Holman QuickSource Guide: Atlas of Bible Lands (Holman)
26. Holman Bible Atlas by Thomas V. Brisco (Holman)
27. The Harper Collins Concise Atlas of the Bible, James B. Pritchard, ed. (Harper San Francisco)
28. The IVP Atlas of Bible History by Paul Lawrence (Inter Varsity Press)

29. Atlas of the Bible Lands, Harry Thomas Frank, ed. (Hammond Inc., Maplewood, New Jersey)
30. Josephus: The Complete Works, translated by William Whiston (Thomas Nelson)
31. The Life and Times of Jesus the Messiah by Alfred Edersheim (E.R. Herrick and Co., New York), 2 Volumes
32. Sketches of Jewish Social Life / Updated Edition by Alfred Edersheim (Hendrickson)
33. The Temple: Its Ministry and Services by Alfred Edersheim (Eerdmans)

Coming Soon

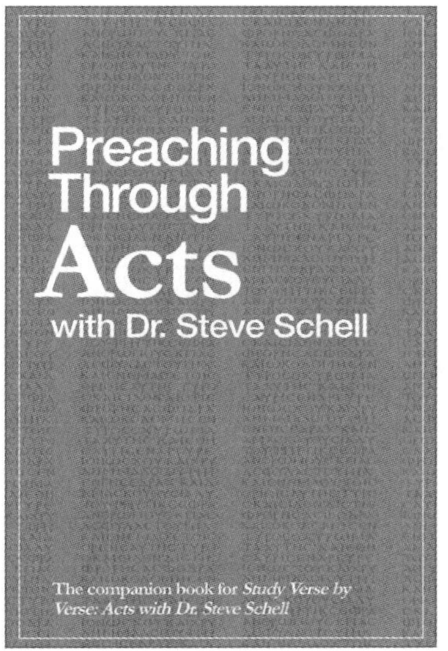

Here is a complete set of Pastor Steve's sermons through the Book of Acts starting at verse one and ending with Luke's closing words in chapter 28. For the man or woman who wants to preach or teach through this great account of the early church, this book contains ideas and insights drawn directly from the text.

Other commentaries

Acts is the second published work in this series of verse by verse commentaries. If you have enjoyed your journey through Luke's account of the early church, you will want to watch for the upcoming study of the gospel of John.

In addition to John, the following commentaries have already been written and will be edited for release: Genesis • Exodus • Luke • Hebrews • Revelation

Additional copies of this book can be ordered from Life Lessons Publishing, a registered trade name of Pastoral Resource Ministry, at:
lifelessonspublishing.com
You can also order copies through Amazon.com.